A Hidden Jewish Child from Belg

Survival, Scars an

FRANCINE LAZARUS

VALLENTINE MITCHELL
LONDON • PORTLAND, OR

First published in 2017 by Vallentine Mitchell

Catalyst House,
720 Centennial Court,
Centennial Park, Elstree WD6 3SY, UK

920 NE 58th Avenue, Suite 300
Portland, Oregon,
97213-3786 USA

www.vmbooks.com

British Library Cataloguing in Publication Data:
An entry can be found on request

ISBN 978-1-910383-28-5 (Paper)
ISBN 978-1-910383-34-6 (Ebook)

Library of Congress Cataloging in Publication Data
An entry can be found on request

Printed by CMP (UK) Ltd, Poole, Dorset

In memory of
my beloved father, Israel Kamerman
1897 Przemysl, Austro-Hungary (Poland) – 1944, Auschwitz, Poland

~

Dedicated to my wonderful and supportive children,
Michael, Cindy and Jason

Acknowledgements

My thanks to:

Charles Kamerman, my brother, who recalled for me some of his painful memories, allowing me to connect a few of the missing pieces of the puzzle of my own childhood.

Phillip Lazarus, my husband, who has shared my decades of coming to terms with my rough start in life.

Haya Oakley, who sent me photos and anecdotes about our family in Israel

Cindy Lazarus and **Jason Lazarus** who provided useful comments on drafts of this work.

Michael Lazarus who enthusiastically took charge of the electronic communications by setting up a website for my work.

My wonderful grandchildren for their love and support.

Dorien Styven repeatedly accessed archival material from many sources within the Musée de la Caserne Dossin, Belgium.

Special thanks to **Dr Margaret McNiven,** my Australian editor, who helped me research and frame this work.

My gratitude to my UK editor and my publisher for their support and help enabling me to complete this work.

Lastly and most importantly, I thank with all my heart all the wonderful nameless Belgian people who selflessly took me in or escorted me throughout the war at the risk of their own and their family's lives. They are the true heroes of this story: without them I would not have survived to write this book.

Contents

Acknowledgements   vi
Foreword   ix
Inberg-Rosenblum family tree   x
Kamerman-Lazarus family tree   xi
Glossary   xii
Preface: Bad Timing   xiii

Chapter 1.   A Jewish family in Brussels   1
Chapter 2.   Attempted escape   21
Chapter 3.   Hiding from Hitler   33
Chapter 4.   Hiding alone   39
Chapter 5.   My father arrested   53
Chapter 6.   Forced silence   61
Chapter 7.   Waiting for my father   65
Chapter 8.   Not wanted   67
Chapter 9.   Foster care   79
Chapter 10. Discovering my family   93
Chapter 11. I have a stepfather   103
Chapter 12. Servant to the family   111
Chapter 13. Education denied   121
Chapter 14. Growing up   125
Chapter 15. In love with Sydney   135
Chapter 16. Revisiting Survival   147
Chapter 17. Was my father still alive?   149
Chapter 18. My name is Survivor   153
Chapter 19. My own family to love   169
Chapter 20. Resuming my education   177

Chapter 21. Family reunited in Australia   181
Chapter 22. Recovery   189
Chapter 23. Ending intergenerational victimisation   195
Chapter 24. Emotional scars   199
Chapter 25. Healing   205

Postscript   213
Appendix: Timeline: Francine Lazarus née Kamerman   215
Endnotes   225
Bibliography   229
Index   237

Foreword

Without the personal tragedies Francine Lazarus née Kamerman faced during the Nazi occupation of Belgium (1940–45) during the Second World War (1939–45), readers would have been deprived of a detailed analysis of what constitutes 'Survival'. It requires courage, luck, trust, resilience and an appreciation for being alive, one day at a time.

Her absorbing description of the Nazi occupation of Belgium from May 1940 details the anti-Semitic laws that would eventually lead most Jews to be arrested and transported in cramped cattle cars directly to their deaths in Auschwitz or to suffer in concentration camps. In Brussels, her family's only hope of survival was to hide, sending their four-year-old daughter to live with strangers where she narrowly escaped death on several occasions. Francine's survival was largely due to the courageous Resistance workers (and a Bordello Madam), the pluck of this child in implausible situations, as well as her ability to hang on when there seemed to be no hope.

Francine has integrated her personal experiences with historical and academic discourse to provide a comprehensive account of the impact of the Nazi 'final solution' on those who survived to tell the world. Other hidden children's recollections help maintain the momentum of the narrative, expanded by research results and recent academic theories about the emotional impacts on Jewish children who were concealed during the war.

A Hidden Jewish Child from Belgium may provide solace to the extended families of the one and a half million Jewish children who died in the Holocaust. Descendants of surviving hidden children will find details that their parents and grandparents may have never mentioned and perhaps discover insights into how current generations remain under the shadow of the worst genocide in world history, still in our living memory.

If following generations are to understand the Holocaust and the bravery of the Survivors, this book will be a worthwhile educational tool. It is a remarkable and timeless story.

Dr Margaret D. McNiven

INBERG-ROSENBLUM

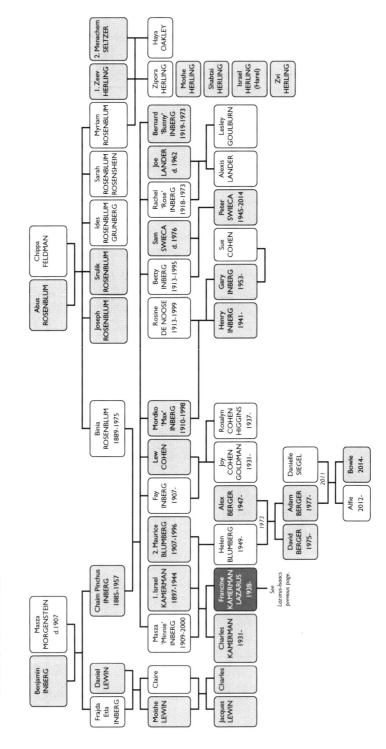

See Lazarus-Isaacs previous page.

KAMERMAN-SCHILLINGER

LAZARUS-ISAACS

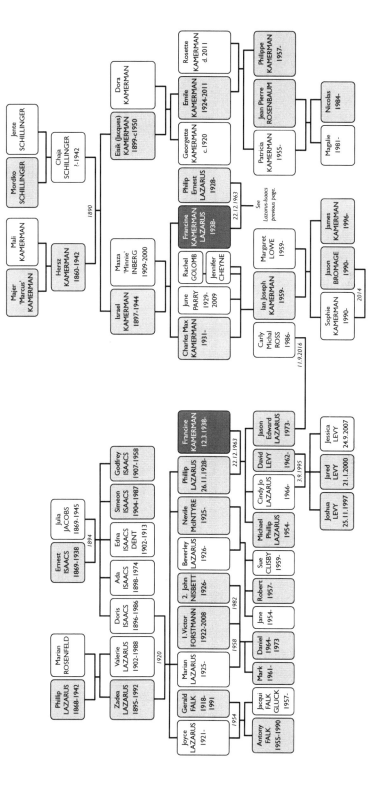

See *Lazarus-Isaacs previous page.*

See *Lazarus-Isaacs previous page.*

Glossary

Shoah   The Hebrew word referring to the specific murder and persecution of European Jewry as part of the crimes and horror of the Holocaust.

Survivor   Capitalised, to honour every witness of the *Shoah*.

Gypsy   Common usage for the Roma before and after the Second World War.

Round-up   The mass arrest of Jews by Nazis and collaborators, followed by deportation to the death camps or forced labour.

Spelling for proper names persons and places vary according to sources, languages, centuries, authors and translations, so the most common usage by my family is used here.

Geographic names vary because Poland, the Ukraine and Russia have had many boundary changes, especially over the nineteenth and twentieth centuries. The Austro-Hungarian Empire (1868–1918) consisted of Austria, Hungary, Bohemia, Moravia, Slovakia, Croatia, Slovenia, Bosnia, Herzegovina and parts of Poland, Ukraine, Romania, Serbia and Italy.

Preface
Bad Timing

Whomsoever saves a single life saves the entire world

Mishnah Sanhedrin 4:9

Nazis ruled the first six and a half years of my life. Memories of the ensuing events would dominate the following seventy years. From my early childhood I felt like I was standing in quicksand, without stability, struggling to keep my head afloat with no way forward. At just four years of age, I became a prisoner of a life-defining secret. During the Nazi occupation of Belgium, to ensure my survival, my father hid me with brave strangers in various places near or in Brussels. I was unable to live with my mother or older brother. I heard the click of Nazi officers' shoes and guns; I saw the blood of my rescuers. For all those years, I was frozen with fear.

After the Liberation of Belgium, my war was not over. I was told to forget anything that may have happened to me and that I was a lucky child because I had survived. I yearned for my father. If I mentioned any of my war experiences, my mother immediately dismissed my words so I learned not to talk about my hidden years. Only many years later could I allow my memories to penetrate my ironclad defences.

Inside me, I built up a terrible guilty feeling about why I survived when the Nazis murdered more than one and a half million Jewish children. As a witness to the *Shoah*, I feel urgency as well as an obligation to record my account. While too young to keep a diary at the time, I have obtained information on my early years from reliable historic and political literature and treasured family anecdotes. I have combed museums and public offices, as well as researching archives and libraries for evidence of my childhood.

Writing seven decades later, perhaps I felt a temptation to impose order on what I had experienced during the war-related chaos in Belgium. However, it remains impossible to put into words all that I lived through as a hidden child and expressing my emotions about those years has been a daunting experience.

Much of what I remember remains dreamy and hazy. In contrast to a magician whose skills present illusion as reality, my early reality feels like an illusion after many decades of repression and forced silence.

Frequently my emotional torment feels raw and fresh, as I repeatedly recall desperate times and the bitter legacies of years of shame, hate, fear and abuse. Often I struggle to recognise myself in those appalling circumstances.

However, my grief for my father and my guilt that I survived have never subsided.

Chapter One

A Jewish Family in Brussels

War is a random series of individual actions. Some have ramifications far beyond their immediate surroundings.

Patrick Lindsay[2]

Hitler made a speech on the day that I was born, not a good omen for this little Jewish girl. While he spoke to millions of cheering Austrians, I came into the world 1,100 kilometres away in Ixelles, a suburb of Brussels, on 12 March 1938. Our little family consisted of my parents, an older brother and me. Only three of us survived the Shoah.

Decades later, I began to reconstruct my family story. Like seeking missing pieces of a puzzle, I searched for clues in the few wartime photographs I had, recalled family lore and learned from other peoples' anecdotes. My own blurred images, a few remembered words from family and neighbours and many facts and hints from serious documents blended and aligned in this quest.

My father, Israel Kamerman, was born in Przemysl on 7 March 1897, in the Province of Galicia. The town was in the Austro-Hungarian Empire, close to the Ukrainian border and was incorporated into Poland after the First World War. His father, Hersz Kamerman, was from Sadowa Wisznia (either in the Ukraine or Poland, so fluid were the borders), son of Majer and Mali Kamerman. My father's mother, Chaja (née Schillinger), was born in Sambor in the Ukraine, the daughter of Mordko and Jente Schillinger. My paternal grandparents married on 19 February 1890 in Sambor. Never would I experience the joy of knowing them.

My father's brother, Jacques (Eizik/Eisik) Kamerman, was born in 1899. A younger, third brother, Joseph was recorded in the 1938 census of Przemysl, where my grandparents were living at that time. I know nothing more of this younger uncle, though one photograph taken in the late 1920s shows a young man alongside Jacques and his family who has a strong resemblance to my father and their parents. It seems likely that this was my uncle.

1. Hersz Kamerman and Chaja (née Schillinger), parents of Israel Kamerman, paternal grandparents of Francine, Poland, *c.*1920s.

The brothers completed high school in Przemsyl, a high standard of education in early twentieth century Poland. They grew up in an enlightened society where the significantly large Jewish community – 30 per cent of the town's population – was accepted, educated and held leadership positions.

A portrait of my father as a young man captures the determination in his direct gaze. The reverse of the portrait bears the stamp of the photographer's location, Lwov (Lviv) in the Ukraine, 100 kilometres east of Przemysl. He wears a gold signet ring on the little finger of his left hand. It is the only item I have that was his. I have long cherished it as a connection with my father and when I put it on my finger, I can almost hold him to me.

2. Portrait of Israel Kamerman as a young man, wearing signet ring, Lwov, mid-1920s (now Lviv in the Ukraine).

3. Signet ring, Israel Kamerman, still kept by his daughter, Francine.

My father was tall, dark and handsome with classic good looks. He wore a black hat and coat whenever he went out. My older brother remembers that my father spoke German, French and several other languages, that he was softly spoken and a very kind person. After he finished high school he planned further studies but, during the First World War, the Kaiser's army conscripted him to fight against Russia. After the Russians captured him, he was held as a prisoner of war, forced to wear Russian uniform and sent out to fight against the Kaiser; fortunately, he managed to escape from the Russians.

Documentation of my parents' separate arrivals in Belgium, and almost every address at which they subsequently lived along with their future family, remains amongst meticulously-kept Belgian government records. At the local level for the Administration Communale, every person in Belgium had to register where they lived, when they left that address and the next address to which they were moving. A special department monitored the *étrangers* (foreigners) and their nationalities were nearly always recorded. There were also departments at the *Arrondissement* (borough of several Communes). From there, notifications went to *l'Office Central des Statistiques* (Central Statistics Office) and to *Monsieur l'Administrateur de la Sûreté Publique Bruxelles* (the Administration for Public Security in Brussels), along with the *Division Centrale de Police Bureau des Etrangers* (Bureau of Foreigners within the Central Division of Police, for the City of Brussels). Even hospital records of foreigners were copied to multiple government offices.

Due to excessive redistribution, such as sending a copy to *le Gouverneur de la Province* (the Governor of the Province), I was able to discover a great deal about my family situation. Copies of the information would have been sent to the *Direction Générale des Classes Moyennes* (Director General of the Middle Classes) within the *Ministère des Affaires Economiques* (Ministry of Economic Affairs). Continuing into the higher government levels, documents went to and from *Le Ministre de la Justice (Sûreté publique)* (The Justice Minister, Public Security for all of Belgium), which scrupulously maintained the *Casier Judiciaire* (police files on individuals). Throughout this paper trail, each person had a specific file number identifying the individual with all authorities. Everyone could always be found.

Tracing my father's journey through government documents, I followed his migration as he left Przemysl on 15 May 1927. Comically, I discovered that the Polish government did not consider my father to be a Polish national as he was born in the former Austro-Hungarian Empire. He had to obtain a Polish transit visa to travel through his own country via Warsaw on 10 June 1927 on his way to Belgium. He arrived in Belgium on 22 June 1927 as a legal immigrant, ready to work. He registered in Antwerp on 28 June 1927. Police correspondence addressed to the Justice Minister on 30 July 1927 noted that my father was a salesman of textiles and clothing and that he travelled to markets. On all my father's Belgian documents his nationality was always recorded as Polish. One year later, he moved to Brussels in July 1928.

Place Jourdan was one of the local markets in which he sold goods. In 1931, the police investigated merchants at Place Jourdan for supposedly not paying taxes. My father's name was in a police document issued on 21 December 1931, containing a list of foreigners selling at the markets a week before Christmas. By then, the worldwide depression affected Belgium so removing competition (foreigners) from the markets may have been an underlying motive for a complaint, along with an official investigation into who may not have been paying the obligatory taxes. This was a time of increasing antisemitism in Belgium. Judging from the names and nationalities listed, of which the majority were Jewish, the report reflected police willingness to enforce rules against Jews.

4. Israel Kamerman working on the markets, standing on right, Belgium, 1930s.

In 1936, my father successfully applied for a permit as a *commerçant ambulant* (travelling salesman) with no opposition from the police or other officials. He moved well above a street pedlar on the business ladder and probably knew that he had to secure his occupation in an increasingly xenophobic climate. 'In 1937, the Eastern European Jewish peddlers and vendors ... had ceased receiving official peddler permits. This was due to a campaign carried out by essentially middle-class Catholic groups against what they alleged to be "unfair competition".[3]

My mother, Masza Inberg, was always called Minnie. She was born in Biala Podlaska, but her birth date was and always remained a mystery. Her parents repeated many times that she was born on the first light of Chanukah, which was 21 November 1909 and that was the birthday that Minnie wrote in 1927 on her application for a temporary visa to Belgium. Yet her 1929 Polish passport, issued in London, listed her birthdate as 21 September 1909, documenting the certification by the Biala Starosta (mayor) in 1927. Later, her 1930 marriage record listed her as born on 15 May 1909 and this third date remained her 'official' birth date throughout the rest of her life.

Minnie exploited the confusion by expecting and cheerfully accepting presents in May and November every year; September never featured in her birth celebrations. Such were the hundreds of mysteries and unconfirmed facts which collectively formed my fragile sense of truth in relation to any matter concerning my mother. Many times I was told to remember something, then on other occasions Minnie ordered me to forget. That was what it was like living with my mother; she was ever fickle.

My mother's father, Chaim Pinchas (Phillip) Inberg (*Chaima Pinkesa Inberga* in Polish) was always known as Zeida (Yiddish for grandfather). He was born on 20 November 1885 to Benjamin and Masza Dwora (Maszy Dwojra née Morgensztern) Inberg in Koden, so Minnie was probably named after her father's mother, my great-grandmother who died in 1907. They lived near the Belarus border with Poland where Jews had lived since 1725 and intermarried with Jews from nearby towns. In one such town, Biala Podlaska, Zeida's future wife, Booba was born. Zeida's story, as told by Minnie, was that he had escaped Russian-controlled Poland and reached London where he established his tailoring business and his home.

One of Zeida's brothers also went to England, settling in Leeds and changing his last name to Greenberg. There were three 'Greenberg' children:

5. Three Rosenblum sisters (from left) Miriam, Booba and Edis with their mother and a sister-in-law, Biala Podlaska, Poland, *c.* 1905.

Mary, Esther and Harry, none of whom married. Another brother of Zeida went to the USA. His older sister, Frajda Etla (born 20 November 1881) married Daniel Lewin and lived in Biala Podlaska in Poland. Their son, Moishe Lewin, moved to Belgium five months before the Second World War commenced, arriving in April 1939 from Biala Podlaska in Poland.

My mother's mother, Binia (Beatrice) Rosenblum was born in Biala Podlaska on 14 August1889 in Russian-controlled Poland. Her parents, Albuck/Avraham/Albus Rosenblum and Chippa/Chupa (née Feldman) were reasonably well off and owned horse studs. Always known to me as Booba (Yiddish for grandmother), she and her sisters were illiterate in the era when it was not considered necessary for girls to read and write. Instead they learned how to be *balabustas*, the Yiddish expression describing a good homemaker among Ashkenazi Jews. By contrast, her brothers were well-educated at the Cheder (Jewish school) as that was the family standard for sons.

6. Binia (Beatrice) Rosenblum/ Rozenblum, or 'Booba,' as a young woman, Biala Podlaska, Poland, *c.* 1910–14.

7. Binia Rosenblumor 'Booba' with her parents, Albuck/Avraham/Albus Rosenblum and Chippa/Chupa (née Feldman), Biala Podlaska Poland, *c.* 1936.

8. Rosenblum family home in Biala Podlaska Poland, 1906.

Booba and Zeida grew up in different towns during a time of restrictive settlement conditions, when the Russian authorities prohibited any travel for Jews. They may have been introduced by a third party such as a family member or possibly a traditional matchmaker, Shadkhin. An extract of their

9. Binia Rosenblum Inberg, 'Booba' on balcony of Rosenblum family home in Biala Podlaska, Poland, early1920s.

wedding certificate, written in Cyrillic, records: 'on 26th December in the year 1906 at 9 in the evening, in the presence of witnesses, the residents of the town of Biała, the [synagogue] teachers … Chaim Pinkus Inberg, residing in the town of Biała, a permanent resident of the town of Koden, a bachelor, 21 years old, son of Benjamin and Masza Dwojra … and Bina Rozenblum, a maiden, a permanent resident of the town of Biała, 17 years old, daughter of Abus and Cipa … by the rabbi of Biała's Jewish community Szlama Goldberg. This certificate was read to the spouses and the witnesses and signed by us.'

They never told me anything about their wedding or their subsequent travel to England. I do remember that Booba told me how her long thick hair was braided, during the war she cut off her plaits because long hair was no longer practical or sanitary. She hid her plaits in the record cupboard under her gramophone. They were taken when the house was unoccupied and plundered, perhaps for Nazi wig manufacturing.

Minnie often repeated her family's story of how, when Booba first became pregnant as a teenage bride in England, she decided to deliver her baby in Poland where her parents provided comfort and care. The family custom, before each impending birth, including my mother's, was for Booba to pack up her brood of young children and undertake the arduous journey to Poland. Then, with the newest baby in arms, Booba claimed that she returned to London with all her children, when the weather and her health permitted.

On reflection, it is highly unlikely that an illiterate, pregnant and teenage Booba would have travelled unaccompanied with one or two small children, across Europe to the western perimeter of the Austro-Hungarian Empire and back again to England. It seems more likely that they lived in Poland following their marriage and that their first four children were born in Poland before they moved to England as a family, where more children were born.

Auntie Fay was their first child, born in 1907 in Poland, then Minnie (1909) followed by Mordko Aron, known as Max (1910, sometimes erroneously recorded as 1911). I have not been able to obtain any verification of their births in Poland or their arrival or residence in England. The English-born children were Betsy, known as Betty, and her twin brother (1913), Joseph (1914), Rachel, known as Rose (1918), and the youngest, Bernard, known as Bunny (1919). Sadly, only six of Booba's eight children survived to adulthood because Joseph died in infancy from meningitis and Betty's twin brother died at birth.

Minnie and her siblings went to school in England. The eldest, Fay, gained a job in an office. As Booba was often ill, the second-eldest girl was taken out of school to look after the household, her younger siblings and her parents. That daughter was my mother who forever regretted being prevented from completing her education when she was young.

The first time I saw all their names and years of birth was on the Nazi-instigated registration of Jews in Belgium in 1940, despite the fact that some no longer resided in Europe. It was a shock to see a document that not only illustrated our family history but was actually part of the Nazi intention to find and kill all Jews.

Booba did once mention going to Portobello Road in London. This was a predominantly Jewish migrant area so they may have lived nearby. One hot July day, she went to the Portobello market and stopped at a stall selling hand-fans. There were fans sold for two pennies and others for one penny. As she was perpetually short of cash, she decided to buy the cheaper one. Returning home, Booba started using her new paper fan which, being flimsy, broke immediately. Now hot and angry, Booba marched back to the stallholder and complained that the fan had broken. The patient stallholder first asked her how she had used the fan. Disdainfully, Booba mimicked the actions of a Spanish dancer fanning herself. The stallholder told Booba that this action was exactly what she could have done with a two-penny fan but, with a one-penny fan, she must hold the fan in her hand and move her head from side to side. Booba loved telling and retelling this story.

Claiming she was ailing, Booba went away from her family to various European spa resorts frequently. Back in England, she had a permanent housekeeper in Minnie who looked after Zeida and the younger children while Booba enjoyed the spas. When I was a girl, Booba told me about the wonders of Piestany in Czechoslovakia to which she travelled every year, despite Jews being prohibited from entering the public baths.[4] She also went to the town of Spa, the place after which the term is named, in Belgium.

Brussels

In early 1926, Zeida left England. Perhaps he had no choice but to leave; I remember overhearing that he was not allowed to return to England, not even as a tourist. For his third country, now with a large family, he chose Belgium.

10. Grandparents' house, 66 rue de la Senne Brussels.

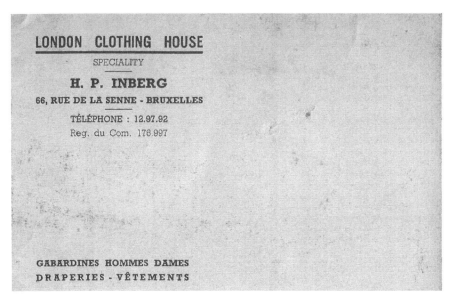

11. Business card of Phillip Inberg, 'Zeida'.

Language divided this country between French speakers in the south and Flemish speakers in the north, closer to the Netherlands. I wondered how they prepared to live in French-speaking Brussels, after growing up speaking Yiddish and English across the Channel. Booba must have been pleased to have one of her sisters, Edis, also migrate to Belgium. In Brussels, Mima Edis married Max Grunberg, a widower, and helped raise his daughter Chava (Eva).

Zeida purchased a three-storey house for their home and his tailoring business at 66 rue de la Senne in Brussels, a building that I would come to know well. Minnie, Max, Betty, Rose and Bunny, all moved to Brussels within a short time after Zeida's arrival. Fay remained working in England where she had met her future husband, Lew.

In 1927, Belgian officials approved Minnie's visa for just one month and she and Max travelled together, arriving in Belgium on 1 February 1927. They shared the same document so perhaps she was in charge of her

12. Booba and Zeida before the Second World War.

younger brother. Almost as soon as Minnie arrived, she applied for permanent residency in Belgium on 25 February. One of her documents stated that she worked as a tailor and helped her parents with that work; it was just what the officials needed to see, although she could never sew. On another document, her occupation was listed as a travelling sales person.

Within the next decade, three of my mother's siblings would migrate to Australia before the Second World War. Betty married Sam Swieca and they left Belgium in late 1937, arriving in Sydney on 20 January 1938; Max married Rosine De Noose in Belgium and they migrated soon after Betty and Sam left Belgium. Rose Inberg migrated alone; she met and married Joe Lander in Australia. Only Bunny and Minnie remained in Belgium with Zeida and Booba. Mima Edis and Max Grunberg, a widower whom she had married, also remained in Belgium. This new uncle Max (my other, Max Inberg, was in Australia) was a skilled cabinetmaker who made Minnie's bedroom suite when she married my father.

13. Francine's parents' wedding portrait, Israel Kamerman and Minnie Inberg, Brussels Belgium, 20 August 1930.

14. Carnet de Marriage for Minnie Inberg and Israel Kamerman, issued by City of Brussels, 20 August 1930.

My grandmother cooked and served meals in her Brussels home as a cash business, which she fondly referred to as her 'restaurant'. Occasionally Minnie helped Booba by serving the meals. By coincidence, my father was a customer and there, according to family history, my parents met.

They married on 20 August 1930. Her nickname for him was Joe. Possibly she felt that his name, Israel, might provoke anti-Semitic remarks. The exquisite Belgian lace in her wedding gown and the veil that fell to the ground were clearly expensive, along with her exotic bouquet of lilies from distant lands. Many years later when dementia had begun to erode her memory, when I showed Minnie her wedding photograph she exclaimed, 'What a handsome man! Who is he?'

Their twelve-year age difference was one reason that I suspect my parents had an arranged marriage rather than a love match. The greatest indication of an arranged union to me was that they could not easily communicate, as she spoke English as her first language and minimal Yiddish but did not master French. My father spoke German, Polish, French and Flemish but never mastered English. Maybe he spoke German and she answered in Yiddish, a derivative of German. Another clue to suggest an arranged marriage was that they came from completely different backgrounds – his was highly educated and hers, sadly, less so. Perhaps she agreed to marry this older foreign man to

15. Francine's Birth Certificate, 12 March 1938, Commune d'Ixelles, Belgium. Extract, 23 October 1963.

16. Israel and Minnie Kamerman, Charles 'Charly' aged eight and Francine, four or five months in Blankenberg, at the Belgian seaside, summer 1938.

escape her parents' authority and also to avoid the endless housework for Booba.

Charles Max Kamerman was born on 15 August 1931 in Brussels and was about to turn seven years at the time of my birth. He adored our father. I always called my brother 'Charly'. Our seven-year age difference determined the brevity of our shared childhood and the memories we held of each other. We were separated by circumstances and decisions, some made by Hitler and others made by our mother. We would share very few years under the same roof – only my first four years and then a brief period after the Liberation of Belgium from the Nazis in 1944. Eventually, we would become better acquainted and closer than ever in a faraway land.

From when I was a baby, my father seems to have spent his rare moments of spare time with me, judging from the early photos of the two of us together taken in my first summer, aged four or five months, when our family was staying at the seaside where my father was selling goods at the markets.

Despite widespread antisemitism, especially in Flanders and the province of Antwerp, Belgian Jews numbered close to 66,000[5] and comprised approximately 6 per cent of the population. Jews who had acquired Belgian nationality had all the basic rights provided by the Belgian Constitution: equality before the law, freedom of religion, freedom of speech and freedom of the press. However, my parents did not have Belgian citizenship.

Too soon, photos showed our grim faces in worsening times, no one smiling. My father's deep concern showed in his riveting gaze.

War against Jews

Already in the Nazi-occupied territories, the 1935 Nuremberg laws effectively cut every Jew from all social, academic, scientific and economic participation. Expropriation, isolation and discrimination were imposed on Austrian Jews in March 1938. When Kristallnacht, the night of broken glass, began on the evening of 9 November 1938 continuing into the next day, I was eight months old. Anti-Semitic riots in Austria and Germany targeted Jewish-owned properties, destroying over 100 Synagogues and 7,500 shops within 24 hours. The Nazis intended to wage war against the Jews until all of us were exterminated.

By the time I was eighteen months old, France and Britain had declared war on Germany on 3 September 1939, according to their respective Common Defence Pacts with Poland, thereby launching the Second World War. Germany had two contiguous wars, one against the Jews and the other against the Allies.

At about the time that I turned two, I was living in increasingly chaotic and hostile circumstances. It is difficult to imagine a people more exposed to conquer, capture and extinction than the Jews who lived in 'neutral' Belgium with no defences, hoping we would be untouched. Frightening stories had already filtered through to the Jews living in Belgium about the Nazis rounding up the Jewish population in Germany, Poland and Austria. There, Jews were brutalised, imprisoned, starved, tortured and murdered. Those Jews who had managed to escape from the invaded countries told these terrible truths on arrival in Belgium. The hope that we would remain uninvolved, as Belgium was a neutral country, proved to be naïve.

One of the world's leading authorities on the Holocaust defined the three stages through which antisemitism proceeded under the Nazis:

Firstly, you can't live among us as Jews;
Then, you can't live among us;
Lastly, you can't live.[6]

Hilberg's succinct analysis described the abrupt end of my normal childhood, the breaking up of an extended family, my isolation when hidden and a constant and very real fear of death. All those experiences left me in an emotional quagmire as a little child. I missed out on having role models, resources or opportunities in childhood, let alone nurturing. These events created such stress that their impacts would dominate the next seventy years of my life.

Chapter Two

Attempted Escape

On 10 May 1940, the Nazis invaded neutral Belgium without warning, as part of their Blitzkrieg or 'lightning war' against France, their ancient foe. As Nazis walked and rode across the nation, many people, including Jews, tried to escape Belgium using cars, carts, donkeys, horses and wheelbarrows that clogged the roads, while others began to walk to freedom over the border. After eighteen days, Belgium surrendered and the government leaders fled to London where they operated the government-in-exile.

My father procured train tickets for our family, no doubt at great financial cost and personal risk. His plan was to reach England where he thought we would find safety with Zeida's relatives. Our family of four boarded the train in Brussels and successfully crossed into France.

Apparently, my father intended to take us to Dunkirk where we would board a vessel for England but we could not reach the port. We travelled on many trains and trucks, trying to reach safety. We caught a train towards Switzerland but that country refused us entry. Another train trip took us south-west within France, as my father now planned to pass through Spain from where he hoped we could reach England. According to my brother, he paid a *passeur* (people smuggler) to guide us across the Pyrenees to Spain. However, I had whooping cough that could alert French *gendarmes* and Spanish *Guardia* to our illegal presence and the *passeur* refused to help us because of this.

We never escaped from France. We were stranded in a small run-down cottage in Cepet, a village nineteen kilometres north of Toulouse in the Haute Garrone region. My brother explained that we shared this old cottage on the avenue de Toulouse with a young Jewish refugee couple who had also failed to enter Spain. They had to sleep on straw mats in the kitchen. We did our bathing and laundry in an old washhouse behind the cottage. For the first few days, we ate food supplied by a nearby restaurant as part of the fee refunded by the unsuccessful smuggler. Charly minded a herd of cows, receiving a pail of milk as payment each time. A nearby chateau owner allowed my brother to collect firewood for our rustic kitchen and sent a couple of bottles of wine for my parents.

An image of my father at this time remains indelibly etched in my memory. As I entered the kitchen, I saw my father, wearing a shirt and squeezing something in his hands, juicing either an orange or a lemon. He was speaking in a language that I did not recognise. This vague and ephemeral vision was a clear image of my father as a young man. In that moment I asked, 'What language are you speaking?' and Minnie replied, 'Flemish'. Perhaps they did not want me telling anyone that they were speaking Yiddish in a country which had begun to collaborate with the Nazis. This was the first lie I remember my mother telling to mislead me and protect us. Lies became survival tools throughout that period as we tried to stay alive during Nazi rule.

On the first day of September 1940, Marshal Pétain's collaborationist government gave all foreign Jews notice to leave France in order to return to their original place of residence. There was no alternative, as waiting meant arrest by Pétain's government police and removal to Gurs, the main concentration camp for Jews and dissidents. This camp was originally built to shelter refugees from the Spanish Civil War, then those fleeing persecution (from Russia and the Nazis) and, from 1940, it was used as a concentration camp by Pétain and Nazi Germany, holding 15,000 prisoners by 1942[7]. Most were transported to the death camps of Auschwitz and Sobibor in Poland. Within one year, more than 90 per cent had been transported and only 1,200 were still alive in Gurs by 1943, 48 of them Jews.

French police actively transported us in reverse, back to the Nazis in Belgium. Over seventy years later, France's National Archives (declassified on Monday 28 December 2015) revealed details of French police collaboration with Nazi Germany, when we were under the Vichy government (1940–4) jurisdiction in Cepet. Antisemitism had popular French support as the Vichy regime worked with the Germans and introduced anti-Jewish laws that prevented foreign Jews from transiting through France.[8]

Under Nazi rule

Returning to Brussels in September 1940, the conditions for all Jews had become still more precarious. We moved back into the same apartment at 14 rue Gendebien that we had vacated as there were no new tenants. On 8 October 1940, we moved in with my grandparents at 66 rue de la Senne. The four of us lived in one bedroom off my grandparents' apartment, without cooking or bathroom facilities. To wash ourselves, Minnie boiled a pot of water in the upstairs kitchen and walked down the stairs holding it; one day, she tripped and spilled the boiling water over my head, neck and body, resulting in third-degree burns. Fortunately, a nurse, Mademoiselle Becks, visited Booba regularly for her ailments and she treated my serious burns and prevented infection. I carry the scars to this day.

Within a few months after their invasion, the Nazis began their strategy of stigmatising Jews in Belgium, isolating them from the general population and destroying their financial resources. There were eighteen Nazi Decrees against Jews, 'marking step by step, the stages of a process of strangulation towards always more precarious condition of living, leading to physical destruction'[9]. Some Decrees contained more than one law or directive and each of these was enforced strictly by the German military administration, supported by local Belgian government officials.

The first Nazi Decree in Belgium was made on 23 October, 1940 and banned the ritual slaughter of animals. As my family kept Kosher, this rule meant that we ceased eating meat because it was *treif* (unkosher), although we still had fish, eggs and cheese for protein, if we could afford them.

The purpose of these anti-Jewish Nazi Decrees was to identify Jews in Belgium and thereby to exclude them from rightful participation in Belgian society[10]. The title of David Fraser's article, 'The Fragility of Law: Anti-Jewish Nazi Decrees, Constitutional Patriotism, and Collaboration Belgium 1940–1944' precisely defines how the Belgian government betrayed the Jews in its country.

Officially, the government-in-exile refused to allow the measures to be incorporated into Belgian law. 'However, it did permit, under their reading of The Hague Convention, that the Belgian government departments and many local administrations could assist in implementing the German anti-Jewish Nazi Decrees'.[11] Collaboration occurred throughout Belgian society. Ultimately, the edicts intended to send every Jew to his or her death.

Firstly, there was a legal definition of a 'Jew'. On threat of penalties, after October 1940, all Jews over the age of fifteen years were required to register at the *Administration Communale* (local level of government) and have the letter J stamped on their Belgian identity cards (not citizenship documents, as we were not Belgian citizens).

My father complied with the Nazi requirement, signing the new form called the Register of Jews, on 18 December 1940, as he would have been threatened with dire consequences if he had not registered; it listed all our details. How could Jews realise that their registration would soon facilitate their arrest by the Nazis? Part of the information required was a written declaration of possessions, creating an inventory of belongings; eventually, those assets would be collected after the owners were arrested and transported to the death camps.

Included in the Nazi Decree of 28 October 1940 was a ban on the return to Belgium of Jews who had emigrated ensuring that my aunts and uncles in Australia could not have come back if they had wanted to. The establishment of a mandatory official record for every Jew over fifteen years of age, namely my parents, was completed by my father. Then too, the exclusion of Jews from key professions (civil servants, lawyers, journalists and teachers) would have made it difficult to obtain professional help for my extended family.

A few weeks after my third birthday, on 14 April 1941, anti-Semitic actions in Antwerp destroyed two synagogues, Torah scrolls and many Jewish businesses.[12] Within two weeks, on 25 April 1941, Jews were forbidden to enter public parks throughout Belgium, denying us simple and free recreation. I have no memories of ever going to a public park or garden until after the war.

'On May 20 1941, Eichmann's department informed Gestapo [Nazi secret police] branches in France and Belgium "in the light of the Final Solution which will undoubtedly be implemented, emigration of Jews from France and Belgium is to be prevented"'.[13] We had no way of escaping again from Belgium.

The 1935 Nuremberg Laws had already forbidden the participation of Jews in civil society, through exclusion from the legal, medical and educational professions. The following week, on 31 May 1941, a Nazi ordinance required every Jewish business in Belgium open to the public to identify that it was a Jewish enterprise. This would have applied to my father's stalls at the various markets. In addition, the Belgian population was forbidden to patronise Jewish-owned shops, resulting in most of these having to close as they had no customers. My father would have lost many sales and made very little money for our family.

Further laws in that Decree concerned the declaration of real estate owned by Jews. One document I obtained showed the sudden change of official ownership of my grandfather's house. Instead of my grandfather being listed as the owner, a *Monsieur Debloos* was named on a Police document. As Jews had to declare any real estate they owned, my grandfather had become a lessee of his own home. It is unclear whether or not my grandfather really sold the home or whether he made an arrangement with a non-Jew to be declared the official owner. Later, on our family's registration card, we were declared to be sub-lessees of Zeida, his last name misspelled as 'Imberg'.

The Nazi Decree of 29 August 1941 prohibited Jews from living outside Brussels, Antwerp, Charleroi and Liège. On the same date the night curfew was set for Jews, prohibiting us from being outside between 8 pm and 7 am. Fortunately we were living in one of the prescribed cities, Brussels. However, my father could only leave for work after 7 am and had to be home by 8 pm, which would have restricted his opportunities to travel between market towns, something which had been profitable for him. Nor could he travel in one day to obtain supplies from faraway places. Gradually his livelihood was being taken away and the security of our family eroded.

All around us, our daily life began to reflect our trepidation about what the Nazis would do to us next. Jewish New Year on 22 September 1941 was an uneasy time for families.

On 25 November 1941, *l'Association des Juifs en Belgique* (the Association of Jews in Belgium or AJB) was established to control and keep intimate details on the Jewish population. 'The aim was to utilise the AJB in order to facilitate the implementation of the Nazi anti-Jewish orders issued to the Belgian administration … under the constant control of the SS officer responsible for Jewish affairs',[14] to facilitate the arrest and then deportation of Jews. Ostensibly, this organisation provided a social care network, by establishing orphanages for children whose parents had been deported and group homes for older Jews. Such services eventually became the means by which Jewish children and the elderly were gathered for transportation to the death camps.

The Nazi-mandated registration of our family indicated that we had an identity card valid until 27 December 1941; what would happen after that? This was a decision of life or death; if we registered, we would be able to get food coupons but the Nazis would be able to arrest us easily. If we did not register, we were breaking the law –enforced brutally by the Nazis – and food would only be available on the high-priced black market.

Another purpose of the registration information was to identify all the business operators in Belgium and to record their skills and inventories of goods. A Nazi database of 'all possessions of enemies and Jews' in Belgium and France was published sixty years later by the French National Archives in Paris[15]. In Groupe XII, *Feind- und Judenvermögen* (*biens ennemis et juifs*) (enemy and Jewish property), I felt enormous surprise to read my

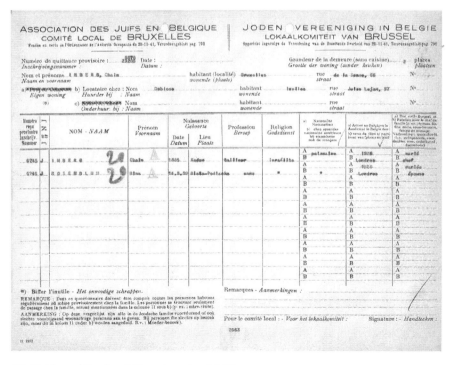

17. Zeida and Booba, AJB registration 1940.

ASSOCIATION DES JUIFS EN BELGIQUE   JODEN VEREENIGING IN BELGIE
COMITÉ LOCAL DE BRUXELLES   LOKAALKOMITEIT VAN BRUSSEL

Numéro de quittance provisoire :   673   Date :
Inschrijvingsnummer :   3342   *Datum :*

Grandeur de la demeure (sans cuisine) 2   places
Grootte der woning (zonder keuken)   *plaatsen*

Nom et prénoms KAMERMAN Israel   habitant (localité) Bruxelles   rue de La Senne 66 N°.
Naam en voornam   *wonende (plaats)*   *straat*

a) Propre demeure b) Locataire chez : Nom
Eigen woning Huurder bij : Naam

c) Sous-loc. chez : Nom Leberg   habitant   rue   N°.
Onderhuur. bij : Naam   *wonende*   *straat*

Numéro reçu provisoire Inscript.		NOM - *NAAM*	Prénom *Voornaam*	Naissance *Geboorte* Date *Datum*	Lieu *Plaats*	Profession *Beroep*	Religion *Godsdienst*	Nationalité *Nationaliteit*	Arrivé en Belgique le *Aankomst in België den*	Signature
8381	J	KAMERMAN	Israel	7-3 1897	Przemusl	vacyageor	Isrl	A B	1897 Przemul	marié
8382	J	INBERG	Maaja	15-5 1909	Biala Podlaska	sans	"	A B	Londres	épodes col
8383	J	KAMERMAN	Charles	15-8 1931	Bruxelles	"	"	A B		fils
8384	J	KAMERMAN	Francine	12-3 1938	"	"	"	A B		fille

*) Biffer l'inutile - *Het onnoodige schrappen*.   Remarques - *Aanmerkingen* :

REMARQUE : Dans ce questionnaire doivent être compris toutes les personnes habitant régulièrement ou même provisoirement chez la famille. Les personnes se trouvant seulement de passage chez la famille, seront mentionnées dans la colonne 11 sous b) (p ex. : mère visitée).

AANMERKING : Op deze vragenlijst zijn alle in de Joodsche familie voortdurend of ook slechts voorbijgaand woonachtige personen aan te geven. Bij personen die slechts op bezoek zijn, moet dit in kolom 11 onder b) worden aangeduid. B.v. : Moeder bezoek).

Pour le comité local : - *Voor het lokaalkomiteit* :   Signature : - *Handteeken* :

18. Registration of our family completed for our family, listing the address of our grandparents' house, 66 rue de la Senne, 1941 (month and day undocumented). Provided to *l'Association des Juifs en Belgique* (Association of Jews in Belgium), established by the Nazis.

grandfather's name, listed as number 468 under *Industrie de l'habillement*.[16] My father's name was entered as number 216 under *Commerce de produits textiles et habillement*.[17] My father and grandfather had been reduced to mere names and numbers in the Nazi 'industry' of discrimination and death.

Legally, the forced registrations of Jews, whether Belgian or foreign, was in violation of the Belgian constitution. While the government-in-exile protested that it was a racist and illegal edict, nothing stopped the increasingly obvious violations of the constitutional rights of Belgian residents and citizens under the Nazis. In December 1941, eighty-three Polish Jewish families in Antwerp were 'repatriated' by the Nazis to Poland. A few months later in 1942, a larger number of Jews were sent forcibly from Belgium to work as slave labour in the textile factories of the Lodz Ghetto in Poland. From September 1942, Jewish children were banned from schools, contravening Belgian law for compulsory education from ages seven to fifteen.

The Nazi Decree of 31 May 1941 banned the possession of a radio by a Jew; any Jew found with a radio was immediately arrested. I have a very clear memory of being in the cellar at 66 rue de la Senne, huddled in the cool

19. 1940 'Registration of Jews', Israel Kamerman's report, 18 December 1940.

kitchen and the adults standing hunched over, listening to a large radio at the back of the rustic unlit stove. They successfully hid this radio for the entire war, even when the house was unoccupied and plundered. After the war, I used that radio as my model to make a pretend radio out of a cardboard box.

If anyone still had a clandestine radio, a gasp of hope would have been heard in Belgium when the USA announced that it had entered the Second World War as an ally on 8 December 1941, the day after the Japanese bombed Pearl Harbour.

Times were tough. Food was very hard to obtain, especially for Jews who were excluded from all ways of earning a living to pay for food and who were also denied coupons to buy food legally, so food was also very expensive. Buying on the black market if one's income ceased and assets were depleted was impossible and so starvation loomed. One of the few war stories Minnie told me many years later was that we once had a beautiful white fluffy cat called Leiele. One day, Madame Jules, my parents' sometime landlady, requisitioned the cat to catch mice or so she said. Leiele was never returned and surely became a delicious meal for some family.

A top secret conference was held in a villa in Wannsee, a suburb of Berlin, on 20 January 1942. It was attended by high ranking members of the Nazi party and some military officials. The aim of this meeting was to coordinate the implementation of the Final Solution to the Jewish problem. The Wannsee Conference laid out the plans for the Nazi attempt to exterminate the entire Jewish population of Europe.

In the wake of the Wannsee Protocol, more Nazi Decrees were issued that restricted further the freedoms of Jews in Belgium. On 11 March and 8 May 1942, Decrees prohibited Jewish workers from receiving bonuses, paid leave including sick leave and requiring them to be isolated from other workers. On 22 April 1942, German Jews who had fled Germany were stripped of their nationality. Then, on 8 May 1942, forced labour was imposed on Jews living in Belgium.

Forced labour was another tool to implement the Wannsee Protocol to gather and murder all of Europe's Jews by shipping them east to concentration camps where they worked in factories for the Nazis until they died or were murdered. The euphemism used by the Nazis was that families were being resettled in the east and many Jews believed this in the beginning. Before long the sole destination was immediate death.

From 27 May 1942, all Jews over six years of age had to wear a Star of David on their outer clothing. In what was possibly our last family gathering in my grandparents' house in Brussels in 1942, no one was smiling. In this photo, each seated person's head was aligned strategically to cover the Star on the person standing behind.

Next to our father, Charly was trying to stand very tall. I sat on my mother's lap, who was not wearing her Star. I kept her hateful Star to this day.

20. Masza Kamerman's Star of David, forced, by Nazi edict, to be worn on outer clothing from 27 May 1942.

Moishe Lewin was the son of Zeida's sister, Frajda Etla. He had arrived in Brussels only three years earlier, in April 1939, from Biala Podlaska in Poland, where his parents remained.

More severe Nazi laws were introduced in the Decree of 1 June 1942, when Jewish doctors, veterinarians, dentists and nurses were banned from practising, thus depriving their Jewish patients of treatment when sick. In addition, there were strict limitations placed on freedom of movement and re-location for Jews.

Towards the end of July 1942, the Nazis re-opened a former Belgian army barracks, the Caserne Dossin in Malines (Mechelen), located halfway between the two major cities of Antwerp and Brussels, where the majority of Belgian Jews lived. Ominously, there was a railway line linking Malines to Eastern Europe, now controlled by the Nazis. Mass round-ups of Jews by Nazis and collaborators commenced in Brussels in August 1942, when arrested Jews were crammed into trucks to be driven to the Caserne Dossin where they were held until they were transported by rail to the death camps.

The intent of the Nazis was to enslave, plunder and murder. The term *Razzia* conveys the intent more precisely than merely 'rounding up' people. It

21. Israel and Minnie Kamerman, Charly aged eleven and Francine, four years, 1942. Francine is wearing her brother's old trousers, hemmed into shorts and braces crossed in front. Her mother's head covers her father's Star of David on his jacket.

is derived from an Arabic term for a raid or military attack, to plunder property or to enslave people, especially as perpetrated by Moors in North Africa[18]. The moment that the arrested Jewish men, women and children entered the Caserne Dossin, their names were typed onto the next deportation list, part of the production line heading to the death camps.

22. Extended family gathering at grandparents' home, 66 rue de la Senne Brussels. Standing from left: Charly, Francine's father Israel Kamerman, Moishe Lewin (Zeida's nephew), unknown woman, uncle Max Grunberg. Seated: Minnie, Francine, Booba and Mima Edis (sister of Booba, wife of Max Grunberg). Brussels 1942. Note strategic seating poses to hide the Star of David on clothing, only one is clearly visible (far right).

For those Jews not alarmed by the Nazi Decree(s) banning access to school or the forced wearing of stars, the brutal round-ups that began in July and August 1942 dealt an insufferable blow. Now it was clear that no Jew, not even women and children were safe. Finally as fear overwhelmed all other feelings, there was a scramble to find hiding places.[19] An atmosphere of threat, physical danger and random violence pervaded our everyday life, along with food shortages and many deprivations. Violent arrest, ambush, torture, disappearance and deportation were becoming a norm for Jews. Nothing here has been overstated.

The Nazis instigated mass arrests of Jews, commencing in Antwerp in August and again in September 1942. Local authorities and Belgian citizens played supporting roles when they dutifully, even self-interestedly, informed the Nazis where Jews lived. According to Vromen, the *Vlaams Nationaal Verbond* (Flemish National League) founded in 1933 was fascist and anti-Semitic in orientation and collaborated extensively with the Germans during the occupation of Belgium.[20]

While the Belgium Government-in-exile opposed Nazi occupation and laws, at the local level, there was direct permission for the local government to obey the Nazi administration. Civilian collaborators came from all socio-economic strata. Comparing the ordeals which Jews in Belgium suffered during the Second World War with Jews in Denmark, Richard Rorty disdained the 'Belgian vice' as compared with 'Danish virtue', in relation to the courage shown by individuals throughout all levels of government in Denmark, compared with the lack of evidence of much courage in Belgium.[21] 'Belgium collaborated with Nazi Germany, and victims' relatives said the state should look more closely at its role', John Tagliabue wrote in 2008.[22]

It was harder for Jews to find hiding places in Flanders or the Province of Antwerp, as Flemish areas were decidedly more anti-Semitic. For the few Jewish children whose parents managed to find places, hiding was just their first test. Surviving any hiding spot was always a matter of luck and subterfuge. Soon after the Van Damme family in east Flanders took in Hersch and Salomon Grunstein, neighbours in their small village called Belsele became curious and suspicious and could have denounced them. Therefore, their rescuers leaked the 'true'(fabricated) reasons why the boys had come to live with them. Supposedly, their mother was in and out of mental institutions and their father was a womaniser who neglected the boys. The Van Damme family cleverly re-positioned these boys as objects of pity and sympathy – a sympathy they already deserved for being hunted as Jews. Temporarily, the danger they were in was reduced.[23]

At first, my brother was happy when Nazis banned Jewish students from attending school in September 1942. He enjoyed spending extra time with our father who was, by then, no longer able to sell goods on the markets. However, Charly missed reading and so he stole books from a shop. When the owner caught him, he must have guessed that Charly was Jewish as he was not in school. The shopkeeper offered him free used books, understanding the boy's urge to learn and possibly making a subtle and individual act of resistance against the Nazis.

Jewish parents gave away their children in the hope that they might live, pleading with neighbours, friends and the dominant Roman Catholic Church. Most young Jewish children caught in the round-ups were deported immediately to the death camps, via the Caserne Dossin.

Howard Kershner, director of European relief for the American Friends Service Committee wrote on wartime suffering in 1940. 'One of the greatest tragedies of all times is the separation of families in Europe today: wives in one country, husbands in another with no possibility of reunion and often no means of communication; babies who have never seen their fathers; scattered fragments of families not knowing if their loved ones are living or dead and often without hope of ever seeing them again. There are multitudes of wretched souls for whom it seems the sun of hope has set'.[24]

Chapter Three

Hiding from Hitler

Les Boches vont venir nous prendre.
(The Germans will come to get us.)

My parents would say this
around the dinner table every night in Brussels.

At four years of age, my childish imagination pictured horrid, painful torture and, even worse to me, separation from my family. Constantly I imagined monsters and I feared terrible things happening to me. We lived in a state of perpetual urgency, a heightened level of anxiety. We always anticipated the ultimate catastrophe: arrest. We were afraid of the unknown that would follow arrest. Those anxieties and fears have remained imbedded in my psyche throughout my life.

When the round-ups of Jews accelerated in mid-1942, it became imperative for Jews to escape Belgium or to find hiding places. The people who took us and other Jews into hiding put themselves and their families at extreme risk, especially as they were threatened with death if they were found hiding us. Many who hid Jews did so as part of the Resistance to the enemy and others out of a deep religious conviction. Some Belgians hid Jews just for the money and a few of those gave Jews up to the authorities.

During the war, our safety and food had to be purchased at increasingly higher prices. In earlier successful years in business during the 1930s, my father and Zeida had each purchased jewellery, an investment considered safer than the banks after the Great Depression and their earlier oppressed years in Poland. Zeida and my father kept some valuables hidden, defying the Nazis, to pay for us being hidden and for the family's sustenance.

Such gold and gems became our life insurance, as pieces were gradually sold to pay for our necessities and hiding expenses. Many times my grandmother told me this fact, always angrily, implying that I had not been worthy of their expenditure. In addition, Zeida obtained cash by taking loans at exorbitant interest, to pay others to keep us alive.

Zeida and Booba first hid with the De Noose family who ran a bakery. They all stayed in the living quarters above the bakery. They were related through the marriage of their son Max Inberg to Rosine De Noose, now living safely in Australia. Nearly two decades later, Auntie Rosine told me about her parents hiding my grandparents, albeit temporarily. Booba's next hiding place was with Mademoiselle Becks, her nurse who had also treated my serious burns only a year earlier. Zeida's home, 66 rue de la Senne, was hardly a safe house, as the Nazis knew who lived there from our registrations with the *Association des Juifs en Belgique* (AJB).

Charly was, initially, protected in a Jesuit seminary, College St Michel. The Jewish boys were hidden within the buildings so as not to put the entire institution at risk, especially when Nazi soldiers came to inspect the seminary's occupants. This happened frequently and at different times of the day and night and the seminarians were told to drop their pants to show whether they had been circumcised according to Jewish, but not Catholic, custom. The Jewish boys received instruction in the Roman Catholic faith and learned the catechism. A few would forget their origins and many converted to Catholicism if their family did not live to reclaim them. A notable case was the French-born Cardinal Jean-Marie Lustiger, son of Polish Jews, who converted to Catholicism during the Second World War when hidden.

Still a small child, I remember going with my parents to a bakery on rue des Chartreux, near my grandparents' house in old Brussels. My parents were pleading about something with the bakers while I stood quietly, shifting from foot to foot, eating a pastry I had been given while waiting for my parents. I could see that my mother was crying but I did not understand then that they were begging the bakers to shelter me. My parents took a big chance, as they had no idea if those compassionate people were genuinely in the Resistance or, in fact, collaborators, thereby risking all our lives. Children, their parents and the Belgian resisters faced so many fears and dangers. As it turned out, those bakers could not help me but this memory remained a vivid illustration of our desperate state.

Moishe Lewin, Zeida's nephew, hid in various places that I gradually uncovered in documents. In the summer of 1942, the Nazis arrested him. He was allowed to remain alive to work as a slave labourer for a German engineering company, *Organisation Todt* (founded by a Nazi supporter) that was building the Atlantic Wall in the North of France. This was a system of defence consisting of bunkers at regular intervals built along the Atlantic Ocean, the length of the territories occupied by the Nazis, with the aim of preventing any possible invasion by the Allies. Just a few years later, after the unexploded mines, machine guns and barbed wire had all been removed, I would be playing alone in those disused bunkers on the Belgian coast. At the end of October 1942, Moishe's name was entered on the deportation list of Transport XVII as prisoner number 475 on that 17th Convoy. His train left the North of France on 31 October 1942 and arrived at Auschwitz-Birkenau on 3 November 1942. However, Moishe miraculously escaped from the train en route and returned to Brussels, probably on foot.

Back in Brussels, for a second time Moishe was arrested when hiding in Zeida's house. Due to registration with the AJB, it was an easy place to find Jews. It is possible that the Nazis were determined to find him because he had previously escaped. When Charly arrived with food for Moishe, he saw men in leather coats standing outside the house next to two Citroen cars and my brother knew immediately that Moishe had been recaptured.

So, on 11 February 1943, Moishe was brought to the Caserne Dossin where he was loaded for a second time into a cattle train bound for the Auschwitz-Birkenau concentration camp. This was the 20th convoy of human beings departing Malines on 19 April 1943. On the transportation list of 1,631 people, he was listed as No. 619: Lewin, Moszko (Moishe in Polish), born in Biala (Podlaska) on 10 April 1921. Three young Belgian resisters stopped that train, using just a fake warning light, a single pair of pliers and one little pistol, creating enough disruption to allow 231 Jews to escape, Moishe amongst them[25]. That train arrived in Auschwitz on 22 April 1943 without Moishe.

After walking back to Brussels, Moishe went to the Jesuit seminary, where my brother was hiding, and banged on the door asking for his young cousin. During the night curfew for Jews, this visit was dangerous for everyone in the seminary. My brother recalled that, immediately, he was told to leave the seminary because Moishe had unwittingly attracted attention to all its inhabitants. Now my brother was like many Jewish teenagers during the war, fending for himself until the end of the Nazi occupation, finding temporary refuge in basements, attics and shops, barns and forests. Sometimes he hid in dog kennels when he knew that the 'occupants' and their owners had left temporarily, sometimes for a summer holiday. His wartime involved 'being hungry all the time', living in fear for his life, alone and abused. To this day he has never told me details of his experiences and he still has nightmares every night.

Minnie never told me where she hid. I had always believed that her English friend Betty Carlier, married to a Belgian, Marius Carlier, hid her. That family myth collapsed when my brother explained that the Carliers had not been prepared to take the risk of sheltering a Jew, even a friend. Many Belgian families must have developed myths about who helped Jews hide, to sanitise the truth, either to protect the innocent or to gloss over decisions taken in self-protection.

One by one, my family members each disappeared unexpectedly, without warning. No reason was given nor was anything said that a four-year-old child could understand or accept. Suddenly, I did not know where either my mother or my brother were, nor do I remember seeing either of them again until after the war. My father took me to a family in the country who hid me successfully.

He never gave me any explanation or warning that he was leaving me there, alone. I suffered an almost-paralytic fear from that and other, repeated separations, never knowing when or if I would see him or my family again.

That feeling of uncertainty and abandonment affects me to this day.

The Bordello Madam

In the public's view, Madame Jules ran a café and hotel called Pax Taverne, located at 2 rue des Boiteux, parallel to rue Fossé aux Loups, not far from my grandparents' house. In fact, she ran a bordello! Her husband, Monsieur Jules De Heyn, engaged Zeida to make his custom suits. Madame Jules became highly significant for our family during the war, as I discovered later from Charly. Among her investments, she owned a house at 26 avenue du Couronnement in Woluwe-Saint-Lambert. Above the top floor of this two-storey house, there was an attic comprising a large room serving as kitchen and living room and there were two bedrooms.

My father paid Madame Jules to hide him and Minnie in that attic. On occasions Moishe Lewin hid there and sometimes my brother slept there as well, lying on two lounge chairs pushed together. The tenants on the first floor were a single man who worked for the German Railways and his sister who did secretarial work for them. The very presence of those other tenants represented a constant risk of discovery and arrest.

In 1944, Zeida was walking on the street and the Gestapo arrested him. Knowing that he tailored for Madame Jules' husband, Charly asked her to help save our grandfather. It turned out that the Chief of the Gestapo was one of her clients so, after she intervened, Zeida was released.

Undeterred, Zeida went outside another day, trusting his fair hair and blue eyes to disguise his Jewishness on the Nazi-controlled streets; again he was arrested. This time, Madame sent Charly to obtain a letter from a Catholic seminary, stating that 'Brother Oscar is deaf and dumb' and the message asked that anyone reading the letter should assist the Brother, enabling Zeida to be freed a second time from the Gestapo. Twice, Madame Jules' connivance and connections saved Zeida from death. He was lucky twice, as was his nephew Moishe.

Why did this bordello Madam help our Jewish family? Given her unusual if not illegal business, she was sufficiently amoral not to feel bound by Nazi laws. Perhaps she was loyal to Zeida as a long-term local businessman who made her husband's suits and maybe she felt protective of some Jews, perhaps only those whom she knew. Possibly, she was securing her future defence whenever the war with Germany ended, as she openly consorted with Nazi customers. We were her 'customers' as well, but only of her protection and discretion, two positive characteristics rarely attributed to a bordello Madam.

Perhaps one of Brussels' most accomplished 'networkers', Madame Jules had a cousin who owned a furniture shop in Tubize. Madame Jules had helped friends of her cousin who were farmers in Saintes by laundering their black market earnings from the produce they sold without Nazi-issued food coupons. The farmers were in debt to Madame Jules.

Exceptional at negotiating, Madame Jules pressed those who were obligated to her, persuading these farmers to hide a small Jewish child: me.

Chapter Four

Hiding Alone

Braving risk of detection, arrest, deportation and death, my father smuggled me to the farm in Saintes, near Tubize, not far from Brussels in the autumn of 1942. He did not explain why or how long I was going to this farm as he knew neither detail himself. My father disappeared from my sight that first day before I comprehended that I was remaining with these absolute strangers in an unknown place.

Only four years old, I felt deposited like a parcel with people whom I did not know. I was disoriented as I had only known the streets of Brussels. Instead of being with my family and my loving father, I was living in a remote farmhouse with strangers and their animals. Feeling very upset, I cried, asking when my father would return and the whereabouts of the rest of my family.

I felt utterly abandoned and was distraught. Dwork summed up the feeling which I shared with many other Jews in Belgium of having 'a fundamental lack of comprehension of why they were forced to leave their homes, their families, their friends'.[26] My crying must have gone on for days and, following many reprimands, I was slapped for punishment and deterrence. Perhaps these farmers were afraid that the Nazis could have heard about a sobbing child or that collaborators, who knew they were childless, would report them.

My father would have known or suspected that my hosts were part of the local Resistance if they were prepared to hide a Jewish child. The owners of this small farm were Auguste, his wife Marie and their daughter Catherine whose husband was Jean: they did not have children. Repeatedly I was instructed that, should anybody ask who I was or where I came from, I must say that I had come to my country cousins to recuperate from tuberculosis that was endemic in the crowded living conditions at that time. When I looked outside, there were no other houses nearby, so we were quite isolated from outsiders: safe but lonely.

Fortunately, I did not have to change my name and lose that part of my identity. After I was born, my mother had planned to name me Frances but, since Catholicism was the main religion in Belgium, the authorities refused to register that name as it was not the name of a Catholic Saint; they did,

23. Francine with her two dolls, outside the farmhouse in Saintes Belgium, mid-1943. This was Francine's first hiding place, 1942 to mid-1943.

however, agree on Francine. With a last name derived from my father's Prussian heritage, it too passed as a Belgian name so I remained Francine Kamerman. Recovery after the war must have been more difficult for hidden children who had been given new identities to protect them. They had the challenges of reconciling their two different names and two life stories,[27] from before the war and with their fictitious names, if they returned to their surviving families. Their psychological turmoil exceeded mine, especially those young children who only knew themselves as the fabricated hidden child with a fictitious family story.

When first in hiding, I did not feel completely removed from my identity, despite my sudden and harsh separation from my family. I only had to pretend that I was a cousin of my protectors as, fortunately, I could keep my true name. It was not enough to stop me feeling devastated, sad, lonely, lost and very scared, and such debilitating feelings were common. Vrome talks of 'Children's struggles with being left by their families and their confusion when arriving at the new housing ... [and] the need to instruct children to avoid discovery or denunciation and their massive efforts to fend off Nazis and collaborators'[28]. My father visited me only once that I can remember, risking his life to travel in and out of Brussels. During the war, I did not know where he was hiding.

Still, I had to lie about who I was, as did my hosts. While they knew some of my identity, obviously that I was Jewish and they knew my father, they possibly had no more details. They definitely knew that my family was under the protection of Madame Jules.

From four years of age, I no longer interacted with my family and, therefore, I could not maintain deep emotional relationships with my parents and brother. In retrospect, I can see how the bond weakened between Minnie and me. I idealised that bond as our relationship but it was never restored between us.

From this time on, I learned not to express my emotions. Sadness stealthily invaded my being. Terrible nightmares came every evening and the following morning I was punished for wetting my bed. From what I recall, in most ways, all four adults gave me good care as I was well fed, enjoyed fresh air, outside play and slept in a clean bed. As I grew, they provided garments to replace my clothes and the shoes in which I had arrived. Their care gave me a firm basis on which to survive for the remainder of the war. The worst feelings were my homesickness and loneliness and the overwhelming confusion I felt about where I was, why I was at this farm and when I would return to my family in Brussels.

While I hungered for warmth from a person's heart, I no longer felt the warm love that I remembered from my parents. I yearned for physical closeness – a hug, a pat on the shoulder or a kiss would have made me feel more wanted. Cumulative trauma, after being left in this hiding place and many subsequent placements, reinforced my acute feeling of being unloved. Soon I thought that I was not loveable; eventually I became convinced that I was not worthy of being loved.

Two dolls were my only toys: one without legs and the other without arms. Eyelids on each doll opened and shut when I tilted the dolls back and forth, revealing incredibly beautiful blue-painted eyes. One made a sound like 'Mama'. A single photo of me with the two dolls, standing next to the farmhouse, is the only remaining evidence of my time in that home and, indeed, of my hidden years. Perhaps the farm owners took the photo for my parents as the reverse shows it was printed in nearby Tubize. It was thrilling to see this image many years later in a box of family photos. It captured how isolated I was as a toddler, physically and emotionally.

Catherine taught me how to play the card game Solitaire or Patience with her during the long winter evenings, the only playtime I remember with another person in the years of hiding. She taught me how to count and to recognise numbers to play cards, so it was my first informal education and I would always be accurate with numbers. Chores kept me busy and helping with the laundry was one of my pleasures. The family used rendered animal fat to make their own soap which looked like honey. Two of us twisted the sheets to wring them waterless before laying them on the grass to dry in the sun. I slept in those sweet-smelling sheets in a bed in the older couple's room. However, I was frightened each night because Auguste snored loudly.

It was the custom for little girls to have their ears pierced at four or five years of age. One day, Catherine threaded a needle and held it over a flame to sterilise it to pierce my ears. She did this by holding a piece of cork behind my earlobe and pushing the hot needle through to the cork, leaving the thread in my ear to keep the hole open. I guess it must have been painful but I was thrilled that I would have pierced ears and one day I would wear earrings just like my mother and grandmother. Unfortunately, the wounds became infected but I was healthy enough to overcome the infection; there was no medicine available. Those scars remain on my earlobes and even professional piercing has ended with infection, so I have never been able to wear earrings for pierced ears as I had once hoped.

Farm animals were my playmates and provided many thrills for a city child. Auguste taught me how to milk a cow but when I first sat next to him on a little stool, my small hands did not bring out any milk. He laughed and took over and then squirted milk in my face; soon I became more proficient. Leaning into the cow's side when I milked her was comforting, her warmth and soft hide providing a primal experience of physical intimacy. I helped to make butter, taking my turn to churn the cream by hand, and I liked the homemade cheese we made.

Outdoors we wore roomy wooden clogs on the farm that we removed and lined up outside when we came in, changing into slippers to wear inside the house. Catherine painted flowers on the clogs that she gave me; soon my growing feet could only fit in my clogs. I fed the chickens, scattering seed while calling out, 'cheep, cheep, cheep'; I especially liked the white hens. The farm pig was my pet but, unbeknown to me, it was intended for food to sell at the market. When it was killed and I saw its blood, I was very upset. In all my time on the farm, I was never allowed to be alone because the family was worried that I might be seen.

My only outing was going to church in the horse and cart, but after the Nazis requisitioned the horse, Auguste or Jean pushed me in their wheelbarrow. Every day I had to go to the church in the village, Sainte Reineldis, with my hosts. It seemed excessively devout but it was probable that adults exchanged family information and relayed messages in the relative safety of churches. If someone had a clandestine radio, war information was shared in the sanctity of this building. I did not learn any of the news that adults whispered among themselves. I did learn to say many of the Christian prayers, yet another means of concealing my true identity and religion. I knelt for what seemed an eternity and became fascinated with the square marks on my knees from the raffia straw prayer kneelers. Several times, Catherine took me with her into the confessional booth, most likely to keep me hidden from an untrusted adult in the church.

Having to keep quiet in church when I had a myriad of questions for which I desperately wanted answers, I became introspective and did not share my thoughts. Such introspection resurfaced as I reconsidered my childhood for this memoir because so many sad memories returned in spite of the occasional catharsis seven decades on. At times I have longed to return to my earlier childhood when all things seemed possible.

Still I had no contact with other children, although some lived nearby and I saw others at church. Perhaps this was another means of keeping me safe, constantly kept at a distance from others. I think it was for the family's security as well, in case their small 'cousin' forgot her story.

The only visit from my father was memorable, not for what we did together but because he left me so quickly again, using subterfuge to leave without me noticing. I felt so helpless. Why could my father not stay with me when I wanted him to be with me and make my life happier? While I often wondered why he took such a risk to leave Brussels and travel to visit me in Saintes, in hindsight he was probably bringing payments for my safety. He would have taken fresh food back to our family in Brussels, braving risks again when returning with his black market supplies.

From the time my father took me to live in Saintes, I cannot remember ever seeing Minnie. Daily, I wondered if she could have visited me at the same time as my father. Did she know that I missed her? Was she waiting for me in Brussels? Feeling abandoned by those I loved and only tolerated by those with whom I lived, my heart ached to be with my own family once again. After the war, I understood that it was too dangerous for her to leave her hiding place and buy a ticket to travel on public transport, especially with her English accent, let alone the Star of David sewn onto her coat.

My father rightly believed that I was safer hidden on that farm under the patronage of the bordello Madam. Daily, my family in Brussels had to avoid the round-ups of Jews that were increasing in frequency and viciousness. Their little girl could have caused all of them to be arrested if I had remained with them.

However, one day, a truck lumbered up to the farmhouse and, as it approached, Catherine grabbed me and pushed me into one of the nearby haystacks that I was surprised to discover was hollow. She hid with me and we saw what was happening through the straw. It was summer time because, from my straw hiding place, I saw beautiful big ripe peaches trained *en espalier*, the fruit trees clinging to the wall of the farmhouse for maximum exposure to the sun.

Murderous soldiers

When the truck stopped, uniformed soldiers and men in civilian clothes, either Gestapo or local collaborators, all jumped to the ground. Whether Auguste and Jean tried to escape or if they were being taken away or a soldier was trigger-happy, nobody told me and I will never know. We heard gunshots and then saw their blood splattered onto the wall and over the peaches. Catherine held me tightly between her legs, pressing her hands over my mouth lest I should scream or make a noise. I was rigid with fear and I could barely breathe. Were the men killed or injured? I never saw or heard of them again. My sole focus was on surviving.

Then our situation became even more terrifying as, following their search of the farmhouse, the soldiers walked outside and picked up farm implements that they pitched into the haystacks, including the one in which Catherine and I were hiding. One pitchfork stabbed my neck just behind my right ear with two tines of the dirty fork. Those scars remain, alongside the one caused by the boiling water a couple of years before. Doubling over with pain, another implement struck me from the other side, digging into my right calf; still I did not utter a sound. They were not looking for a little Jewish girl without valid identity papers. More probably they were searching for hidden arms and munitions or Resistance members. Luckily for us, they did not notice my blood which probably wiped off as the pitchforks were withdrawn from the haystack.

At this critical moment, action seemed to freeze and we waited silently for their departure. All the females were safe for the time being. We had no time to grieve as it was so important to stay alert and to deal with the daily pressure to stay alive.

Treating my wounds to prevent infection was a problem. Since 1942, when non-Jewish doctors could not treat Jews and Jewish doctors could not practice, there was no one who could help. Everyone in the area would have known that the two men had been shot and either killed or taken away. Catherine could not have trusted any doctor to know about our escape from the Gestapo. She treated my injuries as well as she could. Throughout my life, I have remained very grateful to Catherine and Marie for all they did to help me recover and stay alive and safe while hidden. My scars remind me of them, my saviours, and our lucky escapes from death.

Marie and Catherine could not look after the farm by themselves and decided to leave. After the war, as I was still a small child, I was too young to take any independent actions to find and thank them by, for example, visiting Saintes. Later, as an adult, I did not know their full names and I could not find them in Belgium. I wanted to thank them in person and have them recognised for their deeds that saved me.

In my heart, I will always thank and honour Auguste and Marie, their daughter Catherine and son-in-law Jean for being the epitome of Righteous Gentiles, hiding and saving me at great risk to themselves.

Since the fork stab in the haystack I have always had a large scar, two centimetres wide and three centimetres long on my neck. After the war, children at school teased me for my 'dirty' neck, referring to the discolouration of the scar. The scar on my right leg was also visible. As signposts to my hidden years, my scars had a story to tell but I never felt able to volunteer to anyone what had really happened to me.

For many years, I had nightmares about Auguste and Jean's probable deaths and the sight of blood on the peaches. I could not understand what had happened to them. I could not eat fresh peaches for many years, as they always carried connotations of blood, fear and death.

Nazi footsteps

Aged five and a half years, in the early autumn of 1943, I was returned to Brussels after approximately one year on the farm at Saintes. On the day that was possibly my homecoming to Brussels, I was holding my father's hand and we were walking in rue Camusel, near my grandparents' house in the city. Perhaps he was returning me from the farm., as walking on the streets of Brussels in broad daylight was the only time Jews were allowed outside, due to the curfew. Of course, my father must have held something, such as a newspaper, to cover the Star of David sewn on his outer clothing, lest he be identified as a Jew and arrested, captured in a round-up or killed on the spot. I would have been treated in the same manner.

Hearing heavy marching footsteps behind us, my father immediately jumped into a building foyer and pushed me behind its entrance door. Then he crushed himself behind me and our hearts quickened. I was hiding inside his big black overcoat, the aroma of which, mixed with the smell of our fear, remains with me forever.

As the steps receded, we waited until the stampeding in our chests slowed, then tiptoed away from our hiding place. This is my most vivid memory of my father, feeling enveloped by his warmth and protection as he held me closely to him. If he had not acted so quickly we would have been discovered and I might not have survived the Holocaust.

Changing places

Survival during the war relied on being watchful and rapidly adapting to new circumstances and chance. There was nowhere safe to hide but, thanks to an active Resistance in Belgium, I survived. Volunteers, mostly non-Jews, risked their lives to courier Jewish children like me between 'safe' houses. Put yourself in the shoes of these women. Many were still teenagers, knowing that they were heading for trouble each time they walked a Jewish child between two hiding places. They had two incomparable defences: leadership and courage, along with ingenuity to avoid detection.

I was shuttled between many hiding places. I cannot remember even one dwelling or any caregiver or sharing a room with another child. I was moved frequently between houses, seemingly every few days, when an adult, always a female, arrived and then took me to a new hiding place. Like many hidden children, with each move, I 'felt repeatedly overwhelmed by feelings of abandonment' which evoked permanent feelings of rejection.[29] I felt frightened every time I saw the uniforms of the occupiers on the streets and the Nazi flags suspended from buildings.

Only when I was much older did I recognise my latent need to meet and thank those women who couriered me to safety so many times and to show my respect for their lifesaving deeds. Until that time, I was not able to remember, accept or research my hidden years. Perhaps a fear of reconnecting with that high-risk period in my childhood held me back from seeking their names. It was too late to find them and thank them in person by the time I had overcome my fears.

Adeline Fohn's excellent research revealed that the more times hidden Jewish children changed their placements, the greater their anxieties about being denunciated or caught in a round-up.[30] Her findings resonated with me, in the sense that I have always felt anxious. As Decoster concluded, after analysing seventy-two child survivors' testimonies, 'the hidden children, from the youngest to the oldest, lived with the fear of being caught or betrayed by someone at any moment. The older children often knew exactly what they feared, whereas the young children and toddlers feared more in general. Even if they did not understand the exact threat, they knew their lives were in danger'.[31]

When I consider what life was like for a five-year-old child whom the Nazis had vowed to kill, I realise that I was never at home; I merely changed hiding places. I could not live with my family, as they were all in hiding and in constant danger of being discovered and sent to their deaths. Every day and each night was distressing. People had to black out their windows with paint, paper or curtains, so that they could not signal to the Allies. We were in complete darkness at night, not even a star could be seen, adding to the tension. If I heard voices, footsteps or vehicles outside, I could not see who was coming or if they were coming for me.

Neither carers nor children could afford to relax; the tension and mental pressure of that time has never left me all my life. We were preoccupied with surviving in our hiding places, crying silently or worrying about whether we would be alive the next day. One of the most debilitating aspects was always maintaining vigilance and making no noise. This resulted in constant pressure on a small child already suffering deprivation and hunger. Yet, like any young child, I looked forward to what each new day would bring, always hoping to see my family.

I felt abandoned by my parents whom I perpetually longed to be with in this very scary time. I was still in shock from seeing the shooting of Auguste and Jean. As a young child, I did not recognise that many of my feelings were cumulative grief and trauma, feelings that I could not articulate clearly. There was no one with whom I could share my overwhelming and crushing emotions nor was there anyone from whom I could receive guidance.

Yet, there was a pool of courage in me that I drew on to trust and live with strangers, again and again, and to believe that each assault by Gestapo or bombs would not touch me. Now I believe that I used up a good part of my reserve of courage in those war years. This was a great load, physically and emotionally for a child who was not yet old enough to start school. By my late teens, I would collapse under my emotional burden.

In addition to being in fear of death constantly and without reprieve, I was continuously hungry as there was insufficient food during the war. To make things worse, hidden Jews had no food ration coupons that were issued by the Nazis. We relied on our protectors being able to purchase food on the black market, if available, at highly inflated prices. The limited food we ate was not sustaining or balanced, causing physical suffering and psychological trauma with long-term health effects. Most meals consisted of bread and *saindoux* (lard) with soups made from dried legumes. Very seldom was there meat, milk, fruit or fresh vegetables.

The rough living, the freezing winters and hot summers, the lack of food, medicine, soap and water all combined to weaken our hidden bodies. We were pallid from being kept inside all the time, emaciated from starvation and had regularly looked death and disaster in the face. Malnourished, I succumbed to scurvy and developed scabies during these war years.

Lice were also relentlessly biting and itching. The lice were fun; they were my pets. I shook them off my head onto a piece of paper and made them race each other. I squeezed them and then made little colourful patterns with my blood. Materially, we owned the bare minimum. Children changed their one set of clothes with another child's, partly to disguise us when being moved between buildings. As we grew, we needed larger clothes that only became available when handed down from an older child; these were often infested with lice. Clothes were not washed regularly as laundry was the lowest priority when hiding, compared with surviving hunger, round-ups and feeling constant fear. Practically, as laundry was hung outside to air dry, our clothing would have signalled extra children in a house, thus revealing our hiding places and identifying our protectors.

Another debilitating deficiency was the horrendously poor sanitation. I never washed in a bath, only using water from a basin and rarely soap to clean my body. There were no toothbrushes or toothpastes, so I substituted sand as an abrasive and rubbed my teeth with my finger. There was no toilet paper during the war; sometimes there was not even old newspaper to use in the outdoor toilets and I could only wipe myself with leaves. Still, I managed to keep my two precious dolls, my only constants throughout so many changing circumstances.

One hiding place was in an attic in Brussels. One night there was a round-up of Jews occurring in that street. To avoid detection, I was quickly thrust through a little hopper window out of the attic and pushed onto the rooftop to cling to the roof tiles. I heard heavy footsteps running up and down the stairs in the building, no doubt the Nazis checking for hidden Jews. Fright overwhelmed me and I was immobilised on the rooftop.

Incredibly, the safest place for me that night was clinging alone to a steeply sloping roof, hoping the tiles were secure, all the while fearing that the Nazis would look out of the attic or up from the street and see me. Once again, things went from bad to worse when, suddenly, I heard an unmanned missile approaching my location, followed by a mammoth explosion. The flames illuminated a vast area. From my rooftop perspective it looked like a whole city block was alight. I was rigid with fear, as though I had turned into stone, and I cannot remember leaving the roof. Despite many bombings, I remained alive and protected by my carers. There was no question of the Resistance giving me up or giving in to the Nazis.

This extreme episode combined several fears of death all at once. Like every Jew, I feared being caught by Nazis and, like everyone in a war, I worried about being killed by bombs. The risk I had faced of falling off the unstable roof tiles and dying as a result left me afraid of heights at six years of age. Death had loomed over me from when I was just three years old. The intensity of the risks I endured during the war made the description, 'an anxious childhood', inadequate and trite. My degradation contributed to my feelings of shame when I recalled how basely I lived to survive. Perversely, I later blamed myself for living so crudely in these grim childhood years caused by the Nazis and the war conditions.

After many temporary shelters, a slightly more permanent hiding place was provided by Monsieur Mason, formerly my grandfather's accountant. The Masons kept me alive for a few months longer. Nowhere was guaranteed safe but they kept me away from the Nazi killing machine. I remained completely hidden in their apartment, never seen and never heard. To stay alive, it was necessary to cease childish behaviour, never playing or laughing, talking or crying, in order to avoid detection or betrayal which would be followed by death for all of us.

Most probably it was while I was hidden by the Masons that I received a new toy, a miniature porcelain coffee set, decorated with lovely decals showing happy children playing with a train set and other bright toys. I loved pretending that I was entertaining other children and grown-ups, drinking special coffee and eating imaginary biscuits. I kept this set all my life, safe among my few possessions.

Mademoiselle Mason was in her twenties, living with her parents, and I shared her bedroom. She said that she was working for the Resistance. Many times she brought German officers back to the apartment. I was led to believe that she was doing this to help the Resistance not to obtain the chocolate, silk stockings or other gifts which I saw her receive.

When each visitor arrived, I had to jump into her clothes cupboard, shut its flimsy door firmly behind me and then hide on its floor under clothing and in complete darkness, keeping absolutely quiet in that stuffy enclosed space. I was terrified and remember vividly that I could not scratch my scabies which were very itchy. All the while, I would pray that the visitor would soon go away. I heard men's voices talking and laughing. Usually I was required to hide, totally still, for a long time which seemed like an eternity to a child. Only that rickety cupboard door separated me from a Nazi and certain death. After an hour or two of fear, cramped in the dark, I again enjoyed my relative freedom of movement within the apartment – partial respite from my bouts of hiding behind the wobbly cupboard door.

Decoster, in her book on Jewish hidden children in Belgium, comments that, 'Most of the children in this situation experienced extreme fear of being caught'.[32] All the factors were stressful and incomprehensible. I was separated from my family, hidden with strangers, governed by severe restrictions such as not making a sound or being seen from a window. In addition, I suffered the repeated hazards of hearing round-ups and bombings. Constantly, I was exposed to those many traumatic experiences, confronted with destruction, fear and death. They were superimposed on my continuous and underlying disturbances following separation from my family and the absence of basic comforts and the entire repeated and accumulated psychological trauma I have described. Those locked cupboard hours could well have contributed to my adult-onset of agoraphobia that later transformed into panic attacks when driving through a tunnel, over a bridge or whenever I see reminders of dangerous places.

Infrequently, my father visited me, each time very briefly. He would bring a little loaf of bread from Monsieur De Noose, the baker and relative by marriage, who hid my grandparents for a short period. My father did not know that the Masons took the bread from me as soon as he left. Maybe it served as an additional payment for keeping me safe. Of course, it was very dangerous for my father to be out of hiding on the Nazi-infested streets but he cared more about my wellbeing than for his own safety. At the time, I did not know that I had received my final hug from my father when he visited me the very last time at the Masons.

Throughout all my times at these shelters, I never felt that I belonged to these temporary families and, of course, I just wanted to live again with my family. In his 2003 article, Durst described his early hidden childhood in Belgium with such clarity that his experiences appeared almost identical to mine.

Durst wrote that:

> The devastating reality I had to go through required new coping mechanisms, abandoning baby ways and feeling abandoned by my

parents. When in hiding, I kept longing and thinking about my relatives and kept them alive to me at least in fantasy. While my memories of that deprived childhood that included many losses and cumulative traumatic stresses remain vivid, I have never revealed much of my feelings of longing and grief.[33]

All I wanted to add to Durst's eloquent soliloquy, to summarise my feelings when hidden and afterwards, was 'especially longing and grief for my father'.

From June 1944, just after the Allies' Normandy landings, the nightly attacks by the German Vergeltungswaffei (V1) missiles were horrific, possibly the worst assaults during the war. These unmanned flying bombs were developed by the Nazis to strike London but frequently failed to reach their targets over the sea, bombing Belgium instead with devastating results. They caused massive fires and destruction as they fell indiscriminately on housing, schools and open spaces. A screeching sound announced their arrival overhead and it was impossible to gauge where or if they would fall.

Abruptly, the Masons decided that I could no longer hide with them. Charly recalled that he was sent to fetch me when I was six years old, left standing alone in front of the Masons' house in Nazi-occupied Brussels, opposite the Gestapo headquarters decorated with the Nazi red flags, fluttering as I waited. I did not remember having seen Charly since our family went into hiding two years earlier. By mid-1944, I was so accustomed to people coming to fetch me to go to a new hiding place, I would probably have left with anybody. Of course, Zeida knew where I was hidden and sent my brother to collect me from the Masons. Charly must have fetched me just before Brussels was liberated and he took me to our grandparents' house at 66 rue de la Senne. I do not remember who else was living there. By then I was quite weak, both physically and emotionally.

Since I had left Brussels two years earlier with my father to hide in Saintes, I do not remember having seen my mother although I longed for her presence and her love. Less and less did I think about her when hidden for those years. Even after I was returned to my grandparents following the Liberation, it seemed a very long time until I saw my mother again. By that time I was over six years old and I no longer missed her. It is possible that I had forgotten what my mother meant to me. Yet I would come to yearn for her love and approval in my teen years and for the rest of my life.

On or soon after 4 September 1944, Charly and I watched General Montgomery's troops ride in their tanks through the old streets of Brussels. German snipers were still shooting from the rooftops but the joyful crowds ignored them and everyone was cheering. Everyone was happy. I did not understand that there had been a war or what that meant to my family or what its impact would be on the rest of our lives.

24. Francine in the lounge room of grandparents Booba and Zeida, with brother Charly, 1944.

Some soldiers were throwing chocolate bars out to the crowd and Charly caught one. He shared it with me and we were sick very soon after consuming it. We had eaten only basic food for years and experienced starvation; our stomachs were no longer able to digest such rich food.

In spite of the celebrations, my war did not end in 1944. The chain of traumatic experiences for me and my family continued.

Chapter Five

My Father Arrested

Nazi malice had ruled two-thirds of my early childhood, until I was six years and six months of age. Only after the Liberation and when I came out of hiding did I learn a terrible truth. The Nazis had taken my father.

While I never knew with certainty where my family hid during the war, I presumed that my father lived at my grandparents' house, 66 rue de la Senne, hiding there with Zeida. Little coincidences, such as being close to that house when my father and I were walking on my return from the farm, reinforced my childish conclusions. I became convinced, decades later, when I saw documentation from the Belgian Department of Security (the Police Department for Foreigners) that my parents were on record as residing at 66 rue de la Senne during the war.

After I learned that my father was forced to give this address to the *l'Association des Juifs en Belgique* (AJB) I realised that he could not have stayed there all the time as, logically, the Gestapo knew his address and could arrest him. In hindsight, my theory made no sense. I guessed that he may have gone in and out of there but surely he was hiding somewhere safer.

Likewise, I formed an idea or received misleading clues about my mother's hiding place. In fact, our parents lived, unofficially, at 26 avenue du Couronnement, out of sight, in a property owned by Madame Jules.

Possibly, my father knew that the Allies had landed in Normandy on D-Day, 6 June 1944, about 500 kilometres to the west. If so, he would have known that Brussels would soon be free. Why did my father leave his hiding place in daytime and walk on the streets in late July 1944? According to Charly, who was then hiding with our parents, my father left the relative safety of the house in daylight to find food for those in hiding on what would be his last day as a free man.

It must have been horrifying for my father. He was suddenly stopped, searched, facing guns pointed at him and forced into a truck. He must have realised that he was not going home that night and probably would never see his family again.

For decades, I thought I was the cause of my father's arrest and deportation. My long-held and haunting fear was that my father was on his way to visit me in hiding at the Masons when he was caught in a round-up of Jews. I imagined that, if I had told him that I never ate the bread that he brought, perhaps he would not have been on the street that day. I had always assumed that I was responsible for his arrest and death and felt enormous guilt for most of my life.

In another fearful scenario, I wonder if my father could have been a victim of the notorious Jewish traitor who was driven around Brussels in a Gestapo car, spotting fellow Jews whom he denounced by identifying them to the Nazis. Jacques the *Moussa* (Yiddish for denouncer) was blamed for over two hundred arrests.[34]

After his capture, my father would have been taken to the holding barracks of the Caserne Dossin in Malines. Just once, Charly took a parcel there for

25. The Caserne Dossin, Jews unloaded from trucks following arrest by Nazis during the Second World War before transportation to Auschwitz. My father was held here before being sent to Auschwitz. Courtesy Caserne Dossin – Mémorial, Musée et Centre de documentation sur l'Holocauste et les Droits de l'homme.

our father. As he arrived, he saw a family friend and former neighbour, Dina Lewkowicz, who was volunteering with the AJB. She urgently told Charly to run away as he was at risk of arrest if his Jewishness was discovered. In a perverse irony, my brother returned to those same barracks, post-war, to serve his compulsory Belgian military service.

In the summer heat of July, my father and all the prisoners in the Caserne Dossin waited in the open square without shelter or sustenance. Many prisoners were already weakened by the privations from years of hiding and

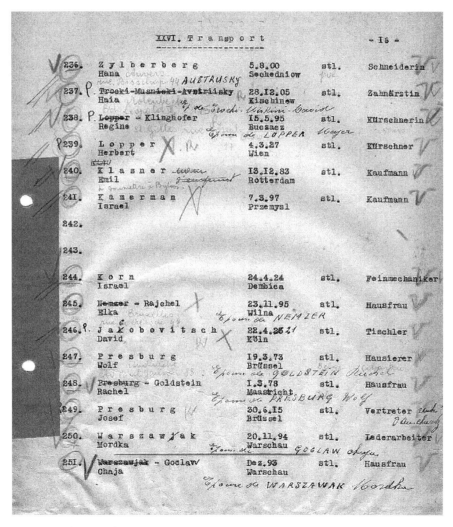

26. Entry for Israel Kamerman in XXVI Transport from the Caserne Dossin to Auschwitz, July 1944, sixth entry, prisoner number 241.

ROYAUME DE BELGIQUE 17 ANNEXE VI.

Commune de Woluwe Saint Lambert

Arrondissement de Bruxelles

Province de Brabant

Numéro du dossier de la Sûreté publique.

POLICE DES ÉTRANGERS

1.482.584

Avis d'arrivée d'étranger (1)

Les ressortissants (nationalité), polonais *désignés ci-dessous, a été*

inscrits le 14 novembre 1944 *au registre* { ~~des étrangers~~ / *de population* } *de cette commune,*

rue Av.du Couronnement,26 , *n°* *venant de* Bruxelles

rue de la Penne,66 *n°*

NOM	PRENOMS	LIEU DE NAISSANCE	DATE DE NAISSANCE	ETAT CIVIL	PROFESSION
KAMERMAN	Israel	Przmysl	7-3-1897	mar.	voyageur commerce
		arrêté par les allemands.			
INBERG	Masza	Biala-Podlaska	15-5-1909	ép.	sans
KAMERMAN	Charles Max	Etterbeek	15-8-1931	fils	
KAMERMAN	Francine	Ixelles	12-3-1938	fille	

Ces ~~cet~~ étrangers sont en possession { ~~d'un certificat d'inscription au registre des étrangers~~ / *d'une carte d'identité* }

valable jusqu'au 27 décembre 1945

A Woluwe Saint Lambert , *le* 27 novembre 1944 *194*

Pr.*Le Bourgmestre,*
(ou son délégué)
l'Agent Spécial,

A Monsieur le Ministre de l'Intérieur,
Office central de Statistique
Bruxelles.

ou

M. l'Administrateur de la Sûreté
publique,
Place Poelaert, 4, Bruxelles.

O 13². — Imp. E. Guyot, s. a., Bruxelles.

(1) Ne peut concerner qu'un seul étranger. S'il est marié, son épouse et ses enfants âgés de moins de 15 ans accomplis y seront mentionnés.

20

27 Registration 'arrested by Germans', 14 November 1944.

some died. The living were crammed together into cattle cars with standing room only, denied food or water for the train trip which lasted many days taking them to their deaths. Many did not arrive alive when the trains pulled into Auschwitz.

Even as the Allies had almost reached Paris, my father was herded into the XXVI (26th) transport. Cruel fate put him on that very last transportation of Jews from Belgium, departing on 31 July 1944. Only five weeks later, the Allies liberated Brussels. Our family knew he was arrested but we all hoped he was not dead and would soon return. For years, I waited in hope for my father to return.

The manifest of my father's transportation documented how zealously the Belgian police and Nazi officials ticked and re-marked each name several times. They strove to make sure that everybody left on their designated train to the Auschwitz death camp and then to their assigned death. The last deportation from the Caserne Dossin in Malines was of 249 men, 268 women and 46 children. My father was Number 241 on the list of 249 men. Did this mean that he was the eighth-last male Jew transported from Belgium? What a wicked fate for him and for me.

About three days' train ride later, 2 or 3 August 1944, my father arrived in Auschwitz. There is no record of him being tattooed with a prisoner number, such was the haste to kill him, nor was his arrival in Auschwitz recorded in the files of the camp as his extermination was the next step after arrival. His journey ended with the steps he took to his death in the gas chambers.

A witness later told Minnie that my father reported to the infirmary, a euphemism for the gas chambers. That was the Nazi modus operandi later in the war, accelerating the rate of murder of Jews as their real goal, regardless of losing the war against the Allies.

I did not believe that my father was dead. At first, I believed and hoped that he would come back home. After all, the Allies were winning the war against the Nazis at the time that my father was arrested and transported to Auschwitz. Steinberg calculated the death rate of Belgian racial deportees to Auschwitz as 63.7 per cent who went directly to their deaths in the gas chambers, while 32.8 per cent subsequently died or were murdered.[35] My beloved father only had a 4 per cent chance of surviving Auschwitz. Of all the Jews in Belgium before the Second World War, 28,900 were murdered or 44 per cent of the pre-war Jewish population.[36]

For years I believed my father was alive. Gradually, belief and conviction faded into a fond hope that he had survived somewhere, somehow. As years passed without him, I never fully accepted that he was dead. Two months after Belgium was liberated, on 10 November 1944, my mother formally registered herself, Charly and me as leaving the address at 66 rue du la Senne and moving, on 14 November, to 26 avenue du Couronnement in Woluwe-Saint-

PROVINCE DE BRABANT

ARRONDISSEMENT
DE
BRUXELLES

PROVINCIE BRABANT

ARRONDISSEMENT
BRUSSEL

Commune de Woluwe-Saint-Lambert
Gemeente Sint-Lambrechts-Woluwe

Extrait du registre ~~aux actes de~~
supplétoire pour l'année 1950.-

Uittreksel uit het register der
akten voor het jaar

N° 6.-Entre le premier septembre mil neuf cent quarante-quatre et
le trente et un décembre mil neuf cent quarante-cinq, est _____
mort pour la Belgique en un lieu indéterminé :_____
Kamerman Izraël, né à Przemysl, Galicée(Autriche) le sept mars
mil huit cent nonante-sept, fils de Kamerman Hersz et de Kamerman Chaja, ayant résidé en dernier lieu à Bruxelles, rue de la
Senne, soixante-six._____

Droits à percevoir :
Timbres . . . . 30.
Droit d'expédition 15.
Total . 45.

Te heffen rechten :
Zegel . . . . . .
Afschriftrecht . . . .
Totaal .

Pour extrait conforme :
Voor eensluidend uittreksel :

Woluwe-Saint-Lambert, le 9 mars 1960.
Sint-Lambrecht-Woluwe, de

L'Officier de l'Etat Civil,
De Ambtenaar van de Burgerlijke Stand,

Délivré
Afgeleverd

J. DE LANNOY

28. Extract of death registration of Israel Kamerman (1950), Belgian government. 'He died for Belgium in an undetermined place.' Issued 9 March 1960.

Lambert. That was the address at which my parents had paid Madame Jules to hide them, from 1942. It is likely that Minnie came out of hiding after the Liberation, just five weeks after my father's arrest, to formally declare Woluwe-Saint-Lambert as her 'current' address, declaring that her husband had been arrested. An official wrote the words '*arrêté par les allemands*' (arrested by

29. Gas Chamber in Auschwitz where my father, Israel Kamerman, died in early August 1944. Visit to Auschwitz, 1999.

30. Memorial candle shines for Israel Kamerman, my father, Auschwitz crematorium. Visit to Auschwitz, 1999.

the Germans) next to my father's name. At the time of writing those words, we did not know that my father was dead.

On 18 June 1946, Minnie again reported to the Belgian police department for foreigners. The documentation declared that my father died '*in Duitschland, Auschwitsch*'. Even this report on his death was incorrectly entered, as he died in 1944 in Auschwitz in Poland.

In February 1947, my father was crossed off the foreign population register at 26 avenue du Couronnement, recorded as leaving for '*destination inconnue*' (destination unknown). By now it appeared to be accepted that he would not return, given that he had been arrested by the Nazis almost three years earlier.

My father was murdered in Auschwitz in 1944. I was left without a father at the age of six.

Chapter Six

Enforced Silence

After the war, I was told that I was a lucky child because I had survived. True, my brother and I were lucky in one respect, in the sense that we were alive when slightly fewer than 6,000 Jewish children in Belgium survived after the war. We two were amongst the 3,000 who lost one or both parents.[37] Barely 11 per cent of the Jewish children who were alive in 1939 throughout Europe survived the war. The Nazis murdered more than one and a half million children in Europe. Chance contributed to my survival.

Forcibly, my mother, grandparents and other relatives told me never to speak of my wartime experiences and to forget everything that had happened to me. It was the prevailing wisdom that young children could not remember. Certainly, we were considered 'lucky' in comparison with children who died and those who had endured the horrors of the concentration and labour camps. This directive created a wall of silence so, even when I met other Jewish children at school or in the neighbourhood, we never talked about our war experiences, keeping our secrets from each other.

Our tacit silence was almost universal according to the study by Ngo & Roos, aptly entitled, *Silence within a world of words: why it took almost fifty years after the Holocaust for 'hidden children' to speak out.*[38]

Of course, Minnie felt embarrassed by my awkward truths and possible inference of any parental neglect and she insisted that I should not talk about my war experiences. 'Nothing happened to you', was her admonition, a tacit threat to prevent me from mentioning anything that I had seen or done. She always refused to answer my questions about our past years, separately and together, and especially about my father.

Prohibited from talking about everything that had happened to me and those around me, I could not express my grief for the loss of my father or begin to mourn his death. Confused about the disjunction between what I knew had happened and being told to say nothing of my war experiences, I felt ashamed and a fraud, as I was no longer telling the truth. I could not talk about Catherine and Marie saving me on the farm nor ask for adult assistance to find and thank them after the war in person.

Because I was admonished not to talk about what happened to me during the war, I had no means of resolving my feelings or making sense of the distinctly scary events that very few other children had experienced. Now it felt wrong to remember those times and I felt bad for wanting to talk to anyone about my experiences. I began to blame myself for my wartime memories. I felt embarrassed and ashamed of everything that had happened to me.

Survivors not telling their stories, or editing the grisly details out of their true experiences, would have satisfied the Nazis. Many of the last witnesses to their atrocities, child Survivors like myself, have yet to share their entire experience. It was the failure of the Nazis to find me in the haystack and thousands of other Jewish children hidden in Belgium and elsewhere that ultimately ruined their plan to kill all Jewish children and thereby leave no witnesses. Their 'Final Solution' to kill all Jews failed: we survived them!

However, my life was altered irreversibly. From my fourth to sixth years of age, I had suffered the anguish of feeling abandoned while living with the constant fear of discovery and death. Uninterrupted isolation, coupled with no permanent relationships drove me into a sustained state of loneliness and left me quite bare of emotional expression, as though I had a hole in my heart.

I wanted to reunite with my father. I had vague hopes for a peaceful life after all this chaos ended. Unfortunately, there was never to be any normalcy for me, marred as I was by many physical and emotional scars of that terrible time inflicted on so many Jews.

My experiences were similar to those of other hidden children. 'Child-Survivors suffered innumerable losses; not only did they lose their parents and other loved ones but they also lost their basic sense of trust and security, self-control, positive self-image, former beliefs, sense of justice, independence and autonomy; it was often difficult to build a new life with a new identity based on a lost childhood'.[39] My brother and I each experienced severe 'humiliations, prejudice, betrayal, and discrimination [which] inflicted demoralising psychic pain, long before knowledge of the killings in the extermination camps flooded [us] … with horror, fear, loss, and mourning'.[40]

I complied with my family's admonition to be silent about my war experiences. As Frieda Menco, a Survivor of Auschwitz, said, 'Because of [my] inability to tell [my] stories and express [my] pent-up emotions, [I] felt like a psychological outcast for years'.[41]

After the war, I developed shame about my hidden years and the deprivations I experienced. It did not seem likely that anyone might believe my real escapes and near-death experiences. It became easier to make up good tales that made me feel better about myself and that might make other people become interested in me.

Family members exterminated

Further misery struck us down when we finally learned that virtually none of our relatives in Poland survived the war. Booba's brother, Joseph, in

Czechoslovakia was murdered along with his family. My maternal great grandparents and all of my grandmother's extended family were murdered. The whole of Zeida's family who had remained in Poland was murdered. The only Inbergs still alive were his two brothers (in England and the USA), their families and one nephew, Moishe (in Belgium), son of Zeida's sister Frajda Etla and Daniel Lewin who had been killed in Biala Podlaska.

My father's entire family in Poland, including my elderly paternal grandparents were dead as well, leaving me just with one photo to remember

31. Uncle Jacques, Aunt Dora, Georgette and Emile and an unknown man, possibly the youngest Kamerman brother, Joseph. France, late 1920s.

them by. Only my father's younger brother, uncle Jacques, Aunt Dora and two cousins, Emile and Georgette in France were alive; somehow they had survived. Of the possible third brother, there was no record.

Anxiety and fear ruled my childhood and crushed my recall of my early years. Perhaps, after being ordered to forget what happened to me during the war, whether hiding or escaping death, I succeeded in never mentioning my experiences by repressing those memories. Bergmann & Jucovy summarised this as a 'Conspiracy of silence'.[42] In this type of shared reaction to psychological trauma, 'intense individual and collective defense mechanisms functioned to ward off preoccupation with, and memories of, traumatic experiences'.[43] So many days and years of my early childhood can only be described by the following words: 'I have no recollection.'

Contagion was an immediate issue with unhealthy, neglected and undernourished children and adults emerging from hiding, many of us barely alive. My skin infections were among the public health problems requiring treatment. At l'Hôpital St Pierre (St Peter's Hospital), my hair was shaved and then I soaked in a sulphur bath after which I was scrubbed. My skin was scoured, especially between my fingers and toes, until it peeled off.

Life must have been very tough for Minnie, looking after two children and not knowing where my father had hidden his remaining money and jewellery which had been whittled down to pay for our hiding and food during the occupation. On 27 November 1944, we officially left Madame Jules' apartment at 26 rue du Couronnement, the place where my parents had hidden, yet I have no memories of that apartment – perhaps I stayed with my grandparents.

During the first year after the Liberation of Belgium, the World Jewish Congress collated names of Survivors and shared those lists with refugee organisations around the world. My name was on a list of children who were described as living with family or friends in Brussels. Almost every Jewish child then alive in Brussels had been hidden.

Thus I was officially declared 'a Survivor' at that time, yet decades passed before I felt that was my true identity.

Chapter Seven

Waiting for my Father

Every child cherished the hope to see its parents again when the war was over

Sylvain Brachfeld[44]

Each day, Charly and I walked to la Gare du Midi, the main train station in Brussels, to scan the lists of names of returnees from the concentration camps. As he read each day's lists, I asked over and over again, 'Is our father on the train?' Oh, how desperately I wanted to hear his voice, see his face and feel his big loving hug again.

Silently, we looked at the Survivors walking off or helped off the trains. They looked like living cadavers. Many of the 'weeping skeletons'[45] were still in the tattered striped clothes they had worn in the camps. To a young child, most seemed hideous and very frightening. Even for those reunited with family, there were no exuberant joyful reunions. One prisoner said after her arrival home from Auschwitz, 'I will not tell you anything, because you would not believe all that I could tell you'.[46] In adulthood I read about the gas chambers, in which Jewish women, children, men and Gypsies (Roma) tried to cling to life for as long as possible. I have had nightmares in which I see my father trying to breathe air as his lungs exploded from the poisonous gas.

Many Survivors returning from the camps had nobody to meet them at the station, as no one else from their families had survived. We did not spare a moment to greet them as we focused on looking for our father. We wanted him to return and hoped that our lives would become better. Gradually, day after day, there were fewer and fewer returnees and still my father did not arrive. Throughout childhood, I believed that he was only detained. Surely he would soon return and make the world a safe and good place for me, as only my father could.

By being told to forget my war years, indirectly I was being ordered to forget my father. This was an impossible demand. Minnie showed no outward feelings of loss or grief, despite knowing that my father was transported to Auschwitz; later she learned that he was murdered there.

My father had disappeared from our home, our conversations as well as from our lives. He was no longer part of our family or our shared memories. It was almost as though he had ceased to exist for my mother. My grandparents said nothing about my father being missing. This imposed silence about my father prevented me from learning more about his personality, likes and dislikes, friends and leisure. I yearned to know anything about him to retain his presence in my life and to strengthen my personal memories of him. It seemed that he was eradicated twice, the second time through censorship and indifference by my mother and her parents: they were trying to expunge my father from my life.

As I could not talk about my father's disappearance, or his visits with me when in hiding, I could not begin to express my grief for him or begin to mourn his death. I felt ashamed that I seemed uncaring about my father. Even worse, I was starting to forget details about my loving father as no one talked about him with me to keep my memories fresh.

Now I know that my father was deported from Belgium barely five weeks before the Allies arrived to free us. He died but we lived. He never had the consolation of knowing that we survived. My personal remembrances of my father remained static from those early years. My most vivid memory of my father was when he and I hid from Nazi footsteps in Brussels, him holding me closely, warm and protective. Most other recollections are of his face, his brown eyes and his hat. Photos preserved him as a young man, a new father and a working businessman. In my mind and in my heart he remained strong and protective, my warm and affectionate father. My father never grew old.

Chapter Eight

Not Wanted

If you grow old you will know
In letters soaked with blood
For you shall feel and you shall hear
The lamentation and the wailing that will not be silent

Jewish folksong

Minnie was liberated too and she intended to make the most of her newfound freedom. She had spent her life looking after her siblings, her parents, then an older husband and their children. 'She'd been sheltered excessively by her husband and then, midway through her life, cut loose and told to earn a living. It was as if after hobbling around with bound feet her bandages were suddenly removed and she felt she could become a marathon runner'.[47]

Charly and I were both awkward, sad, naughty and streetwise kids, and Minnie was not going to let us spoil her fun: she did not want us around. I did not like the atmosphere when her friends came to visit at the apartment. I was afraid when she went out late at night and left me alone. Under these new home pressures, I was very sad and achingly lonely, possibly the earliest signs of depression. Rudy Rosenberg described himself very much as I felt, '... my heart [was] in pain and my spirit badly bruised'.[48] I pretended that I was strong and did not need a mother's love. Perhaps what I really wanted was the love of a mother, any mother, to feel wanted, protected and cherished.

Soon Minnie commenced full time employment and I was left alone to spend each day by myself. There was no one to play with, as children my age were all in school making new friends. I owned no toys nor could I read or write to fill in my time, so I wandered the streets looking for items to scavenge as playthings and for food to eat. Living next door were two older women who saw me outside one day and asked me what I was doing on the street by myself. I said that my mother was at work and that I was hungry. They invited

32. Francine (seven) and Charly (fourteen) Kamerman after the war, *c.*1945.

me in for a wonderful meal and kept bringing food to me. I must have looked so famished that they served me an extra bowl of soup after the end of the sumptuous meal and I had no difficulty eating this extra course. It was the one and only time I encountered them and I still wonder why I never saw them again.

Toys existed in my imagination. Once I created a radio from a cardboard box at my grandparents' house, in which I sat and pretended to be the 'announcer'. I spoke to whomever walked by and asked them to turn a pretend dial; each time they did, I began a different program, sometimes singing, sometimes being a weather announcer. Cardboard made a great toboggan to ride down snow-covered hills in winter but, eventually, melting snow saturated it and it no longer supported me.

I had no protectors. After avoiding the Nazis who wanted to kill me, I had a well-honed sense of self-protection. I remained terrified of the Gypsy (Roma) camp located very near to our apartment as I had heard that they were stealing children: being stolen or arrested was a very deep and realistic fear of mine. However, I enjoyed their lively music in the evenings.

Hunger

Charly, then fourteen, had returned to school. Minnie found him an after-school job scaling fish at Delhaize, an expensive food emporium where she had worked before she was married, fifteen years earlier, and had worked again for a short time after the Liberation. Paradoxically, they were surrounded by fine food that we could not afford to buy.

Most days, Charly arrived home very tired at the end of his shift at the food store following his day at school. Then he made some food for me. On good days, it was chips and a fried egg; as a young child, I thought that he cooked the most wonderful chips. Once he made a soup but it was too thin as there were not enough vegetables, so he decided to thicken it with flour. The soup turned solid and, so that the pieces were small enough to eat, we had to hack pieces off to gnaw. Charly called it *ciment romain* or Roman cement as it was as hard as the roads the Romans had built.

With little money for food, the only meat we could afford was the cheapest offal. Minnie sent me to the markets on Place Sainte Catherine to buy two kilos of lung, which tasted awful and had a horrible texture. I was embarrassed to reveal that we ate it and so I always asked for '*Deux kilos de poumons pour mon chat*' (two kilos of lungs for my cat). To reach the markets, I walked along rue des Chartreux, past where my parents had begged the bakers to save me in 1942. On the way back, I would stop to look at the beautiful display of Val St Lambert crystal where the sun shone on the glassware, refracting rainbows and shining brightness into my bleak existence. Because I was severely anaemic, the local health clinic gave me a weekly voucher for a horse steak redeemable at the *boucherie chevaline* or equine butchery. I did not know that it was not Kosher nor did I care as I was malnourished and still bordering on starvation.

Each morning I woke up hungry, or more accurately, hunger woke me up each day. Inventively, I devised a 'milk hunt' in those early hungry hours. This consisted of trawling the streets soon after milk deliveries to homes. The milkman went down streets on a horse-drawn cart, dispensing milk from his big barrel using two measuring cups, for 1 litre and ½ litre. People left a pot or jar outside into which the milkman served the required amount of milk. I drank a small amount of milk from many containers in turn and, each day, I followed a different route to avoid detection. It was time consuming but very nourishing. This was proof of the cunning I had acquired, along with independent thinking, so early in life.

From my early childhood, short of food, with less and less to eat and finally experiencing starvation, I developed an obsession with food. Eating always made me feel better. My only source of good feelings or positive emotions was when I ate. Whenever I felt sad or upset, I overate to comfort myself. I mistook that satisfaction for love. Since those lean times, I have stockpiled food just as squirrels do for supplies during their harsh winters. My obsession developed into a love affair with food. The downside of this relationship with food was that I became overweight in later years. Even more negative feelings developed as I hated myself for being weak-willed and berated myself for not controlling my urges to overeat; I disliked my appearance for many years.

Fantasies and falsehoods

In wartime, I was taught to lie about who I was and why I stayed in strangers' houses in order to disguise my true identity as a Jew. Never could I reveal who my parents were or where they lived, nor the names of my brother and grandparents. In particular, I hid the fact that I was Jewish. Those lies were a highly rational component of my defence to stay alive. There was no escape from lying during the war. Truth would have had me killed.

Now I was afraid that other people, children and adults, would not believe my extreme war life spent hiding with strangers, hungry and dirty, and frequently close to death. Therefore, I continued to hide my real self from others and to block memories from myself. Soon I decided that I had to invent my life and identity, despite the war being over. I made up stories about my family, my home and myself. I did not tell people that I no longer had a father or that my family was poor and I never admitted that I felt no love at home.

Surely other children and adults would find me interesting with a make-believe and more glamorous life? Then they might like me and I might even fulfil my great goal to find a friend. At times, I believed my stories and fictitious life. Constant lying built up more guilt inside me as I knew it was all false. I really wanted my father back living at home with me.

By then I was a prisoner of my own deception, forbidden from telling the awful truths while longing for my fantasies to be real.

Emotional suppression

We seemed so busy getting on with life, living together as a family of three, that I suppose I put many of these fears, memories and emotions out of my mind just because there was something new or urgent to do. Only as an adult did I gradually reflect on my war terrors and losses.

My capacity for feeling and showing emotion was minimal. Tears rarely came to my eyes, even when I was deeply upset. This restriction in my range of emotional expression was a lasting consequence of being hunted and hidden, even being punished for crying as a four-year-old in case I revealed my existence, nor did I laugh very often. Once concealed, my expression of passions and sentiments did not resurface as though they had been permanently removed from my being.

Minnie and her parents always appeared displeased with me. I believed that I was naughty, as I was criticised repeatedly for being so. According to the adults, everything I did was incorrect, disruptive or disobedient. Minnie claimed that I caused problems and she punished me by withholding things that she had promised me, a mental punishment rather than a physical penalty.

Tiny fragments of self-reliance that I had developed during the war and after the Liberation were shattered in this relentless environment of criticism. I began to believe Minnie's harsh words and that I deserved her reprimands. I believed that I was guilty of misconduct and that I was worthless.

One day when I met a little girl who said she was hungry, I brought her home and served whatever snack I could find. When Minnie returned, I said that we were going to keep this little girl. I was longing to have someone younger to play with who respected and liked me, unlike my peers. My mother spent hours looking for the little girl's home and both mothers were very upset with me.

Mother goes to work

Soon after the Liberation in 1944, Minnie began to work as a sales assistant at Delhaize, a luxury food store. In December 1945, she had applied for a licence to work as a *commerçant ambulant* or a travelling sales person, selling stockings at markets around Belgium. The bureaucratic police records enlightened me about my mother's post-war activities, about which she never spoke directly to me.

In late 1946, Minnie found a new job as an interpreter with the Navy Army and Air Force Institute (NAAFI) – a recreation and entertainment service for the British troops, located in the Palais du Centenaire. We moved closer to her workplace on 14 February 1947 to a larger apartment at 19 rue du Heysel with three rooms that seemed luxurious: one bedroom, a sitting room and a small kitchen at the top on the second floor. There was a communal toilet for all the building's residents. Our clothes, fruit and vegetables, dishes and bodies were all washed in the same kitchen sink. We lived in the last street next to the Parc de Laeken, the King's residence, although he did not live there. Our infamous neighbour remained in exile in Germany.

Collecting abandoned ordnance was one of Charly's hobbies. His most prized possessions were two bombshells that he displayed on the mantelpiece. Sometimes he wedged them between his knees and polished the brass nozzles, which had many numbers engraved on them; sometimes I would play with the control knobs. One day, when Minnie brought home a friend, this soldier recognised that the mantelpiece decorations were unexploded bombs, so their removal was promptly organised. Charly also had a rifle; one day he raised the gun with both hands, threatening to hit me on the head. Luckily for me, he hit the ceiling light first, smashing it into many pieces. Minnie punished him for the breakage not for his aggression towards me.

That year, the NAAFI was giving a Christmas party for some children of the staff and Minnie was in charge of its organisation. When I arrived, I overheard my mother tell a co-worker that every child was going to receive a jar of sweets but there was one child too many for the number of jars provided. These jars appeared enormous, decorated with shiny ribbons and filled with the most wondrous confectionery of all colours. It was difficult to imagine that every child would receive a whole jar when leaving the party.

Armed with prior knowledge and eager to receive the jar intended for me, I positioned myself well at the front of the line when the jars were distributed. I held one for a brief few seconds until Minnie pulled it back from my eager hands, declaring, 'Francine doesn't really need one.' I often think of this very small and seemingly insignificant incident and I still yearn for that enticing jar to this day. That original jar is what I long for, even though now I could buy many jars filled with sweets. I was so sad but also very angry with Minnie, my mother. It was part of her job to ensure every child had the gift of a jar of sweets, yet I was not treated like the other children. I still feel pain, even all these years later, when I recall how Minnie treated me that day. She did not register how I felt or show me any sympathy later when I went home empty-handed. I was never able to forgive her for this.

There were fleeting happy moments when we lived in rue du Heysel. When a tango played on the radio, Minnie and Charly danced, narrowly avoiding knocking the furniture in our small apartment. I watched them and applauded their elegant performance. I loved to listen to my mother sing. Minnie had a lovely voice and often sang popular songs such as *Twas all over my jealousy*, made famous by Vera Lynn, and *I sat seven years in a prison*.

One Mother's Day, Charly and I walked to the Parc de Laeken where we began to pick a nice bunch of flowers for our mother. Seeing park rangers approaching, Charly ran away, leaving me holding the stolen flowers. The rangers took me to a police station as I refused to give them my address. It was much later in the day when Minnie angrily arrived to claim me but not

33. Charly and mother still dancing, 1986.

before the policemen had fed me a very nice dinner and allowed me to keep the flowers.

Minnie spent very little time with either of her children. As a rule, Charly, as the elder child, was the one punished if we fought, which was often. Sometimes out of boredom, I would start screaming for no reason and when Minnie marched into the room, she slapped Charly as punishment. When he finally became tired of my blackmail, he decided to take me on an outing on the lake in the Parc de Laeken. I was thrilled that he was taking me in a rowing boat.

34. Auntie Betty Swieca née Inberg, visiting Brussels from Australia with Zeida and Booba Inberg, immediately after the war. Natacha, Francine's cat posed for the photo, 1947.

Charly rowed to the middle of the lake then stood up and made the little boat sway from side to side. I was terrified as he rocked the boat; he knew that I could not swim. He promised not to drown me if I swore never to call out to our mother to get him into trouble and if I vowed to complete a long list of chores for him including cleaning his boots. I promised to do as he asked. I was so terrified that I would have promised to steal the crown jewels. I kept my promises to him. I remained frightened of water for decades. I cannot remember ever going out again with my brother when I was little after that incident. Many years later Charly told me that it was a flat-bottomed canoe, that the water was less than a metre deep and that other boats were around us and he could not have drowned me. The fear of him remained for a very long time.

In 1947, Auntie Betty, who had migrated to Australia before the war, visited her parents, Booba and Zeida. She brought her son Peter with her, one of my Australian cousins who was nearly two; I was already nine years old.

Auntie Betty brought presents for everybody. I received a soft white cardigan that amazed me, as I had never owned anything new and definitely nothing white, as it was difficult to keep clean. Minnie took that lovely cardigan, saying that she did not want it to become dirty; then she sold it and I never wore it. Betty also gave me a box of many coloured pencils with which

35. Francine with Auntie Betty Swieca, her son Peter, Zeida and Booba, Brussels, 1947.

I would draw for many years. It was the best present I ever received as a child. I loved spending time with her and Peter. Before Betty returned to Australia, she gave me a Christian Dior suit that she no longer wanted (worn in her photo with my grandparents and cat). I wore it very many times. When it was no longer wearable, I carefully picked off the label and sewed it onto another garment so I could still claim to own a Dior in my pitifully limited wardrobe.

It is a great pity you did not go with your father

At about that time, Minnie had fallen in love with a widower, Georges Berlinblau. She said he would have married her except that he did not want any encumbrances, namely somebody else's children. Minnie was very distressed when he ended their romance. That day, she uttered the poisonous words which have remained engraved in my mind for nearly seventy years. 'It is a great pity you did not go with your father.' I cannot forget her very angry face as she spat at me her brutal wish that I was dead. My war had not ended.

However, at the time I did not understand the depth of meaning of her words and the venom she felt in her heart against my existence and me. Her words have festered in my mind, reminding me that my own mother neither wanted nor loved me. It was the only time she showed me that she was relieved that my father was dead.

My mother often said that my brother and I looked like our father; it was meant in a derogatory way. I believe it is true, as people often tell me that I look very much like Charly and I think this is because we are similar to our father.

Love of a pet

Walking down the road one day, I saw one of my neighbours bent over a cardboard box on the footpath. I peered into the box and saw a litter of new-born kittens, they looked like fluffy black balls of fur and were meowing, obviously hungry. I asked the man if I could touch one and he replied 'you can pick whichever you like and keep it'. I cuddled the tiny black kitten as I walked home. I named it Natacha, as I liked the name. At the time, I did not know that there were male and female cats. Natacha was a male! Minnie refused to let me keep the cat in her small three-room apartment, so I took him to Booba's home and she agreed that the kitten could stay there despite the risk to her chicken coop in the back of her garden.

Minnie sent me to live with her parents, intermittently. Charly lived with my mother on and off. Perhaps these arrangements were made because she was working and her parents were able to look after me. No doubt she also wanted some privacy. My grandparents never mentioned my father to me nor did they talk about any other family members when I lived with them.

There I slept on a little fold-out camp bed next to Zeida and Booba's bed, listening to their various body noises. I inhaled their medicinal-like scents, mixed with the overpowering smell of naphthalene that my grandmother used in copious quantities to keep the moths away.

When I began living with them, I was school-aged but Minnie never enrolled me in school and my grandparents did not give my education any thought. On Thursday afternoons, when all the schoolchildren were free from lessons, movie tickets were reduced in price to entice children and their parents to attend. Zeida occasionally took me to the cinema on Place Anneessens, a half kilometre walk along rue Camusel from his home. One time, I sat behind a woman wearing a hat, as was the fashion. Hers featured a single large feather, directly in my view, so I could not see the screen properly. Of course, my grandfather was proud of his tailoring profession and was always ready with a tiny pair of scissors kept in his suit breast pocket and a threaded needle under his lapel. After hearing my repeated complaints, he quietly withdrew his scissors and snipped off the offending, if valuable, feather and we enjoyed watching the movie in full view.

Too soon, my grandfather was bedridden, possibly due to heart problems. In addition to standard medical treatment, Zeida's friends treated him with traditional 'old country' medicine that included cupping and attaching leeches to his skin. When they sent me out of the room, I would peek in from behind the door and I was fascinated to watch the leeches drop off his skin when satiated with his blood.

Auntie Fay sometimes travelled from London to visit her parents. She saw, with much dismay, the way I ate. We never learned table manners at Minnie's house where the cooking pot was placed directly onto the table and we quickly helped ourselves straight from it. Habits learned when one has known long-term hunger were ingrained and hard to beat. Fay set about doing a good deed: she taught me how to eat 'like a lady'. She explained how to handle implements and when to use each type. She motivated me by saying that, if I did not have perfect table manners, she would not take me to the Dorchester for afternoon tea. My manners improved dramatically but Fay never took me to afternoon tea in London.

One day I was playing with my cat and I decided to teach him a trick. He would not sit still to be taught, just like any kitten. I looked around for something with which to anchor him and I found a saucepan with a handle and plenty of string. I tied the saucepan around the cat's legs and body and imagined him to be a horse pulling a cart when he pulled the saucepan. Natacha became terrified, especially as the saucepan was making a devil's noise as he moved about more and more. Then, he took off at high speed around the house with me in rapid pursuit. In a panic, Natacha raced upstairs to

Zeida's bedroom where he tried to hide under the old-fashioned metal wire springs of my grandfather's bed. As I chased the kitten under the bed, the saucepan became wedged between the metal springs. Angrily, Zeida turned as red as a beetroot, shouting, '*chameau, chameau*', (camel) which was a big insult in French.

This was another fateful moment when my life went from bad to worse. My grandparents decided that they could not handle such an unruly child. Minnie did not want me living in her apartment again. She had to go to work and could not look after me.

Their joint decision was that I must be placed in foster care.

Chapter Nine

Foster Care

For the next few years, I was placed with foster care providers. I would be moved frequently between carers, yet I was never far from where Minnie and Charly lived. My wartime years of recurrent placements with strangers were replicated with foster carers from when I was eight until I was over eleven years old. Although I lived without the constant threat of death, my 'peace time' living situation lacked love and personal concern for me. I cannot imagine that my father would have approved of or allowed me to live in such austere and lonely circumstances.

Most carers were elderly, retired couples who were paid to care for children, whether orphaned, unwanted or needing time away from their families. They were not government-supervised. I was termed a 'difficult child' as my unhappiness was expressed through naughty and unruly behaviours so the carers became frustrated. Few carers could handle me and most terminated my placement as they did not understand how to handle behavioural problems; each, in turn, demanded that I be moved elsewhere. Repeatedly I was sent to another set of strangers with an occasional short stay at my grandparents. All I really wanted was to go 'home' as I imagined it had been before our family had been broken apart in hiding.

Hence I moved very often, and my life replicated the unsettled times when I was hidden in my early years. For a second period in my life, I was living with strangers and never felt accepted or loved, just criticised and unwanted. I probably did naughty things to get attention from the carers, misinterpreting the reaction for affection, even if it was really condemnation. I have no memory of a hug, kiss or any other sign of warmth.

There were many carers and very many places. I remember very little of this time. In *No Time to Say Goodbye: A Memoir of a Life in Foster Care*, John Tuohy spoke clearly of that 'impersonal and often mercenary taint of the foster care system'.[49] His comments reminded me of my own experience in the system.

Optimistically in adulthood, I requested my childhood records to guide me back to those places to allow me to recall the people but nothing has been found in Belgian archives, not even in my personal file kept by *La Direction*

36. Francine with foster carers and their grandchild, *c.* 1948.

Générale (DG) des Victimes de la Guerre (Director-General of Victims of the War). However, as the police department kept track of changes of address, I found one record of an address of one set of foster carers.

37. Francine in primary school, *c.* 1948.

Late start at school

At eight years of age, I had never been to a primary school and could neither read nor write, two deficiencies that contributed to my unruly behaviour. During the war, I had started kindergarten in September 1941 but, three months later, Jewish children not falling within compulsory school ages (between seven and fifteen years) were banned from official schools by the 1 December 1941 Nazi Decree. By the time I was four and a half, no Jewish children were allowed to attend school after the September 1942 Nazi Decree. Within the next month, I was hidden and had no further schooling.

But now, two years had passed since I was freed; however, my mother had never enrolled me in school despite the legal requirement for every child of my age to attend. If my father had been alive, he would have ensured that I commenced school on time, not just because he was educated as had been his own mother, but because education was essential for every child's future. All surviving Kamerman children received adequate schooling, my brother resuming school up to his mid-teens and each of Jacques Kamerman's children completing their schooling in France after the war.

Why did Minnie and her parents not enrol me in school? Perhaps after receiving sparse schooling themselves, Minnie and Booba were insufficiently educated to value education for a girl. It was not as if they could just choose not to educate a girl in my generation, as it was legally required in Belgium. Minnie had very few interactions with me and I only saw her at night if she came home before I went to sleep. Because I was not always living with Minnie after the Liberation maybe she overlooked the fact that I was now of school age, while she was preoccupied with working, running the home and her social life. She really did not consider my needs, including my education.

One of my foster carers suggested that I needed to go to school. When I was enrolled at *l'école communale, rue Gaucheret*, I had no idea what a school was, what went on there or why children attended. My first day of school, after the carer left me at the entrance gate, remains vividly in my memory. I was dressed in shabby clothes and I felt that I stood out. I am certain to this day that I did. So, when the bell rang, all the other children lined up in their class groups because it was mid-year and the pupils were trained in the school routines.

Due to my illiteracy, the teachers decided to place me in the first class with the five-year-old pupils. The little children in my class laughed at this big, stupid, ignorant eight-year-old sharing their lessons. Then, my age peers sniggered, made nasty remarks and tortured me in cruel ways as I was in the 'baby' class. That first year of school was hell, combining humiliation with frustration every day.

Worsening my first experience of schooling, I was born left-handed and I was denigrated by the teachers as non-conformist. As soon as I instinctively tried to use my left hand, I was in trouble at school. Either the teacher hit my hand with a ruler or else strapped my left arm behind my back for many painful hours when physical punishment was routine in the Belgian school system. Most of the time I forgot that I now had to use my right hand but, after more ruler strikes from the teacher, my knuckles were persistently bruised black and blue. I learned to write with my right hand but felt confusion if differentiating between right and left. In fact, so impaired was my spatial cognition that I cannot trust my own directions to this day and nor does anybody else.

Being myopic, I could not see properly, something which impeded my ability to learn and to catch up educationally with my peers. Frustrated, I became disruptive in the little children's class. The teacher placed me at the back of the room where I could see even fewer of the instructions on the board at the front of the classroom.

Finally and quite embarrassingly, my clothes were always torn and frequently dirty with buttons missing, as I wore second-hand items until they were quite tattered. Female pupils wore a pinafore over their clothes, the equivalent of a uniform. It was pale blue for this school, an impractical colour for active schoolchildren; mine was grey in hue and was covered with stains and rarely washed. My only semi-regular source of clothing was when Auntie Fay sent parcels of odd clothes for me from England, after my cousin Rosalyn had outgrown them. Her feet were smaller than mine but, regardless, I squeezed into her beautiful leather shoes.

Overall, I was the school standout, alone and lonely. I was one of two Jewish students in the school. The rest of the pupils had never experienced our levels of suffering during the war. None of them were hidden or separated from their parents and siblings nor had the Nazis slaughtered their families. The other pupils would not have believed our life stories. Neither of us told our war experiences. They were our secrets, even from each other.

In my first eight years of life, I had rarely interacted with other children and really did not know how to behave or communicate clearly with children or adults. If students made fun of me, teased me or laughed at me, I reacted physically by pitting my fists against their taunts. I did not start fights. Nobody tried to help me in those attacks and no adult tried to counsel me. Fighting back led to my being in trouble at school and I gained a reputation for being unruly that continued through my school years. I had been transformed from victim to villain, at school and at home.

From so many awkward beginnings, I had become a girl whom none of the pupils played with or liked. As an adult, I understood that I was rejected and ignored because, when young, I had experienced no loving peer relationships nor had I received guidance on how to act in a classroom or how to play with other children. I became a ball of reactions to any responses that I felt were unjust or critical, without any capacity for reflection or analysis and no help on how to cope with difficult interactions. I had received insufficient nurturance to develop adequate self-esteem that would have enabled me to reject the negative encounters.

During my second year of schooling, I won an annual prize for attainment, coming third in my class examinations, having completed five years of education in just two years. I had no understanding that I should be proud and enjoy this new, positive recognition at school. This prize introduced a new problem because I was required to wear a white dress to the prize giving. Most girls could comply as every Catholic girl wore a white dress for her first communion in Roman Catholic Belgium. Being Jewish, I did not have one and did not have any hope of convincing my mother to buy me any type of dress. In a creative move, I borrowed Minnie's white petticoat to wear when I received my hard-earned prize. I proudly walked to the front of the class group but I remember feeling very self-conscious about my garment that was obviously not a dress.

All the while, I wished that someone from my family was present to see me on this momentous occasion as a first-time winner, proud of my educational attainment. Neither my mother nor my grandparents attended the prize giving. I really missed my father witnessing my achievement. I comforted myself with the thought that he would have been proud of my educational progress.

Once a week, all pupils were ordered to stand in one line in front of the school head teacher who stood at the front with a bottle of *huile de foie de morue* (cod liver oil) and a single spoon. She administered a spoonful to each child, serving every class in turn. This procedure was a dreaded torment with the horrible tasting oil sliding down our throats 'for our own good'. It was worse than the taunts the other children directed at me. It felt cathartic in a devilish way because all the students went through the same sickening ritual, all of us on equal terms at least once each week.

By now, I had perfected my ability to steal. With neither school equipment nor money to buy the necessities, I began to take pencils, rubbers, sharpeners and slates from fellow pupils. When I became bolder, I stole from the teacher's supplies. I became very adept at concealing my crimes and I was never caught. However, the fact that I was so good at the bad thing I was doing did not diminish the guilt that I felt about stealing and my self-loathing increased. I rationalised that stealing was the only way I could obtain school materials that other students were given. This was how I was able to participate at school, forced to steal what other students rightfully received and even took for granted.

Using the stolen chalk, I drew a hopscotch game on my grandparents' back patio and, on their freshly painted wall, I drew 'lessons' for my cat. Once, I wanted to show my family members who were visiting the house that I could write, so I wrote their names but misspelled Uncle Max's name as 'macs'; I had not yet learnt the letter 'x'. When the adults came outside, they laughed at me and I felt embarrassed at their making fun of me. But how could I have done any better? Adults laughing at me felt demeaning and disappointing when all I wanted to show was that I had learned something new and that I was proud that I could now write most of the alphabet.

School provided me with my first experience of antisemitism specifically directed at me. I remember that students would encircle me and chant, '*Tu as tué Jesus*' (you have killed Jesus). No matter how many times I tried to tell them that I had not, that became their routine at playtime until I flattened the leader with a good punch. Their anti-Semitic jeering went unpunished. A Jewish boy who was hidden in Brussels during the war, Rudy Rosenberg, described being confronted with antisemitism in a streetcar on the first day after the Liberation of Brussels. 'He insulted me, "*Youpin*" for all to hear. It was not written on my face, I thought. And no one had come to my help'.[50] Similar incidents reinforced my increasing concern that I should hide my Jewishness whenever possible, another self-criticism. The Nazis had not introduced antisemitism to Belgium but they normalised and institutionalised and enforced it through their Decrees. I felt that my classmates had been brought up during the war with consistent and vindictive hate against Jews.

I changed schools frequently when moved between foster carers, so I began not to dwell on the fact that other students did not like me or include me in their games. I pretended not to care; I denied my true feelings about my frustrating and friendless circle of negative experiences. Truthfully, I felt deeply hurt as I was repeatedly ostracised, not included in groups and never had any friends at school.

Emotionally, I began to wear an imaginary mask that protected me from bad feelings caused by others directing their negative moods at me, including anger, threats, malice or taunts. Hiding my feelings and refusing to show a response became my lifelong defence against other people's malice, hurtful conduct and ill intentions. Using my imagination, I taught myself never to feel lonely. I conjured up a dream of the perfect world in which I lived. I was living a sad life yet my dream life was perfect. I created an idealised sense of 'home' from books and women's magazines that I read surreptitiously at bookstores or newsagents.

Shunted between foster carers in different areas, I did not know or understand the security of living a stable family life. Nor did I know how to behave appropriately in a variety of circumstances, especially when with other children. I was always with old people or simply left alone. I never learned to play games with others. Despite having the bravado of a street kid, I was a wild and ignorant child, antisocial and with very bad behaviour. I pushed people away.

While I soon caught up educationally with my peers, I could not form lasting friendships despite my longing to talk and play with other children. Growing up in devastating circumstances of fear and trauma damaged me, leaving me unable to communicate or socialise with others. Because I was frightened of rejection, I did not dare ask another child to play with me. Never did a girl or boy invite me to play with them or with a group of playmates.

Whether at school, in any of the foster homes or with my mother or grandparents, I cannot recall a conversation with an adult who showed interest or concern for my ideas, opinions or troubles. Mostly I just received orders. I heard 'sit down', 'Get up', 'Eat your food', 'Go wash your hands', 'Naughty girl', 'Do this', 'Do that', and each day ended with, 'Go to bed.' Criticisms were delivered by accusatory questions such as, 'What have you done again?' 'Why did you do this or that?' Nobody was interested in anything I had to say, whether feelings or ideas nor did anyone appear interested in understanding me.

Fourth class

In spite of changing schools frequently, by fourth class I was achieving more than many of my peers. My schoolwork was excellent but my presentation was poor, to the point of being grubby. My handwriting was not legible after being forced to write with my right hand nor could I ever perfect my natural inclination to write with the left hand. While noting my achievements, teachers' reports emphasised my shortcomings with phrases such as 'Could do better' or 'Francine is disrupting classes.'

The headmistress of my school in rue Marie Christine was Mademoiselle Simonis, an older single woman with a fat body and skinny legs who always wore grey dresses and her greying hair tied severely in a bun. She decided that I was too immature to advance to the fifth class, despite my excellent school results. When told that I must repeat the fourth year, I was devastated. I begged Minnie to intercede. However, my mother wholeheartedly accepted the fat headmistress' decision, confirmed when Mademoiselle Simonis was invited to dinner at our house where I was living with Minnie (following foster care) at avenue de la Reine.

Intentionally, I set the principal's place with a broken knife handle; when it split, Mademoiselle Simonis was very embarrassed. My mother was furious with me as she knew that the knife handle was broken and she knew that I was aware of the breakage. My table placement appeared very deliberate in order to humiliate the headmistress. The two adults agreed that forcing me to repeat fourth class was the best way to control the intractable Francine.

My mother did not champion me, by helping me or supporting me, to overcome this dire set back in my education which felt like an unnecessary halt to my learning that defied all principles of education. There was no one to whom I could appeal without my father alive and if my guardian, Mr Lewkowicz, was aware of this matter, he always agreed with what my mother wanted. I do not think Minnie understood my desire to learn at a higher level nor did she appear to have any appreciation of my potential.

Already at the top of the fourth class, I was not struggling educationally yet I was about to repeat the entire year again. I hoped she would object to this terrible waste of a year of my life and loss of educational opportunities. I had passed the fourth class curriculum with high marks so I was uninterested and I felt very humiliated for being held back a year. If I was naughty during my first year in fourth class, it was evidence that I was bored or had ignored the teacher. How much worse could I become when in fourth class for the second year in a row?

Could I have become even more delinquent? Repeating the fourth year became a year of self-directed learning as I immersed myself in reading the classics, I discovered poetry and I really enjoyed reading novels. Books offered me an easy and immediate escape from my very basic life as well as providing boundless challenges for my intellect and restless nature. After I finished school for the day, often I did not return immediately to my foster home but walked to the public library where it was warm and welcoming and there I read many books. Over time I became a regular borrower and the librarian remembered my name. I appreciated this friendly gesture hugely and the acknowledgement of my interest in reading.

Fortunately, this librarian began to suggest books for me to read, instead of the children's stories I selected. One of the first books I read was *Le Comte de Monte-Cristo* by Alexandre Dumas *père* (senior). As volumes two and five of the seven were missing, I made those stories up for myself. To this day, I have never read the complete set, fearing to spoil my private, magical version.

My mind expanded with each book I read and my resourcefulness grew. Now I knew there were other ways of living and I began to imagine myself far away from this sordid life. I decided that, one day, I would produce something wonderful for humankind. My second year in fourth class was beneficial for my personal development even if it held back my formal education.

Much later I was to read Anne Frank's short stories, *Tales from the Secret Annexe*. She too lived in hiding, in Holland, but sadly did not survive. She died in a Nazi concentration camp. I realised how much more she would have attained had she been allowed to develop her writing talent. However, as an adult, I heartedly disagreed with her conclusion, 'Despite everything, I believe that people are really good at heart.'

Ups and downs

To celebrate my ninth birthday while in foster care, I was instructed to meet Minnie at her parents' house for a special birthday tea. Minnie had promised to buy me roller skates which were the craze – every child in Brussels seemed to be skating about the streets. I was waiting impatiently for her to arrive. On this occasion, I was allowed to invite one friend and I was looking forward to this first-time experience of asking another child to share my birthday. Robert Carlier was a couple of months older than me and a 'friend' by association because he was the son of Minnie's best friend. In truth, I did not have any other person to invite. Booba baked a beautiful butter cake with almonds placed on top but when Robert saw the cake he said dismissively, 'You call that a birthday cake?' I felt devastated, guessing that I failed to attain an expected social standard even though that was the special cake always made by Booba. I also felt extremely disappointed that it was not an acceptable cake and that Minnie had not arrived in time to see it before it was served.

Deepening my shame, I did not have any toys with which to entertain him, yet I remember going to his house where there was one room filled entirely with toys including a vast train set. With nothing to bring from my foster home, I could not find anything suitable for children to play with at my grandmother's home. I waited for my mother at my grandparents' house after the birthday cake disappointment but when she did eventually arrive, Minnie told me that I did not deserve roller skates or any birthday gift. She never gave me a reason and I never learnt to skate. This was not a happy birthday. My next birthday cake was twelve years later and very far from Brussels.

Not quite ten years old and in my second year of schooling, one Saturday in mid-January 1948, I started feeling severe pains in my stomach. The teachers decided that I must have been eating too much and that there was nothing wrong with me. My always-red cheeks were considered an indication of good health so the teachers concluded that I had no illness and accused me of faking symptoms. My foster carers also thought there was nothing seriously wrong with me and sent me to bed. By that time, I was screaming in agony and vomiting.

Much later that evening, a doctor was called to the house and he diagnosed acute appendicitis. I had to go immediately to l'Hôpital Brugmann (Brugmann Hospital) for urgent surgery. Because I was a legal minor, a responsible adult was required to sign the authority for my emergency surgery. The carers managed to contact Charly, who was not of legal age, about the approval. He searched high and low for Minnie but could not find her at her home or in any of the places that she went dancing or at the movies.

By the middle of the night, my appendix burst. Finally Charly begged Zeida to come to the hospital to sign his consent for my critical surgery. Minnie did not visit me in hospital until a couple of days after surgery. She gave me a book, *The Little Prince* by Antoine de Saint-Exupery. I re-read it many times because I loved it so much. It was the very first new book I had ever owned and it was neither second hand nor stolen. While I was in hospital, everyone from my school went to see *Holiday on Ice*, the first ice show performed in Brussels. I remember feeling great disappointment at missing what would have been my first school excursion.

I did not realise how close I had been to death. For ten days I remained in hospital, being treated for peritonitis after my appendix had burst. Miraculously, I survived the serious infection and the delay in surgery before penicillin was available. I was discharged to my mother's address, 19 rue du Heysel. It must be the case that the hospital workers had not been told that I actually lived elsewhere in foster care.

Records of the hospital episode revealed a momentary glimpse of my early life, as the 17 January 1948 admission document provided the address of my foster carers, 8 rue de la Royauté. This was the sole foster home for which I have found an address. My only memory of that abode was the foster carers' grandson, who visited from his parents' home, and my first music lessons.

Introduction to music

> Music is a moral law. It gives soul to the universe, wings to the mind, flight to the imagination, and charm and gaiety to life and to everything.
>
> Plato, Greek philosopher
> (428 BCE–348 BCE)

Creativity helped divert and even sooth some of my worries. Close by to rue du Heysel, where my mother lived from 1945, there was a large communal hall near the tram terminus. Operettas were performed in this barn-like structure. Without money to buy a ticket, I would sit on the footpath in the darkness, listening from outside to the wondrous happy music and laughter. I heard some operettas so many times that, although I did not know their plots, I knew all their tunes and mouthed the words, even if incorrectly. When an adult, I attended performances of these operettas and realised that they told a story. It was a happy revelation when my mother told me years later that my father had loved opera.

Betty Carlier, my mother's English friend, played the piano whenever I visited her cozy home. I especially loved Mozart's *Turkish March*, which she played often, giving me some of the happiest times in my childhood. Inspired, I immediately decided that I wanted to become a pianist. It was a warm loving household and Mrs Carlier talked with me and seemed interested in what I had to say. The Carliers sometimes invited me to their home at Christmas time and under their festive tree there was always a gift for me. There I saw the many toys that Robert owned, more treasures than I could imagine one person could possess.

The grandson of my carers at 8 rue de la Royauté was taking piano lessons and, one day, I went with my carers to hear him play. After I hinted that I was keen to learn the piano, to my amazement, someone paid for me to have one piano lesson each week. However, there was no piano for practice at the foster home. I devised a substitute, by drawing a keyboard on a piece of paper, placing it on the table and then practising on my paper 'keyboard'. The piano teacher was, at first, not aware of my method of practice. I loved to practice my way and I learned two short pieces that I still play today, bringing a smile to my face. One day I may resume piano lessons.

The old male teacher touched me inappropriately but I never objected in case he stopped giving me the lessons which I wanted very much. I just continued with each lesson despite his hateful touch as I really wanted to play the piano. Eventually he found out that I could not practise and he told me not to return – at least that was the excuse he gave to my foster carers.

At one of my schools there was a Jewish girl, Lydia, the only friend I made at school. Once, she invited me to her house where she played Beethoven's *Für Elise* for me on her piano. I thought her musical performance was wonderful. She was also Jewish and, luckily, both of her parents had survived the *Shoah*. Hers and the Carliers were two of the private homes into which I was invited as a guest and where I had a wonderful time. I was amazed that people could live in such clean, bright and warm homes with loving parents.

Music and reading provided comfort, inspiration and liberation from my earliest school years. Through the arts and literature, I have escaped life's stresses, if temporarily, and experienced happiness and discovered beauty outside of my own daily life.

Friendless

Another Jewish girl I met at school was Esther Kremer who had also lost her father in the *Shoah*. Her mother doted on her daughter and worked very hard to support the two of them. Esther's appearance was consistently spotless. She completed all her schoolwork perfectly and on time; she was the top student in our class. I was very jealous of her and of her loving mother and covetous of her clean clothes. I hated that she could take time to study and that her mother helped her with her homework. My desire for Esther's home and her devoted mother turned to spite. I was beginning to detest my hateful and hurtful life. I was in foster care, neglected by an unloving mother, I wore worn and grubby clothes and received neither help nor encouragement for school studies in my foster care placements. Sometimes, when nobody could see me, I pulled Esther's pigtails to cause her pain.

Still I could not understand why people did not want to befriend me. My social and psychological development had been stunted as a hidden child and by being separated from my parents. In later life these experiences came back to haunt me as feelings of worthlessness as well as the burden of loss and guilt. From my deprived background, the other students were privileged, not just average, so I felt jealous of anything that another child owned or experienced, as I could not imagine or hope to have similar items, experience or capability. In addition to all these invidious comparisons, I had no power to make changes in my own life or to experience connections with any adult who could respond positively to my needs and wants.

How could I grasp cause and effect in communication skills and relationships? My only experience of closeness was long ago when I was a toddler living with my father, brother and mother. Following the fearful war years under the Nazis, my post-war life had been fractured, whether I was roaming the streets or living with foster carers. So many barriers prevented me from developing values, communication skills, emotional bonds and, most importantly, the talent of forming friendships.

In about my tenth year, a teacher asked children to write about someone from our class and to describe what was different about that pupil. Most of the students wrote about me and my first reaction was to feel proud that so many selected me. When asked to explain their choices, students said they had chosen me precisely because I was different. Whether it was my Jewishness, appearance or my behaviour, I did not know how they defined difference. Most wrote disparaging things about me. I remember the teacher reading their essays about me out loud to the class; I cannot imagine why. It was very cruel to hear myself criticised by my peers and then made fun of by the students sitting around me. I felt worthless and stripped of any sense of identity as their criticism and comments rained on me, a mental bullying that affected the rest of my life.

The teacher's cruelty extended further. She picked up my written paper and then held it by the corner at arm's length. She said, 'This is a disgusting rag and I am not going to read it' and dropped my paper into her rubbish bin. My chosen subject was a girl who, like me, had no father and had African parentage, unlike any other pupils.

That very public instance of humiliation and malicious rejection by an adult in front of my peers was like a knife cutting into me, a sharp rebuke that I continued to feel for many years. True, my essay was scribbled and there were finger and ink marks because it had been written on the kitchen table after all my chores were completed, not at a tidy desk in good light in the quiet of a clean bedroom as many children studied in. Nevertheless I knew that, even though my essay was not presented in a pristine form, it still had merit. I don't know whether the teacher knew that she took away any self-confidence and core belief in myself that I possessed. My feelings of being rejected, based on that malicious teacher criticising my paper without even reading it, together with my peers selecting me as a negatively different student, fuelled the vicious cycles running inside me every day. I knew I could never belong to this classroom or school. My hopes for a successful education within the scope of my abilities were undermined and nearly extinguished.

Discrimination and torment did not end with the war as far as I was concerned. 'The most outstanding psychological effects of persecution are the loss of identity and feelings of being worthless, accompanied by a lifelong sense of bereavement'.[51] Repeatedly, I was told that I was useless and worthless, both by my mother and at school where teachers assaulted me psychologically and with corporal punishment (which was permitted and condoned by society). Outside school hours, I also endured much brutal physical violence from many people who reluctantly accepted responsibility for my care. As I became more naughty and unruly, I was repeatedly told that I was the problem. I often believed that I deserved other people's nastiness towards me and the hurt that I felt as a consequence. I was being worn down and broken.

Emotionally, I became stalled, unmoved and unresponsive to the events around me. I retreated into my head and pretended the rejection and horrid words did not hurt my feelings. That was my way of resisting giving satisfaction to the perpetrators. Nor did I allow any of my feelings free expression, despite sensing deep hurt and trauma, nor could I share my worries with any other person.

Dissociation from feelings became my primary protection, until the walls of my defences collapsed in my teens when I suffered a nervous breakdown.

Chapter Ten

Discovering my Family

Very few of our relatives remained in Brussels following the war. Gradually, as I searched for them, I discovered more family members scattered worldwide.

Kamerman family

The beautiful handwritten record of the marriage of my father's parents on 19 February 1890 in Sambor in the Ukraine revealed that my grandfather,

38. Marriage entry for Hersz Kamerman (son of Marcus) and Chaja Schillinger (extract), my father's parents, Sambor Ukraine. Courtesy Polish Archives.

Hersz Kamerman, was three years younger than his bride, Chaja Schillinger, daughter of Mordko and Jente. My father's mother was born in Sambor, had a university education and was a professional official translator, *ein Dolmetscher*. She was exceptional in a period when women were rarely educated or practised a profession. My grandfather was a *menuisier* (cabinetmaker), son of Majer and Mali Kamerman (my great-grand-parents).

39. Uncle Jacques Kamerman, my father's younger brother and his son Emile visiting our grandparents in Przemysl Poland, 29 August 1931.

Minnie once recounted that, when she was first married, her mother-in-law used to write to her in *Hoch Deutsch* (High German) calligraphy. After my father had read his mother's letters, Minnie threw them away as she could not read German. She obviously did not think they were of any value to family members; therefore, I never read my grandmother's thoughts directly nor saw her beautiful handwriting. The only thing that remained of her and my grandfather was one photo. I feel sadness that I never met them, an accumulated expression of unresolved grief for my father and all the family connected to him. Nobody from our Kamerman family who remained in Poland survived the *Shoah*.

My father's brother, Jacques, married Dora in France. They and my cousins, Emile and his wife Rosie and sister Georgette, were my only Kamerman relatives to survive the war. Emile told me about the trip he took with his father to Przemysl in 1931. Emile vividly remembered that our grandmother was very loving towards him and that she was quite tiny. When they departed at the end of their visit, she ran alongside their train as it pulled out of the station, waving to him with what looked like a scarf. This family anecdote helped fill the void I felt never having met my extended family and having lost my father who would have been a source of stories about his family.

When I was twenty in 1958, I finally met these sole remaining members of my father's family; I was too late to meet Jacques. Travelling to Paris, I met my Kamerman cousins and their widowed mother. Dora was loving and kind, smiling and very happy to meet me. Emile made me feel extraordinarily welcome, almost overwhelming me with his affection, as did the entire family. I felt a fantastic affinity with them, experiencing a feeling of being with this genuine family that I had always craved. We were our fathers' families. If only my father and Jacques could have been there to enjoy this Kamerman reunion. Subsequently I visited Emile and his wife Rosette whenever I was back in Europe from Australia with or without my husband, Phillip. Several times he invited us to dine in his favourite restaurant, Le Relais de l'Entrecôte. We always enjoyed each other's company. Emile spoke no English and Phillip, no French. Through Rosette and I doing the translating, Emile said to Phillip: You and I can never have an argument, let's be friends! Emile's enthusiastic hospitality extended again to my son Jason when he visited Paris decades later and they became firm friends, later meeting Emile's daughter, Patricia Rosenbaum Kamerman in 2016.

Inberg family

Four of Minnie's five surviving siblings lived outside Belgium during the Nazi occupation of Belgium. Fay was in London, Bunny a prisoner, and Betty, Rose and Max Inberg lived in Australia. Each had married and had children. I did not meet my Inberg cousins in England and Australia until well after the war.

Bunny was the youngest sibling. He had been arrested by the Nazis in Belgium as a 'civilian alien', being a British national. He was lucky not to have been arrested as a Jew or he would have been sent to a death camp. He suffered torture and much deprivation when transported to Italy as a slave labourer. After the war, he told me that the Germans had placed him on the tops of buildings in Italy along with other prisoners of war, where the allies could see them from their aeroplanes: the Germans hoped that no bombs would be dropped, as did their prisoners. Surviving each day was entirely a matter of chance, like playing Russian roulette. His war experiences contributed to the terrible 'shell shock' that he suffered for the rest of his life, no doubt shortened by his war traumas.

Following his release at the end of the war, Bunny lived for a time with Zeida and Booba in Brussels. Like millions of other military and civilian victims, he was never debriefed nor offered psychological help. He sometimes acted strangely and shouted things that were incomprehensible to me. He was especially frightened of loud noises. I saw him daily when I lived with my grandparents. Despite his own sufferings, he was always kind to me. The only trade he had learnt was pressing clothing, working with Zeida before the war.

Bunny would soon join his three siblings in Australia, arriving in Perth in 1952 and settling in Sydney. Bunny lived in a boarding house. He resumed his trade as a presser of clothing.

An opportunity to meet more relatives occurred in my twentieth year, this time in London. I was the guest of parents of a friend. I had not forewarned Auntie Fay, my mother's older sister, that I was coming to London. It was an oversight. I certainly would have liked to have met my cousins, Joy and Rosalyn. When I called Auntie Fay, she said that both daughters were away from London. She did not invite me to visit her home. I did not see her nor meet my uncle, Lew.

The next year I stayed briefly at Auntie Fay's with my mother and grandmother when on my way to Australia but I did not see Lew or either of my cousins. The only time I met Lew was when he and Fay visited Australia in 1966. A decade later in 1977, planning my first visit back to Europe, I took the precaution of sending an airmail letter to Fay, advising her that my husband Phillip and I would be in London for a few days. After we arrived, I telephoned and Lew told me, 'It is not convenient for you to visit.' I was upset that I had come all the way around the world with my Australian husband Phillip and been disappointed in my hope to visit my relatives in England. I subsequently learned that Fay had been very unwell at the time.

On several later occasions I attempted to contact Auntie Fay. I had always admired this aunt, and been grateful to her for having given me one great asset – the knowledge of how to behave in a proper manner. However, sadly I was never able to meet up with her again. My disappointment at not seeing her was accentuated because I considered her a role model in a young life which had had so few. She was so unlike my mother, Minnie; Fay was a lady.

On many subsequent visits to England, Rosalyn, Fay's daughter, and her husband always welcomed us in a most generous, affectionate and kind manner. It has been my good fortune to renew ties with them despite the long distance separating us and our infrequent visits to one another. I am always sad when it is time to say farewell after we have been together, either in England or Australia. Rosalyn is my closest cousin in age as well as the very closest in my personal history. She has always been very kind to me and I love spending time with her.

Rosenblum family

It was surprising to find out how many siblings Booba had. Auntie Edis, Booba's sister had survived in hiding with her husband Max Grunberg along with his daughter Eva in Belgium. Booba and Edis had arranged for a notary to prepare a declaration. It stated that the six people listed [Joseph in Czechoslovakia, Srulik in the USA, Binia (Booba) and Ides (Edis) in Belgium, Soura (Sarah) in the USA and Mania (Miriam) in Israel] were the sole heirs to the estate of Albuck Rosenblum and his wife Chippa Feldman in Biala Podlaska, Poland.

Possibly, at the time of signing this document on 2 October 1946, none of the siblings knew if anyone else was still alive, other than the two former Rosenblum sisters, Booba and Edis (Grunberg), who had survived in Belgium. At about this time, a Survivor Proclamation was lodged in Poland, presumably

Monitor Polski Court Announcements
The Government Gazette of the Republic of Poland
Survivor Proclamations & Family Searches
no specified Region / no specified Province
Last updated December 2012

Searching for Town BIALAPODLASKA
and Surname ROSENBLUM
(D-M code 946786)
in no specified Gubernia
in ALL data

Surname	Given Name	Maiden Name	Father	Mother Surname	Mother	Born	Town Born	Death Date	Town Died	Living	Relation
ROZENBLUM	Abus'									Biala Podlaska	ma\z*
ROZENBLUM	Cypa									Biala Podlaska	z*ona

40. Monitor Polski, extract.

by one of the surviving siblings, in the *Monitor Polski Court Announcements* (The Government Gazette of the Republic of Poland). It named Albuck and Cupa Rosenblum under 'Survivor Proclamations & Family Searches'. The family had already presumed that every relative living in Poland had been murdered in the *Shoah*.

All of Booba's sisters, whom we called Mima (auntie in Yiddish), had survived the war. Around 1930, in Brussels, Mima Edis Rosenblum had married Max Grunberg, a widower, and she helped to raise his daughter Chava (Eva). My new uncle Max (the other was in Australia) was a skilled cabinetmaker who made Minnie's bedroom suite for her marriage to my father.

Eva was about fourteen years my senior. She was one of the few persons who showed me affection when I was young. I could visit her on my way home from school and, after she had welcomed me, she would make me a cup of hot chocolate to drink – a warming winter luxury. I loved her very much. Eva chose me as her flower girl when she married a Polish soldier who had fought

41. Rosenblum family Kiddish cup, engraved silver, Moscow, *c.* 1870.

with the British Army. I held a little bouquet of flowers as I stood and recited in Polish what Charly had coached me for almost a week to say. However, as a very bad joke he had taught me to say, 'Please sir, kiss my arse', when I believed I was saying, 'Congratulations and a long happy life to you.' After I had been slapped across the face, Charly disappeared to avoid punishment. I hope it was not an omen; they divorced soon after the wedding. She and her parents migrated to Canada in the 1950s and there Eva married again and had two sons.

Before Eva's death in the 1990s, my brother Charly visited her in Canada and she gave him a family cup made of silver and showed him the original accompanying documents which described the ancestor giving the cup to a son. It had been passed on through the generations to my great-grandfather Albuck Rosenblum. In 1929, Mima Edis (Grunberg, née Rosenblum) had visited her parents in Biala Podlaska and her father had given her this treasured Kiddish cup which had belonged in the family for many generations. My great-grandfather, Albuck, stipulated that this cup should always be passed to one of his descendants who blessed the wine on Friday night ('making Kiddish'). Almost 100 years later, my younger son Jason would be the family 'keeper' of the cup.

Mima Sarah had migrated to the USA before the Second World War and lived in New Jersey. She married a Rosenshein. They ran a chicken farm and had a large family but I never met any of those relatives. My cousin Rosalyn took an opportunity to visit them once but, soon after her trip, our families lost touch. Mima Sarah knew a young American GI who had been stationed in Germany with the post-war occupation forces. One day this man showed up unexpectedly at Booba's house with an introduction from my great-aunt.

While Booba did not know what to do with a young handsome American man, she asked me to take care of him. He came regularly to visit Brussels, a full day's travel from his base in Friedberg near Munich in Germany. When his furlough was cancelled one time, he invited me to visit his base. There he introduced me to one of his buddies with the unusual name of Elvis Presley. I did not know the reputation that went with the name. Our popular French singers at the time were Yves Montand and Charles Aznavour and I had not heard of Elvis. How I rue my ignorance. I wonder now if I would have asked him to sign his autograph or maybe two or three to share.

Mima Miriam moved to pre-war Palestine (Israel) and there married Zeev Herling, having five children before her husband died at a young age. Later she married Menachem Seltzer and raised his five children as well as their own child, Haya. All eleven children were raised in Israel: hers, his and theirs. Poignantly, Haya wrote, 'My mother (Miriam) went back to Poland after her first husband died to visit her parents and to try and persuade them to sell up and migrate to Palestine. When she told her father

42. Zipporah and her brothers, children of Mima Miriam (née Rosenblum) and Zeev Herling.

about the stories being passed around about what the Germans were up to, he said to her that she must have been sitting for too long in the sun in Palestine to believe these fairy tales.' He said, 'We have been persecuted by the Poles, the Russians, but the Germans are the most enlightened nation in Eastern Europe ...'

My heart leapt and sank again at the thought of their opportunity to leave Poland, an opportunity they had forsaken due to their belief in German enlightenment.

Another time, when he was standing on the balcony she called out to him, '*Abba*' (father in Hebrew). He thought she was calling him by his first name (Albuck or Albus, a shortened form of Avraham), further proof to him of how uncivilised those who went to live in Palestine had become. Every member of Booba's family who remained in Poland was murdered.

The eldest of Miriam's eleven children, Zipporah Herling, became something of an enigma due to her unconventional leadership and her mysterious activities for the State of Israel. She was treated as though she was the 'godmother' of the Israeli Air Force base at Hatzor, for which she raised enormous amounts of money. In 1977, Zipporah invited me to visit the airbase where I was allowed to sit in a Kfir, an Israeli warplane, and my Australian husband was 'allowed' to donate a sizeable sum of money. It was a remarkable day.

All of my extended Israeli family contributed to Israel's welfare and fought to defend its right to exist. One of Miriam's sons, Israel Herling, was a founding member of the Palmach, Israel's irregular army. He changed his last name to Harel, after the name of his brigade in the Palmach. I met him and his family in 1977 when his little son, Rami, entertained us by playing the piano. In May 2016, I had the pleasure of meeting Haya and an extended family group in Israel, including her nephew Rami Harel who is a renowned composer and performer.

American dreams

Minnie applied for visas for her, Charly and me to go to the United States of America. She applied through the American Jewish Joint Distribution Committee (AJJDC), dubbed 'the Joint', an organisation that arranged visas and paid refugees' fares to America. Already it had provided us with food parcels immediately after the war and I remembered the exotic taste and smell of the Del Monte cans of pineapple from Hawaii. Minnie did not usually let us eat them but sold these luxury goods.

Family members in North America were ready to welcome us – Mima Sarah (Rosenblum) Rosenshein in New Jersey, my cousin Eva who was soon to move to Canada with her parents, Max and Edis (Rosenblum) Grunberg and, unbeknown to me at this stage, one of Zeida's brothers and one of Booba's brothers who were possibly both in Texas, since before the war. Practicalities provided by the American Joint included paying for housing, food and education costs in the USA.

Minnie decided to accept our visas. However, her three sisters, Fay (in London), Betty and Rose (in Australia) all berated her, telling her how selfish she was to abandon her elderly parents in Brussels. These sisters, who all lived comfortably and far from Belgium, feigned horror that Minnie even considered going to America to make a new life for herself and her children. Yet all they did for their parents was to send an occasional parcel of goods and write occasional letters. They insisted that Minnie's duty was to remain in Brussels and look after their parents. Our USA visas were never used. My hope of completing an education in my youth disappeared with our unused visas.

Research uncovered that, in 1946, relatives in Australia had applied for visas for all of us living in Belgium to migrate there. Whatever the Australian visa decision was at that time, we remained in Brussels.

Minnie's Belgian Police file revealed our refugee registration number with the United Nations High Commission for Refugees, approved on 29

November 1954 when still living in rue du Progrès. Original records no longer existed to reveal further details. A personal response from Ms Patricia Williams stated that 'Unfortunately UNHCR in Brussels no longer holds individual refugee records. All individual case files were transferred to the Commissariat Général aux Réfugiés et aux Apatrides (CGRA) in the nineteen eighties.' She continued, 'Just to add a personal anecdote, my father was a 21 year old British soldier who helped to liberate Brussels and I am currently living in Ixelles (author's birthplace)! Fortunately the period in history which you witnessed and which had such a devastating impact on your family is over but our work to help victims of persecution and war still goes on as crises continue to emerge or fail to end.'

Chapter Eleven

I have a Stepfather

In 1948, two years before she was officially declared a widow, Minnie married Maurice Blumberg in a Jewish ceremony. I was not invited to attend. They never had a civil marriage to ensure their legal recognition as being married under Belgian law and recognised internationally.

I hated Maurice with a vengeance because he took my father's place. Every night I prayed before going to sleep that he would die in the night, so badly did I seek retribution against him, as well as retaliation against my mother. I was especially worried that, when my father returned, he would find this stranger occupying his bed next to my mother, using the same bedroom furniture that uncle Max Grunberg had made for their marriage. Of course, I longed to see my father there again close to me too.

Maurice had survived the concentration camps where the Nazis murdered his wife. He only talked about those years of suffering decades later. The sole possessions that he brought to the home were a large black cupboard in which he kept his threadbare striped camp suit. It gave me nightmares. In an act of masochism, I would go into his room, sneak a look at his old camp outfit and then feel even more frightened.

At the age of eleven and a half, after living in many foster homes, I was called back to live with my mother and my stepfather. Minnie was pregnant and that made me feel embarrassed as only a pre-teen can feel. I was recalled because they needed my help at home as Minnie was soon to deliver her baby.

I resented what my family had become. I felt as though I was still living in a household of strangers, just as I did for three years in foster care and for two years in wartime hiding places. At the end of that year, my sister Helen was born.

The adults criticised me many times each day; they blamed me for everything; they accused me unjustly. Sometimes I was deliberately naughty to get back at the domineering adults and because it made me feel better to see them upset. Wayward actions included swapping the tube of toothpaste with a tube of shaving cream; Maurice would come rushing out with bubbles foaming out of his mouth and I could not suppress my laughter. At other times, I might intentionally not wash Maurice's laundry properly and that made him angry. Sometimes accidents led to trouble. One day when I was supposed to be ironing, I was so absorbed in reading whilst the iron was heating and crouching over my book that I was oblivious to time passing. I smelled nothing as the iron scorched through the cloth and, next, burned right through the wooden kitchen table on which I did the ironing; only when the heavy iron landed on the floor did I pay any attention to the situation.

Maurice always wore a very wide belt to hold up his trousers. When I was a nuisance, he grumbled and threatened to flog me by pretending to unbuckle the belt. Then I would run and hide from him. I was terrified of him and his belt and I did not stay around to see what he was going to do with it. To his credit, he never hit me. Apparently my brother stopped Maurice from hitting me with the belt one time and used blackmail related to the war to persuade our stepfather not to hit me, ever.

Just after I turned twelve years old in 1950, Minnie received a government document that stated the presumption of my father's death. The Belgian Government declared that Minnie was his widow. Officially, my brother and I were fatherless as we had already feared for the preceding six years since the Liberation. To me, that government letter did not seem true and I still held onto my belief that my father was living somewhere unknown.

My hopes that my father would return diminished but they were never totally extinguished.

My sister Helen

When Helen was born on 23 December 1949, I did not gain a little sister but almost a child of my own. At just eleven years old, I was charged with complete responsibility for her, every day and most nights certainly after she was weaned.

For the first few years of her life, I was quite convinced that Helen thought I was her mother. I did everything: washing, feeding and clothing her. I helped Helen feel better when she was unwell and chased away any nightmares. I washed vast numbers of her cloth nappies by hand on a washboard, in addition to the whole family's laundry. I was overjoyed when the household acquired a manual wringer, ending my years of hand-wringing wet laundry.

I missed quite a lot of my own education looking after Helen when she was ill, before she started school. Then, Minnie was often away for work and later on holiday, so she left me a sheaf of signed paper notes. All I needed to do was think of an excuse for missing school, write it above my mother's signature, date it and give the letter to my teacher whenever I returned to classes. These extended absences reduced my educational achievements.

When I took Helen to the park in her pram every day, often I just read alone. I also met all types of unsuitable people and if I met other teenagers, I

43. Francine Kamerman (thirteen years) and sister Helen Blumberg (eighteen months), outside the Blankenberg train station, Belgium, 1951.

sometimes made social plans, knowing that Helen could not tell on me as she was only a baby. At other times, her baby habits, especially her nappies were not attractive to potential new friends. Charly knew that older boys loitered at the park and would come and find me there at weekends, berate me for my choice of company and then force me to take Helen back home.

Maurice adored Helen. The only way he could show his love was through food. Each week he went to Antwerp to obtain market supplies and his final purchase would always be at the Jewish bakery where he bought the most amazing chocolate-topped almond biscuits. He sat Helen at the dining table and made her eat the whole box of biscuits. I would hover nearby but he would dismiss me saying, 'You don't need them.'

My relationship with my sister was just that: she has always been my sister, not a stepsister and I have always loved her. I believe she has reciprocated these feelings all her life.

My brother Charles

Charly has, for decades, been my only connection to my father. Through circumstances beyond our control, we did not have a steady upbringing. My life of separation and concealment with strangers in dire conditions was far from stable. It was decidedly abnormal for our mother to neglect us. We shared few common years, fewer mutual memories and we never shared any good times. In my imagination, he was the idyllic older brother, seven years my senior and my protector. Yet I did not know him well, especially after we were separated a second time, by half a world, when I was aged fourteen.

When Charly was fifteen years of age, our mother required him to leave school for a full time job that she chose for him. He was apprenticed at a leather goods factory and worked six days a week. On his day off, he woke before dawn to help Minnie and Maurice work at their Sunday market. First, he would collect a large four-wheeled cart from where it was hired for the day. Usually such a cart was hauled by a horse, but Charly brought it back to our grandparents' house, where the market stock was stored, and loaded the cart high with goods. Then he pushed this heavy load to my mother's and Maurice's market stall, through harsh winters and hot summers. He spent the day working at the market, then packed and returned unsold stock to our grandparents' house and, finally, returned the cart to its owner. He was always exhausted at the end of his 'day off'. Charly spent his annual holiday helping Minnie and Maurice at their summer markets. He was never paid by them.

In the summer of 1951, when I was washing Helen's nappies, Charly told me that he was going to Australia. I cried and I felt devastated. From letters and later conversations, it appears that Charly was exiled, expunged from my mother's newly re-married life. Friction between him and Maurice probably hastened his departure, soon after he completed the mandatory Belgian military service. Despite her rejection, Charly kept in touch by writing letters and sending photographs that sometimes made our mother cry.

The following year, when Charly was twenty-one, he left Belgium with not much more than the clothes he stood up in, clearly insufficient for a six-week voyage, let alone to start a new life in a different country. Only Zeida saw him depart from the Brussels train station where he gave Charly a little money for his voyage from the port of Genoa, Italy. Surely financial assistance should have been provided to him. Was there not assistance for orphans from the Belgian government and from German reparations for the death of our father? Charly arrived in Sydney in April 1952, a few months after our uncle Bunny had arrived. My brother rented a room in the same boarding house to which Bunny had moved a few months earlier and soon found a job.

Only as adults could Charly and I recommence our relationship, feeling almost like strangers when we met again for the first time. Sharing intimacy with him remains difficult. We still talk about what we have in common, mostly by email or phone. We sometimes meet and share a meal. He tells me that he has many nightmares about his youth but does not want to discuss anything specific, not even with me.

I really appreciate the many details of my father's life and interests that Charly has shared. We know we are made of the same flesh. He is my brother and I love him. We just never had the joy of sharing a home or good times when we were growing up.

War reparations

For fifty-five years until her death, Minnie received a pension that the German government agreed to pay widows of those killed in the *Shoah*. She could only continue to receive that pension as the widow of my father. Therefore, she never had a civil marriage ceremony with my stepfather because it would end her widow's pension.

Unbeknown to us, having lost a parent in the Second World War, my brother and I were also eligible to receive reparation payments. Instead of passing them on to us, my mother collected our payments for the next fifty years. When Minnie required me to sign papers from the German government, I did not know what I was signing when I was only a child and obviously a minor in legal terms. Only after she died did I see my signature on the document which granted her my rightful reparation payments. Suddenly I realised that, for the previous five decades, she had continuously collected several pensions: hers, Charly's and mine. My father's death provided her with a lifelong income. It was devastating to realise that my mother received money from my father's death. She never acknowledged that Charly and I should have received this money.

Money, however, was not our goal. My brother and I would rather have felt love from our mother and wished that our father had remained alive.

Living in an attic

Minnie and Maurice, Charly, Helen and I moved from rue du Heysel when I was about twelve years old (*c.* 1950). We moved into a larger flat at 175 avenue de la Reine, a building called *le petit Château* as it was built in the architectural style of a miniature castle. The roof section under the narrow turret was where I slept through bitterly cold winters and suffocating summers. It felt like a stronghold, my prison cell perched high above the street. Sometime Charly and even young Helen slept in this roof cavity.

On the floor below, the apartment door was locked at night for Minnie and Maurice's security, barring me from entering if I needed to and especially from our only toilet. In the turret, there was no hope of any urgent assistance during the night. A bucket was the night-time toilet that had to be emptied each morning. At about this time I commenced menstruation without appropriate sanitation.

Despite Minnie and Maurice's security-consciousness for themselves, the door to my turret was always unlocked. I was left vulnerable to anyone who entered the unlocked space from the stairs when I was asleep or alone, excluded from the warm apartment below me. Without electricity, there was no light and, because I was very afraid of the dark, when I heard the wind howl, I was very scared. Our laundry was hung on lines to dry up there, where even a slight breeze through the roof tiles caused it to sway; then I awoke afraid and often remained sleepless for the remainder of the night.

The childless couple living on the first floor took a personal interest in me and I enjoyed social interactions with them that I did not experience elsewhere. They treated me as their guest. Georgette occasionally made pancakes that she filled with jam, rolled up and presented to me on a plate. I would eat this delicious treat faster than she could make them. Her husband was a glassblower whose studio was in the basement of *le petit Château*. He allowed me to watch him work, creating the glass tubes for the newly-fashionable neon shop signs. I was fascinated by his skills and his creative transformation of raw materials into colourful glass. He made and gave me tiny coloured glass animals.

First family car

After Charly left for Australia in early 1952, Maurice bought a glossy new American station wagon. He only used the car to drive to the markets and for business trips to pick up new stock outside Brussels. The vehicle was strictly for work transport, never to carry back the shopping nor for family outings, so we never once went anywhere in the car for pleasure. One of my chores was to help Maurice clean it every week and polish it every three months. Not a speck of dust was allowed to remain inside or on his car that was always kept in 'as new' condition. The restricted use of his vehicle seemed so unkind compared with the choices of other parents who drove their children to school and extra-curricular activities, as well as on family outings. I really wanted to ride somewhere in that station wagon, if only once to feel happiness and pride as a passenger. My wish was to come true once; I was a passenger in his car when he drove me off on my involuntary departure from Belgium.

When I was almost fifteen years old, in January 1953, we moved to 381 rue du Progrès. I was registered as living with my mother who was still listed as the widow of Israel Kamerman in her Belgian Police file, even though she and Maurice were now married and had a child. Helen and Maurice must have been on another document, probably his registration card, because we all lived at the same address.

Clearly, Minnie did not want to reveal to the authorities her marriage to Maurice or the fact that she had a child with him, let alone disclose that she was living with him, as she might have lost her widow's pension from Germany. Minnie's additional fear was that she may have been discovered collecting the war pensions paid for Charly and me as orphans.

Jewish identity

Each of my parents grew up in religious families, observing traditions including keeping Kosher. After the Holocaust, many Jews lost their devotion to their beliefs and the traditions. Before the war, Zeida was an active member of the Orthodox Synagogue in rue de la Clinique in Brussels. After the war, the Inberg family no longer observed daily Jewish customs. We did not keep the Sabbath or light candles on Friday nights or holy days so I never participated in observing any of the commandments relating to all of the Jewish holy days. Yet I knew I was Jewish. My school peers did not let me forget as they occasionally spat, 'sale juive' (dirty Jewess). Poignantly, I remembered all the good non-Jewish people who had hidden me, fostered me and who were protectors of Jews.

There was no Jewish education at home. Fortunately, Zeida insisted that I attend Sunday school when I was ten or eleven, even more belatedly than commencing my primary schooling. He would walk slowly to synagogue and I went with him a few times. The school was adjacent to the synagogue. I loved listening to the wonderful stories where we, the Jews, were not victims but heroes: Queen Esther who saved her people, David who beat Goliath, the many battles where the Hebrews always beat the Philistines and other stories.

Another aspect that appealed to me was the unlocked stationery cupboard from which I helped myself to a modest selection of supplies, weekly. One day, the teacher caught me and asked what I was doing. I lied that I was just tidying the cupboard. The teacher, without uttering one word, took a big brown paper bag and filled it with exercise books, rulers, pencils, crayons and everything that a child might need and gave it all to me. After this teacher left and the new teacher locked the stationery cupboard, I lost interest in hearing the biblical tales. Besides, I could only attend sporadically due to a weekend full of family chores.

We kept two major holy days. One was Yom Kippur, the Day of Atonement, during which Jews fast and pray for twenty-five hours. After a brief early meal, we would walk for about thirty minutes to the Orthodox Synagogue at 67A rue de la Clinique, before night fell. This was the same synagogue to which Zeida had belonged for most of his life in Belgium. I only went inside the Synagogue briefly because we had no special seats. I struggled to find meaning in the service as I did not understand Hebrew and had no familiarity with the rituals which I watched. Without knowing what was going on and with nowhere to sit, I began to prefer staying outside and finding some young people with whom I could to talk. It seemed to mean nothing more than a day off school or, in later years, a day off work.

The other holy day we observed was the Passover Seder, commemorating the Exodus from Egypt of the Jewish people, held at my grandparents' home. Zeida prayed for a very long time in Hebrew or Yiddish. Without knowing its meaning, I recognised that I must remain perfectly quiet, as was required in that house. Praying was followed by a meal but, by that time, both Helen and I would be sound asleep. When I was awoken at the end of the evening, we all trudged home, Maurice carrying Helen. I never looked forward to Seder night – it seemed a long and tedious event.

Decades later, I rectified my ignorance, motivated by a wish to raise my own children in a Jewish home. In terms of symbols, I learned what could and should be done. I continue to acquire more understanding and to embrace the customs but not the beliefs.

Soon after the upheaval of the Liberation, Jewish youths provided respite camps for Jewish child Survivors, providing us with good food and fun for a week at a time. The American Joint was instrumental in funding these camps. I enjoyed sleeping in large tents and hearing one of the *madrichas* (female leaders) reading wonderful stories, only the second time that someone had read aloud to me. I waited with great anticipation for the next reading. Then I was briefly happy with vivid mental pictures of those fun times. It was a magical experience of sharing, caring and learning where I felt an equal. I enjoyed the feeling of belonging to that group.

At that time, various Jewish youth movements were offering Jewish orphans a better life in Palestine and, from 1948, in Israel, after the State was declared. I went to all the youth movements such as Hashomer-Hatzair, Betar and Gordonia, but not for their political indoctrination. I loved to do the dancing and learn new steps. The food they supplied was enticing as well as generous during post-war shortages. It was particularly important to me given the poverty of my family. I also went to the youth groups because they made me feel secure because I belonged and was wanted. Now I felt proud to be Jewish.

Planning an escape from Minnie and Maurice, I ran away with a group from Betar. We travelled through France, as far south as Marseilles. It was so much fun being with them, changing trains frequently and sleeping in different places. French police were checking the documents of all people boarding ships as, at the time, the British had imposed an embargo on shipping to Palestine. When I was discovered without any identification, the French police stopped me from boarding the ship. The Gendarmes returned me to my mother and stepfather in Brussels who did not care for me. This was the second time that the French police had sent me back, the first time to the people who wanted to kill me and, the next time, to the people who did not want me.

The camaraderie and friendships I experienced with the Jewish youth groups rekindled my sense of self-worth.

Chapter Twelve

Servant to the Family

Minnie and Maurice's business was selling goods at the North Sea coastal markets in summer and every Sunday in Brussels throughout the year. Markets were located on various central squares that had hosted traders for centuries, surrounded by hotels and cafes (but we only went into those premises to use their toilets). On Mondays and Fridays we were in Blankenberg, Wednesdays in Knockke, Thursdays in Ostende and Saturdays in La Panne. Year-round we sold on Sundays in Brussels at la Gare du Midi. Tuesdays were when Minnie and Maurice purchased goods in St Nicolas, a small industrial town with many knitwear factories and wholesalers. Initially they sold stockings and later they peddled a range of knitwear.

Market hand

The first time that I worked as unpaid help on the summer markets was in 1950. Minnie and Maurice rented a three-room apartment in Blankenberg, the most central town on the Belgian coast. We took turns to wash ourselves at the kitchen sink, the same place that we washed food, dishes and clothes. There was an unplumbed outhouse for our toilet.

For the first two summers of Helen's life (1950 and 1951), while I worked on the markets, Minnie paid women to look after her baby. They stayed with our family. One had a wooden leg that creaked and which, to my horror, she took off at night. She was extremely smelly and I had to sleep in the same bed as her. I hated her but not as much as the second woman who arrived with a big cage from which a parrot commanded attention. She fed the parrot by putting bits of biscuit between her lips; the parrot would grab the food. One day she showed Minnie two of her old dresses that had been cut up with scissors; she claimed that I had done it and then demanded compensation. Minnie believed her, although I swore repeatedly that I was not responsible. I wanted revenge on that woman who lied but I did not have the courage to act on my anger. I was punished unjustly, without any chance to clear my name. As always, my mother sided with other people against me. Bit by bit, my trust in myself was being undermined.

Tuesday became the longest day of my week because I had complete responsibility for Helen's welfare at the coastal apartment while Minnie and Maurice collected new stock to sell. One day I dressed Helen up and entered her in a singing competition. She was wearing a lacy slip of Minnie's and a new white cardigan from the selling stock which I intended to repack for sale after one use. I hoped to win the competition prize that was on offer as Helen sang with a lovely voice. Struck by stage fright, she did not perform despite my encouragements, threats and prodding, so that was the ignominious end to my impresario career.

From the 1950s, my cousin Rosalyn came from England each summer to visit our grandmother and in order to improve her French, accompanied by

44. Summer in Blankenberg. Francine with her cousins Rosalyn Cohen and Mary Greenberg.

Mary Greenberg who lived in Leeds and was a cousin of my mother. Their fathers were brothers but Mary's last name was anglicised from Inberg. They holidayed and visited us in Blankenberg after we finished working on the markets.

Bands played in the square in Blankenberg on Tuesday nights when people would dance. I loved to dance and have continued to feel great joy in movement all my life. Some hawkers would be selling big yellow sheets of paper with the lyrics of the songs and people would sing along happily with the bands. The bands were local groups whose music was enjoyed by everyone. Maurice would come to find me early in the evening when the dancing and music were still going on, as if to spoil my one night of fun. The next, and every day, I had to be ready to work before dawn because, on market days, we departed from the apartment at first light for the markets, returning exhausted at two or three in the afternoon, after which Minnie and I prepared the family's evening meal.

Working the market was a less than prestigious occupation so, if I saw any school peers who arrived to shop at the markets when they were on holiday, I tried to hide behind the stock. I felt ashamed to be in such a lowly occupation. At the same time, I felt envious that they were at the coast enjoying a holiday in our long summer break away from our studies.

When making change for customers, I became adept at stealing surreptitiously from the cash box. I justified this thieving because I was not paid for working every day throughout the summer. With this small amount of money, I would buy an ice cream or a wonderful grenadine-flavoured yoghurt at Stassano. There I sat at the window alone, eating this delicacy slowly, to make the pleasure last as long as possible. I was happy during those brief interludes, enjoying a rare treat and time alone. Again, food created a small experience or expectation of what I thought was happiness. Food was taking the place of real happiness which I could not feel in any other way.

Another use of my stolen small change was to hire a bicycle on Mondays and Fridays, as those days were spent at the local Blankenberg market. On those days, as our apartment was in Blankenberg, we did not have to spend time travelling back from another town. I tried to finish my after-market chores earlier in the afternoon on those two days. Then I would hire a bicycle and walk to an isolated abandoned building site where I taught myself to ride. After many bleeding knees from quite a few falls on the uneven concrete ground, I was a successful bike rider.

On the Blankenberg promenade facing the sea, there was a games arcade where I loved to go as often as I could. It was dark and full of automated gaming machines that lit up enticingly, the precursors of modern slot ('poker') machines. All of the flashing lights, sounds, bells announcing that somebody had won one of the amazing prizes such as a plush toy, a fake gold bracelet or a ring, fascinated me, even if the prizes were broken or discarded quickly. I was entranced and put most of my (stolen) money into these machines. I could have become addicted were it not for the fact that this amusement parlour was also the place where my brother met his friends. He certainly did not want his little sister spying on him so Charly went to the manager to report that I was under age. Ratcheting up his complaint, Charly threatened the manager that if I were ever allowed to enter the arcade, my brother would personally report the manager to the police. Banned, I never returned, even when old enough to enter legitimately. Instead I walked past, longingly remembering the mindless fun I enjoyed, pushing coins into the voracious machines. This forced interruption cured me of gambling and the lesson has lasted throughout my life.

My grandmother's maid

Soon after I was brought back from foster care in 1949, when I was eleven years old, my mother assigned me as the domestic servant for my grandparents. Each day after school, I trudged to my grandparents' house. It was on four levels, three floors above ground and a full-sized basement apartment. The ground floor was Zeida's tailoring business but, by then, he was too ill to work so that level was no longer used. He and Booba lived on the next level and they leased the top floor.

The basement apartment had been inhabited in previous summers, when the cooler cellar rooms provided welcome relief. Early in the war, when three generations of our family were living together, we gathered down there and lit the iron stove for heating and cooking. Post-war, the bathroom and toilet no longer functioned because the water was no longer connected. My grandparents could not walk down the cellar stairs any longer. Each day I descended repeatedly to carry up coal for their upstairs fireplace. Down to the basement I also carried their dirty laundry, stoked the fire under the big old copper pot to heat water and washed everything by hand on a scrubbing board. I hung their laundry outside, on a patio.

Just one toilet on the ground floor served all the inhabitants of the building. As my grandparents could not manage the steps down one floor to the toilet, they used chamber pots. Very, very carefully, I would carry those uncovered smelly pots down the stairs to empty in the toilet each day and then I would wash then return them for my grandparents' convenience. Booba bandaged her lower legs but, although she removed the bandages during the night, I doubted that her bandages were ever washed. When I rolled them up and then re-wound them around each of her legs, they were very smelly. She also used talcum powder very liberally, which made me feel nauseous.

On hands and knees, I cleaned the floors throughout their apartment. Booba demanded that all the house steps be cleaned weekly, from the entrance up to the third level. I scrubbed each step starting at the top level, drying them individually with a cloth and, finally, covering them with newsprint so they would not get dirty again, at least not too quickly.

Each day I walked to the nearby shops to buy their fresh provisions, purchased daily as they did not have a refrigerator. My brightest daily moment occurred outside the newsagent's shop, where I took a clandestine look at the daily paper on display, reading a serialised story as my temporary escape from the drudgery. That was how I first read Dostoyevsky when *Crime and Punishment* was serialised in French.

Zeida and Booba's fireplace was in constant use because my grandparents' home was cold inside and they remained in the house most of the time. Coal was delivered through a chute from the street, directly onto the floor of a storeroom in the basement. I cleaned their fireplace each day and, after carrying sufficient coal to keep the fire burning until the next day, I started a fresh fire each evening as my last duty for my grandparents.

Following all the cleaning and scrubbing, carting and shopping, I trudged home through Brussels' variable weather and, in winter, I arrived home after dark. Then I helped prepare dinner and performed whatever other duties I was assigned. Only late at night was I allowed to do my schoolwork so my education suffered from my being extremely tired following hours of labour after school. I was barely rested each morning when I returned to school.

During those hours of cleaning, I wore my only clothes, the same garments that I wore to school the next and every day. With hands grubby from dirt and coal and my nails always black, the children's question, '*Êtes-vous en deuil pour le chat?*' (Are you in mourning for the cat?) could have been made up for me.

My grandparents possessed two items made of silver that I had to polish. One was a samovar, a large metal container of water that was boiled and kept hot all day. It had a little tap from which I could fill a glass to make tea for adults whom I then served. Booba always requested a slice of lemon and a lump of sugar on the side. It was ornate with beautiful designs, which made it more difficult to clean, as the silver paste would lodge in the decorative grooves. Booba was very attached to it as it reminded her of her childhood home in Biala Podlaska.

They also had a tantalus, a lockable frame holding bottles displayed on the sideboard. It was a silver stand that locked with a little key, holding three beautiful crystal decanters filled with alcohol. Zeida was not averse to a drop or two of whisky but Booba kept the key in her apron pocket and she seldom released it and then only to serve guests or on special occasions. When I polished this delicate silver cage I had to avoid smearing polish on the bottles locked within the tantalus.

Only after the war did I see their magical gramophone hidden in one of the little side cupboards. Zeida would occasionally let me crank it but otherwise I was not allowed to touch it. He especially enjoyed playing old

Yiddish songs which made them both cry. I was always puzzled about why they would go to all the effort of turning on the gramophone so that they could cry.

As Booba was illiterate, I was her scribe. 'Sit down and write a letter', Booba would say to me in Yiddish and then she would begin her dictation with '*Mein dear kinder*' to her adult children who lived in other countries. I wrote her letters in French. Her ailments were her key news, so I tried to jazz up her letters with a bit of local news and commentary. Had she known, she would not have approved of my creative editing.

During the summers when we worked on markets at the coast, Minnie paid somebody to help my grandparents. Yet, once we returned to Brussels and I recommenced school, it was again my duty to clean and care for them every day, mind Helen daily and help with family chores. Any acknowledgment would have felt like recompense to me but not once did I hear 'thanks' from my mother, stepfather or grandparents, let alone receive a hug or a kiss for my work.

Nobody ever questioned my labour relationship with my family, least of all me. When thinking about those years now, the term 'child labour' springs to mind without any premeditation. I had never used that phrase previously to describe myself. Reviewing the International Labour Organisation's rules, I felt shocked that each type of work I did was outlawed. The demeaning and disgusting cleaning I did for my grandparents was mentally and physically challenging to me; being required to attempt to combine school attendance with excessively long and heavy work was exhausting while, later, I had many long absences from school when looking after my sister. Underage children working and anyone working without payment were both already illegal during those years, yet I was forced to work at the summer markets for no wages.

Booba took no interest in me as a person and never greeted me with a welcome or even a smile. She was consistent in that she was only negative towards me, reprimanding me with unreasonable meanness and frequently criticising me over irrelevant matters. I felt that she resented my existence. She never thanked me for anything I did for her and Zeida. She never gave me a little pocket money as payment for my chores nor did my grandmother give me a single birthday present in my lifetime.

Her days were spent embroidering, something she continued to do until her eyesight failed. She sent me to buy the linens, pre-printed with a design to 'fill in' with predetermined coloured thread. She considered each piece to be her personal creation despite it being an embroidery kit. Many times Booba told me that she was making the 'very next' tablecloth for me. She never gave me a tablecloth except to wash or to iron for her. For sentimental reasons, I salvaged one of Booba's large tablecloths from my mother's estate, despite it being damaged and no longer suitable for use. It reminded me of Booba's many worn promises.

Zeida, my grandfather

In my childhood, I believed that my grandfather loved me. I was so hungry for love that a pat on the head from him felt like a sign of love. He also showed minor interest in me, such as walking me to Sunday school and occasionally taking me to see a movie. My grandfather used to correct me but I always believed that I had inconvenienced him or been naughty, as though I caused his anger. Now, I doubt that he ever loved me.

Zeida had friends and a social life external to our family circle. Once I saw him with a woman at a trendy restaurant, a complete surprise to me as he and Booba never went out to eat. When he saw me staring in the window, he beckoned me into the doorway of the restaurant. He told me not to mention the encounter and I have never disclosed it until now. His private times possibly compensated for his fractious home life with Booba.

Two clear images of Zeida are etched in my memory. Once, his face was contorted with hate and malevolence for a little girl who was too young to have been able to predict or understand the consequences of her game with a kitten. The other image is of a very old feeble grandfather standing in front of his bedroom window wearing pyjamas, prayer book in hand, mumbling and entreating his god, probably about his impending death: he seemed to me already in another world. What he wished for I do not know.

Zeida was out in the city when a heart attack struck him and Minnie was contacted. She told me that he was very frightened of dying and she held him in her arms as he lay in hospital in Anderlecht, a suburb of Brussels. While in the hospital, he gave Minnie a pearl necklace that, to my child's eyes, signified his love for her. When I was in my twenties, Minnie gave me the necklace and I subsequently discovered it was fake. It was not worthless, however, because it was the only thing he had with him to give her. I have a lingering feeling that his gift to my mother was heartfelt but hardly comparable with the many diamonds and gold that his wife, Booba, owned. My grandfather died on 18 October 1957.

A few weeks after his death, the doorbell at Booba's house rang. I answered the door and there stood my grandfather: I swore that Zeida was back from the grave! This man had the same physique and features as Zeida but his face was severely scarred. I felt frightened as I thought a ghost was standing in front of me. I tried to shut the door in his face while my heart beat rapidly. This man spoke English with an American accent.

Here was Zeida's brother, a great-uncle whom I had never heard mentioned. He had searched for Zeida but, unfortunately, had arrived at his brother's door too late to see him alive. He lived in the USA where he owned oil wells in Wichita Falls, Texas, he said, and eventually explained that his face had been burned in an oil well fire. Booba forever referred to him as 'the oil can', somewhat dismissively. Our 'new' Inberg great-uncle was a fun, indulgent and worldly adult, the greatest relative in my eyes for a long time, although I did not remember his first name. He was a bright addition to our family at that sad time. Also visiting was my English cousin, Rosalyn, on her annual visit to improve her French, chaperoned by Mary Greenberg.

At the time of our newly-met American great-uncle's visit, the 1958 World's Exposition (Expo 58) had opened in Brussels. This exciting global event was the first Expo in eighteen years due to the war. A large array of exhibition halls and fairgrounds and so much excitement were very near to where we lived. My great-uncle took Helen and me, with my cousin Rosalyn, on exciting outings to the Expo, seeing many exhibits and treating us to thrilling fair rides. These were several magical days for us, stimulating

45. Visiting World Fair in Brussels (from left) Maurice Blumberg, Mary Greenberg (English cousin and chaperone for Rosalyn), sister Helen Blumberg in front of our Texan great-uncle, Francine and her mother, Minnie Blumberg, 1958.

46. World Fair tickets, 1958.

in a fun and childish way, while informing me about the cultures of many nations.

Our great-uncle offered air tickets to Rosalyn and me to visit him in America. My mother did not allow me to travel to the USA. Rosalyn went as his guest, chaperoned as always by Mary Greenberg, one of Minnie's three cousins in Leeds, a daughter of Zeida's brother in England. They met Mima Sarah and her family in New Jersey. Rosalyn never told me any details, even though I longed to meet my Rosenblum relatives in America and to know more about them. I was left with no trace of information about those relatives. I felt disappointment, jealousy and loss.

Now, all our family males were gone. Zeida and my father were deceased and Charly and Bunny were far away in Australia. I never considered Maurice my family; he was Minnie's husband and Helen's father and never meant anything more to me.

Chapter Thirteen

Education Denied

In my family nobody was in the professions. Only my father had finished high school and he remained my inspiration in education and everything that mattered in life. Our female family doctor became an important role model, as a woman who was educated. The sight of Docteur Martin carrying her big brown leather bag, her dishevelled brown hair streaked with a few grey strands, amazed me because I saw in her a woman who had a good education, having finished high school and achieved university qualifications. She inspired such deference and admiration and had a highly respected position in society. I dared to dream that I would study and that, one day, I would become a doctor just like her. Docteur Martin remains one of the few people in my early life whom I can visualise precisely as she meant so many things to me, from being a caring doctor to an inspiration. In fact, I saw her rarely as the doctor was only consulted if one of us was almost at death's door, necessitating a home visit. Minnie did not take us to the doctor's office for small ailments as she complained that the fee was very high.

My education was forcibly terminated just after my thirteenth birthday. Despite starting school late, at eight years of age, I completed seven years' education in four and a half years. There were four study options following primary school. *Greco-romaines* was the stream for students demonstrating academic aptitude and likely to qualify for one of the professions; *études modernes* was somewhat less esoteric; and for the least academically capable, there was a domestic training program. Another option was to learn vocational skills at a business college or a trade.

Teachers nominated me for *Greco-romaines* based on my high marks, for which I felt very proud. Their recommendation made me feel optimistic and this was the highest accolade I achieved in school. Money would not be a barrier, as the government paid fees and expenses for formal secondary studies for each *orphelin de guerre* (war orphan).

Therefore, I felt sure that my mother, when she saw my excellent results and the recommendation to enter the top stream at no cost to her, would agree to me continuing in secondary studies. Secretly, I hoped to prove to my family that I was as intelligent as my cousin Rosalyn when I made the most of my study options. Already I was dreaming of all the wonderful things I might achieve, all the great personalities that I would meet as equals and all the good things that people would say about my future contributions, perhaps with admiration and maybe with awe.

Minnie refused to allow me to undertake my option for secondary studies. Here was my educational dream in reach and an offer confirmed in writing and only needing her approval. With the advantage of hindsight, given that Minnie's education had been curtailed and that she had not bothered to enrol me in primary school, she obviously did not consider education to be a valid or necessary option for me. She declared that I would not continue studying in secondary school.

Yet I felt driven to learn more and as much as possible about every subject that I could access. Without the challenge of high school to look forward to, it seemed like the end of my world and my opportunities. My persistent longing to learn sowed an idea that, sometime in the future, I could enrol myself in formal education.

Before the last term of primary school, all students were grouped according to their study options for the year ahead. As I could not accept my place in the top stream, I spent my last full term in primary school in the lowest class. We followed a program of very elementary basic learning, boosted by classes in 'housekeeping'. Some of the more interesting topics were washing, ironing, mending, making paste to clean the silver, knitting and crochet. I passionately hated them. I felt angry as well as embarrassed that I was forced into the very bottom class after earning a place in the top class. When I saw my former peers at school, I longed to go with them to their interesting classes, where I would learn new ideas and read exciting books.

I felt sure that my father would have expected and supported me in pursuing high school and further education, as he was well-educated as was his mother. If he had survived I would have had his support and advice on these important matters. Decisions such as ending my schooling were the result of the family dynamics in which I now lived.

Minnie announced that typing school was a good enough goal for me. She dictated that I must undertake the shortest course at l'école Funck, a business college, to learn basic typing and shorthand. Pleading, crying and begging her to allow me to continue my education made no impact on my mother. She was unmoved and stated more than once, 'You cannot expect my husband to support you.'

Her own stunted education blinded her to the value and potential financial advantages of pursuing higher studies. Paradoxically, she admired her niece Rosalyn for her academic achievements in England. Minnie's choice of typing and shorthand for me could only lead to low-level office work, not sufficiently well paid to allow me to become self-supporting. She probably thought that I would marry, have children and not go out to work, mirroring her early life with my father who was the sole provider. She did not have any hindsight about her own situation, ill-educated and widowed with small children. Minnie never understood that women needed more education.

There was no celebration of this important transition in my life, when leaving school. Disappointment was an understatement with regard to my feelings throughout that summer as I spent working, unpaid, on the markets for Minnie and Maurice.

Deprivation of education confronted me each summer when Rosalyn visited Belgium from England. Her parents sent her to improve her French because they valued learning. I ached to be treated in the same way as her and to enter secondary school. My illiterate grandmother used to compare me unfavourably with Rosalyn, calling me '*nahr*' (idiot in Yiddish) as she pointed out my cousin's most recent achievement. I did not dare remind my grandmother that I had been prevented from continuing my education.

Even after I commenced training at l'école Funck in the autumn, I still pleaded with my mother who did not reverse her decision to cease my formal education. My new peers were girls destined to work in typing pools. L'école Funck was in Place Anneessens, a twenty-five-minute walk from my grandparents' home where I still did all their cleaning and chores every afternoon. That walk took me through rue Camusel where my father had hidden us in a porch during the war, not that I dwelt on that lucky escape now that I was thirteen years old.

Whether I refused to learn or I was hampered because I had been forced to use my right hand for tasks in spite of my left-handedness, I never mastered touch-typing and have always had to look at the keyboard as I type. Shorthand was harder still and I never achieved the dizzying speeds of my colleagues, but I did learn the mysterious symbols. I decided to keep a secret diary in shorthand and promptly forgot all I learned. Who knows what I wrote in these diaries as I certainly have never been able to read them.

When I finished my half-year at l'école Funck, it was springtime in 1952, just after my fourteenth birthday. I did not learn much nor was I motivated at typing school as I resented the work Minnie had chosen for me when my mind yearned for intellectual stimulation. My heart ached for a chance at a better life and I was mourning for my lost opportunity to learn for a few more years. Straight after completing that short course at the secretarial college, I worked once again all summer in the grubby outdoor markets, while Charly was far away in Australia.

Chapter Fourteen

Growing up

In the autumn of 1952, despite being slow at typing (that never improved) and without sufficient shorthand skills, I found good employment. Working in a clean, bright and efficient office was a revelation about employment conditions that I had never experienced on the markets. Here I only started relatively late, at nine in the morning, and I worked set hours. I had daily morning and afternoon breaks with free cups of coffee and biscuits. For the first time in my life, I had a daily lunch break in a subsidised cafeteria where I sat at a table, eating prepared food, served to me and enjoying pleasant adult company.

47. Francine working in an office typing pool, Brussels Belgium, mid-1950s.

Occasionally, free tickets to movies and other entertainments were distributed. I made new acquaintances and revelled in the social life among my colleagues after work hours. I especially loved the Christmas celebrations and other parties. There I met people with an education who lived in nice homes, behaved with good manners and treated me with respect. The contrast with my life up to this point was blinding, as now I could see how others lived and socialised and spent their leisure time and money. I was inspired to succeed in my new job.

Minnie required that I give her a large part of my weekly income. Her preoccupation with money was complicated. Despite being in a good job and paying her a substantial weekly sum, when the next spring approached after I turned fifteen in 1953, my mother demanded that I resume unpaid summer work at the markets for her and Maurice. That meant resigning from my first office job that had been my entry into the adult world and which had provided a learning experience about money, social options and friendships.

This was the first time that I had been paid for my work. Of course, I had laboured daily for my family without any payment. The downside of Minnie's financial management of me was that I worked, unpaid, to help her and Maurice to make their good income. Neatly devised, with no direct cost for my labour, their profits were higher. Each summer I must have earned more than my weekly board payments from my office job in the other nine months.

My personal costs were not taken into account, such as losing income three months each year, missing further training provided on the job and the opportunities for advancement, let alone achieving work satisfaction and personal growth. Each time I settled into a job that I liked, nearly nine months' employment passed and then I had to resign at the beginning of summer and begin to work again, unpaid, on the summer markets. Tied up at the coast from mid-June to mid-September, I had to find another new office job for the balance of each successive year. I could only obtain entry-level jobs, again and again, as I never accrued sufficient experience or seniority to attain a better position. Beyond all those occupational dilemmas, each time I found stable employment and a social base for myself, I was wrenched out to another temporary summer flat, social isolation and unpaid hardship.

One of my best jobs was at Unilever, a large multinational enterprise where all staff received American employment benefits. I loved the subsidised cafeteria that served great food. Best of all, employees were issued each month with a list of products available at wholesale prices. There were still shortages in Belgium and many of the products available were relatively luxurious compared with my rugged home standards. Next spring, I was forced to leave this positive work environment again to work for my mother and stepfather without earning money. By that time Maurice had stockpiled enough Unilever soap, toothpaste, canned food, toilet paper and numerous other items to last through a ten-year siege. He stored most of it in his large black cupboard and stacked the rest on top.

Whatever my mother told me to do, I did. Every summer I repeated the disappointment of giving notice and quitting a job that I liked because I was required to help her at the markets. I experienced a cruel imbalance, from being paid for working in positions that were respected and eagerly sought, followed by grubby, low-status, unpaid work for three or more months every year, living in rough conditions. Each autumn I applied for and commenced another office job. I resumed looking after Helen and our grandparents before and after work.

From autumn to spring, Minnie and Maurice worked just one day per week during their nine-month 'off season', at their regular Sunday market in Brussels at Place Jamar near the Gare du Midi. Charly had been their unpaid help every Sunday, the only day he had free from his paid work. Following their financial success over the summer, in addition to their combined four reparation pensions from Germany (three collected by Minnie, one by Maurice), their income for the following nine months included a portion of my weekly office income once I commenced a new paying job.

Soon Minnie and Maurice began to go on exotic holidays to warm places during their off-season, such as the south of France, Madeira and the Canary Islands. They stayed in wonderful resorts which they described when they returned. I was left in charge of Helen and my grandparents, while working full time in an office. After Helen started school and I was working, I helped her with her homework. I hoped that one day I would have my first family holiday together. If we were lucky, Maurice returned with a suitcase full of fancy cheeses and, after many had gone bad (we still ate them), he bought our first refrigerator.

Just before my fifteenth birthday, we moved to 381 rue du Progrès in January 1953, a dismal flat in which the bathroom lacked plumbing fittings. Maurice used that 'bathroom' to store his vats of homemade pickled cucumbers (to which I would help myself), jars of fermenting cherries and shelves of fruit; the market stock was in another room accessed via three steps. His brother in Israel occasionally sent us a case of Jaffa oranges that smelled like perfume to me; they were so rare that we were only allowed to eat one orange shared between all of us, juice running down our faces.

Before Helen began school and after I started office work, Minnie employed a live-in maid. Jadwiga spoke Polish (as did Maurice) and I learned to converse with her in Polish because she did not speak French. She had Sunday off when she went to church and I minded Helen. Before too long, Jadwiga met a Polish man at church whom she married. When she left to get married, I was forced to take on the work of running the family again. I would lose days of work and pay when Helen was sick and I had to stay home with her because there was no adult in the house.

All my life in Belgium I never objected out loud nor queried or refused to do what my mother and her family told me to do. Compliance was expected of me and I did as much as I possibly could. I wanted to show my mother that I was her 'good girl'.

Inside, I did not want to do what Minnie told me to do; I wanted to revolt and yearned to object. Whatever I felt was not shown, so I was always quiet and well-behaved. Yet I believed what I was told – that I was badly behaved. I was labelled a 'problem' and was treated as a villain. 'Naughty Francine' became an accepted fact, neither a fair assessment of my behaviour nor of my personality.

Secretly, I was hoping, craving, begging for her acceptance and love. I hoped that, one day, my mother would say, 'I love you', if only once. I held onto that dream until her death, by which time she had dementia and no longer recognised any of her family. I never heard her say those three important words to me.

Becoming Belgian

Although I was born in Belgium, I was deemed to be Polish as Belgian law ascribed to a child the same nationality as the child's father. Therefore, I was neither considered Belgian nor legally entitled to citizenship when born in Belgium. At sixteen years of age, I could choose between Polish and Belgian nationalities. This was called *opter* (to opt) or *option de patrie* (choice of nationality) that led to naturalisation. I passed all the police investigations into my character, good behaviour and morality. On 20 October 1954, I was granted Belgian nationality, which I still hold.

Cultural awakenings

A work colleague, Mary George, introduced me to opera. We bought cheap tickets to La Monnaie, the Brussels opera house. We waited to buy our tickets until the performance was about to commence, just before curtain call, when the ushers allowed students to sit in any unoccupied seats, known as 'student rushes'. We went to a few operas together and although she lost interest, I continued to attend operas on my own. I cried at the sadness of the stories and laughed when an overweight aging soprano sang *J'ai quinze ans* (I am fifteen years old) in *Madama Butterfly*.

When I arrived back home after seeing *Tosca* by Giacomo Puccini and told Minnie about it, she said matter-of-factly, 'That was your father's favourite opera', and seemed uninterested in hearing any more about the performance. I did not know that he had liked opera nor had I ever seen Minnie attend any

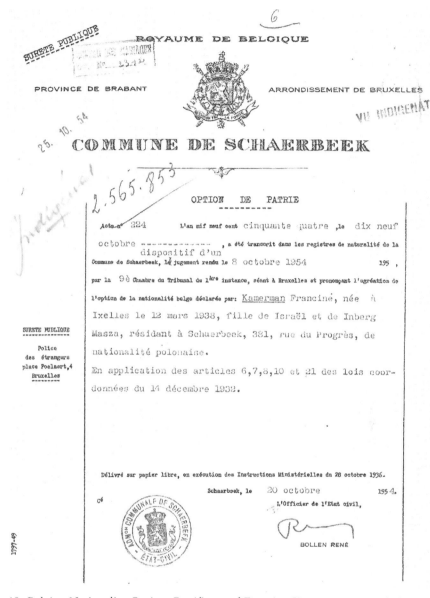

48. Belgian Nationality Option Certificate of Francine Kamerman, provided by the Commune of Schaerbeek on behalf of the Kingdom of Belgium, 1954.

creative performance. This was such a strange and happy revelation and it felt great to discover one more thing about my father; I felt close to him knowing that we shared at least a passion. I longed for more details about my father just like this opera anecdote but no one ever spoke to me about him.

Tosca became my favourite opera, along with Carmen. Many years later, when visiting Rome, my priority was to go to visit the Castel St Angelo where much of *Tosca* takes place. There I made a silent prayer to my father and I experienced a form of spiritual union with him. I knew so little about him. Since that first *Tosca* experience, I have always left a performance with tears streaming down my face, not only for Floria Tosca but also for my father with whom I shared so few years.

Soon I discovered where discount tickets were available from the Concert hall. After attending a few concerts, I began to appreciate what I was hearing. At one performance, the soloist was a child prodigy who played the piano to great acclaim and, for weeks afterwards, I dreamt of marrying him: he was my first romantic crush.

Apart from forays to concerts and the opera, my favourite outings were to meetings of various Jewish youth movements. Although I did not adopt their political aims, I went because I loved the camaraderie, especially when we went camping, sitting around the fire and singing until late into the night, as well as the wild dancing of *horrahs* (Jewish dances). These were the few activities that I enjoyed and which I could afford.

Suddenly, my mother started to impose curfews on me, requiring me to return home by a certain time each evening. I found this constricting and antagonistic. I considered her new restrictions highly hypocritical given that she had left me alone, year after year, to roam the streets unsupervised, and now left me to mind my baby sister (and the household and grandparents) when she and Maurice went on holidays to exotic countries. She was restricting the few activities which I enjoyed and that I could afford. Finally, I revolted and frequently broke her deadline out of sheer bravado to show my mother that she could no longer control my every minute.

At one of the Jewish movements, I met Henri Gurman who became a lifelong friend. He imagined that he was my boyfriend and he tried to endear himself to the family by doing some chores such as helping my stepfather empty heavy bundles of knitwear out of the car. I had become very fond of a type of sausage that was available only from a butchery far from my home. Sometimes Henri arrived with a gift of these sausages and he had to watch me eat them without sharing. They were delicious and made me feel good, just as most food temporarily eased my emotional turmoil (but with weighty consequences in later years).

Henri's childhood was also very tough but he never showed it. His brother André had fallen out of a tree when he was twelve and his lower body remained paralysed. Henri happily pushed the wheelchair and André was included in all activities. Henri was always telling jokes, making people laugh and making the world around him a better place. I was so happy to see him in recent years and felt particularly devastated when he passed away in 2013.

Only after his death did I see his name recorded as a hidden child (in Andrée Geulen-Herscovici's *Notebooks*) in Yad Vashem, Israel. I discovered his secret too late for us to share details of our hidden years.

Often one does not really know one's own hometown. The emblem of Brussels is a little naked boy urinating, based on a stone statue, *Manneken-Pis*, on display close to the Grand Place, Brussels' main square. At eighteen years of age, I first saw this statue when hosting my Swedish pen pal, Monica, with whom I had corresponded in poor English from my primary school days. Monica wanted to see *Manneken-Pis*. After getting lost several times, we finally found him tucked in a little niche and I exclaimed, 'Isn't he small!' All the other tourists laughed as, in the French language, there is no difference between 'he' and 'it'. I felt embarrassed at my innocent mistake.

Nervous breakdown

For my entire seventeenth year in 1955, I was terrified of leaving the safety of my home: I suffered from agoraphobia. I only felt safe in the apartment at 23 rue Vandeweyer in Schaerbeek. I barely left home and then, only with my mother. Anxieties surfaced and I was constantly jumpy, teary and fearful. That summer, I still had to go to the coast markets with Minnie, Maurice and Helen, where I stayed physically close to my mother and worked a little less than in previous summers. My condition was referred to as 'an incident', not a mental health crisis, another battle in my on-going war.

In hindsight, my breakdown was an expression of all the emotional turmoil, deepened through the many physical and social deprivations that I had experienced continuously from early childhood. In addition to trauma and isolation as a hidden child, I still felt inconsolable grief for my father. It was a long-suppressed cry of the anguish of hiding from Nazis, unrelenting grief after my father's murder, rejection and serious abuse in my home life as well as my antagonistic school years.

Among my tribulations in foster homes and relatives' homes, I was physically, mentally and emotionally abused. I longed for a loving touch, not the evil and exploitive touches from adults that left me feeling soiled as a predator's victim, confused and quite traumatised. I spent most of my first two decades without love or care and concern. These circumstances of abuse and neglect left indelible emotional scars. Also, I felt resentment that my mother did not care for me as my father had done and that she obviously cared more for Maurice and Helen. I felt that I was looking outside a window on to others' lives. I was puzzled about why my existence was so different from theirs. It was bewildering.

Minnie was relatively kind to me at that time. She was probably embarrassed by my fearful and panicky behaviour on the rare times she took

49. Francine in her first new gown, aged seventeen years, 1955.

me out in public. A neighbour recommended a non-standard healer to help me and, although he had a respectable plaque outside his office, he had no staff and I never encountered another patient. He would be called a 'quack' today. He tried unsuccessfully to hypnotise me, among many unorthodox 'treatments'. He gave me intravenous injections that left a terrible metallic taste in my mouth; I never found out what he injected into me. I endured electric shocks through earphone devices. The electricity hurt me, shook me terribly and then I would fall asleep in the chair. My mother arrived following each 'treatment' to take me home. I slowly recovered but never ceased experiencing occasional panic attacks.

During this anxious year, the family was invited to a wedding. The bride, Liliane, was the niece of Helen Rejzner who was my sister Helen's godmother; both of Liliane's parents were murdered by the Nazis during the war and her aunt and uncle raised her. Amazingly, Minnie bought me a beautiful gown, expensive and stylish, to wear to the wedding. She rarely purchased me any new clothing apart from the basic necessities. Spending all that money on one dress for a single event was in glaring contrast with her usual expenditure habits for me. She implied that, by her spending an enormous amount on one fabulous dress to wear for a few hours at a wedding, I would become so happy that I would automatically return to good health. Buying me new clothes, even if for the first time, was not my cure. I needed love, emotional support, reasonable leisure time and further education. I wanted new interests, maybe a hobby instead of a task.

Around this time, Maurice must have consulted a matchmaker for me because a young man, about whom I knew nothing, came to our home. I overheard them talking in Yiddish but I was not introduced to him nor invited to join their discussion. When he departed, I saw from the window that this young Jewish man was dressed in a very religious style, wearing a big black hat, black clothes and with his hair in ringlets. He never set eyes on me and nothing was ever said directly to me about him.

By the time I recovered, then about eighteen years old (1956), someone applied for a visa for me to migrate to Australia without consulting me. I later discovered that, ten years earlier, Auntie Betty had applied to be my sponsor in Australia in 1946 (National Archives of Australia).

An Australian visa entailed substantial paperwork. I was required to learn English but, as I did not have much spare time to attend classes, I did not achieve adequate fluency although I had learned some words from looking at the English magazines that my mother purchased and read at home. Oddly, though Minnie was raised in England, she did not help me learn the foundations of English when growing up nor help me now that speaking English was necessary to earn a visa to Australia.

Alarmingly, the required medical report revealed that there were shadows on both of my lungs. They were most likely from tuberculosis that was endemic in the crowded unhygienic housing in which I hid during the war and in which my family lived post-war. It took some time for my lungs to clear, although I do not know how I recovered, and the subsequent x-rays proved that my lungs had returned to complete health.

Really, at first I was blithe about the entire Australian proposition but later I began to look forward to the trip, considering it in the order of a ferry ride to visit relatives in London. I truly expected it to be a brief visit and then expected to return to Belgium. I secretly looked forward to being away from Minnie and Maurice. As the wait for the visa approval took a long time, Australia seemed just an idea not a life-changing event that could actually happen to me. In retrospect it should have been obvious to me that Minnie and Maurice wanted me out of their home.

Chapter Fifteen

In love with Sydney

An opal-hearted country,
A wilful, lavish land ...

Dorothea MacKellar,
My Country [52]

Never did I dream of leaving Belgium, let alone migrating to Australia, a country about which I knew nothing. My Australian visa must have taken so long to be approved (medical re-checking, English competency and so on) that I had forgotten about the spectre of leaving Belgium let alone going to Australia – about as far as one could journey from Brussels.

Zeida died when I was twenty. Soon after, it was decided that widowed Booba would migrate to Australia. Family correspondence provided clues about the thinking behind the decision. My mother and her sisters decided that Booba, then widowed, would be happy living among her family settled in Sydney, namely Auntie Betty, Auntie Rose, Uncle Max and their spouses and children, as well as Bunny and Charly. I understand now that she wanted to be where most of her children lived, even if that was far from Belgium.

Coincidentally, I was about to become obsolete as Helen's carer. She would turn ten at the end of 1959 and Minnie and Maurice announced that Helen would be enrolled in a boarding school. In a decision which was not unrelated, Minnie and her 'coven' of sisters made the decision that I would be Booba's companion and chamber maid on her migration journey.

I'll never know whether my departure with Booba was decided first and, therefore, without me as a built-in carer, or whether Helen was enrolled in boarding school so that I would no longer be needed as her carer. Either way I would be sent to look after my grandmother on the long journey to Australia. I was more upset that Helen would live my dream, going to high school, making friends and achieving her potential, than I was about leaving Brussels. I would be separated from everything that was familiar.

Whatever the decision-making pathways, I was never consulted about leaving Belgium. I had no intention of migrating anywhere, let alone to

Australia. I wondered who paid to send me away. Very soon, I was packing a small case with my few possessions for a long ocean journey to an unknown country. I was only provided with a one-way ticket and my Auntie Betty sent me a picture book on Australia.

In late January 1959, Maurice drove Booba and me, with Minnie and Helen, to our departure point. For the very first time, he broke his self-imposed condition to use his car exclusively for markets and work. This was the only time he drove me anywhere. At the port of Ostend, I said goodbye to Helen who cried. After Helen and Maurice said farewell to us, they returned to Brussels, our ferry having departed for England.

My mother, Booba and I arrived in London after the ferry trip and spent two nights with Auntie Fay before travelling to Southampton to board our ship. I was disappointed that I saw nothing of London because all three women

50. Maurice and Helen Blumberg say farewell to Francine Kamerman and Booba at Ostend, Belgium, as they leave for Australia, February 1959.

decided to remain at the house. For these two nights, I slept with my mother – she never shared any hugs. She never said she was going to miss me or gave me any reassurances during our last few hours together. Minnie was sending me away from her life with Maurice and Helen.

On the third day, Minnie stood on the Southampton wharf to watch us depart for the other side of the world. On the MS *Oranje* from the Netherlands, a former wartime troop hospital ship, we travelled second class in an inside cabin.

With hardly any money, I was leaving for a six-week voyage to start a new life, traversing a vast distance far away from all I knew. Minnie handed me a small amount of cash with strict instructions that it be entrusted to Auntie Betty on my arrival. Minnie decided that there was no need to provide me with spending money for the journey because the cost of my meals and amenities was included in the ticket and she decided that port tours were unnecessary. The paltry amount of money that I had saved from my office salary I spent on trinkets to give to my Australian family.

Yet it was a holiday because, for the first time, I did not have to do any housework. We had our own bathroom. This was where I had my first shower and I luxuriated in taking two or three each day, even if it irritated my grandmother, throughout the journey. I loved so much the sensation of the warm water running down my body and the satisfaction of feeling completely clean.

There were plenty of culture shocks, beginning with being offered Dutch cheese at every meal. It was amazing to see the aquamarine water in the Suez

51. Francine Kamerman and Booba dining aboard the MS *Oranje*, February 1959.

Canal and to view Egypt from the ship's deck. I enjoyed the port stops at Colombo in Sri Lanka, Penang in Malaysia and Singapore. Crossing the Equator was a surprise, with people being thrown into the ship's swimming pool to celebrate the occasion. Because I could not swim and I was very afraid of being in water, I had to be rescued from this frivolity, leaving me feeling embarrassed about my inability to swim during the remainder of the voyage.

Perth was our first Australian port. Auntie Betty met us there after flying from Sydney and joined our ship to cruise with us back to Sydney. Her reason for this excursion, travelling first class, was so that she could ascertain whether I was worthy of being offered a room in her home. Her two key concerns regarded my cleanliness and whether I used proper table manners. I passed both tests and earned an invitation to live in her house. When the ship stopped in Melbourne for a day, we were invited for a meal with relations of Betty's husband. There I discreetly removed all the black pips from the passion fruit on the pavlova (a meringue cake topped with whipped cream and fruit) as I had never seen, let alone eaten, that fruit. I would try many novel foods in my new country.

There are still insufficient words to describe the happiness and awe that I felt when our ship passed between the Sydney Harbour Heads and proceeded to its berth at five o'clock on the morning of 8 March 1959. What a sight! The sun was just dawning and the shores were covered in beautiful gleaming little houses, gardens and green parks. Sydney lay sprawled in all its beauty. It was a glorious morning, the dawn of my new life.

I fell in love with Sydney and I have never ceased loving her. I have travelled to many places but, for me, this remains the most beautiful city on earth. Each time I have been away, as my returning plane circles before landing and I see, sprawled below, hundreds of magnificent beaches, coves and escarpments, I catch my breath and remind myself how fortunate I have been to live in this paradise on earth. When I go to the Sydney Opera House on the Harbour's edge, I see the city standing, mischievous, glimmering – a young and happy city. The clear blue of the sky in Sydney remains unique on this planet. I never take Sydney's welcome for granted.

One week before my twenty-first birthday, I stood on a Sydney wharf with a small suitcase containing all my possessions: a few clothes, basic toiletries and a child's coffee set dating from my hidden years during the war. Since Auntie Betty had decided that I would live in her home, I handed her the money Minnie had entrusted to me before leaving Belgium, as instructed. Even then, I was not sure that I would or even could be happy living in Australia but I had no means to return to Belgium.

Minnie had given me a bottle of Eau de Cologne 4711 to give to Auntie Betty. I also purchased a carton of cigarettes at the ship's duty free store for my Uncle Sam. When I offered it to him, he ungraciously told me that he did not smoke the brand I had purchased and told me to keep it – he smoked only Du Maurier, a more expensive brand. The cheap cigarettes lay in a drawer for some months until I decided to teach myself to smoke, believing it to be the habit of sophisticated people. I opened the carton, took out a packet and, looking in the mirror, I practised and practised holding a cigarette and lifting it to my lips. At first, I could not tolerate the smoke and I coughed but I soon perfected a smoker's 'style' and, unfortunately, I was hooked. In those days, there was no public knowledge of the dangers of tobacco and very many people smoked.

My few clothes were not adequate for the warm weather nor suited to the fashions in Sydney. My aunts and uncles operated the Belmode Knitting Mills and Belmode Millinery in Newtown, an inner suburb of Sydney. They manufactured knitwear and other garments, from which Auntie Betty sold me some clothing at a discount. I was lucky – I could fit in the sample garments which were original designer clothes which the business had purchased in order to copy and sell their local versions throughout Australia.

Family in Australia

Betty and Sam Swieca and their son Peter lived in a lovely three-bedroom cottage on Edgecliff Road in Woollahra. Peter was thrilled to have me staying

52. First Passover with Australian family, April 1959
Seated from left: Booba Inberg, Edith Swieca, Francine Kamerman, Betty Swieca née Inberg, Sam & Peter Swieca, Joe & Lesley Lander
Standing from left: Albert Swieca, Bernard (Bunny) Inberg, Rose Lander née Inberg, Gary Inberg held by Rosine Inberg (née De Noose), Alexis Lander and Max Inberg

and adopted me as his 'big sister'. Without any complaint, he dismantled his train set which occupied the third bedroom so that I could sleep there. For the first time in my life, I had a room of my own, my first experience of privacy, personal space and a peaceful haven.

Taking me into her home, Betty gave me more than a place to stay as she also shared her social position and network with me. She was well respected in the community and her position reflected positively on me as 'Betty Swieca's niece'. I met some young people and settled down comfortably. My command of English improved daily and soon I had no problems communicating. Those were heady, happy days.

All our family lived within a four kilometre radius. I saw every cousin each school morning and, on Friday evening, the family gathered at the home of Auntie Betty for *Shabbat*.

Her sister-in-law, Edith, and brother-in-law, Albert Swieca (Sam's brother), welcomed me wholeheartedly. They were the kindest to me among the entire family. They took me to a nearby beach called Camp Cove on Sydney Harbour on summer Sundays to have a great day out and to meet other young people.

Auntie Rosine and Max occasionally invited me to join them for a meal. I became very close to them and to their sons, Rickey (Henry) and Gary. I never passed over the threshold of Auntie Rose and Joe Lander's home, however, despite her living just across the small green park from Betty's house. I never learned why they did not invite me into their home.

Sam Swieca (Betty's husband) owned a large car, a big eight-cylinder Dodge with protruding tail fins. I acquired my driving licence after passing the test on my sixth lesson. Then I was put in charge of driving and collecting all the cousins each morning and dropping them at their various schools. After that errand, I would return the car promptly, so that the aunts and uncles could drive to their factory in Newtown near the city.

Rushing back one day from the school run, I missed the garage corner – part of the car went in and part of the car did not. I was terrified that, since I had done such a terrible thing, they would throw me out of their home. However, all Sam asked was, 'Are you hurt?' and when I said 'No', he replied, 'That's okay then – the car can be fixed.' For a time, everyone travelled by public transport to school or work. I was amazed that nobody complained at me about anything.

Friday evenings after the family dinner and again on Sunday afternoons, Auntie Betty held an 'open house', when friends were welcome to drop in for a chat and enjoy a cup of tea. It was a very little house, yet somehow Betty managed to accommodate a large number of guests. I invited a young man to tea one Friday night and he arrived with a large bouquet of flowers for Betty and a box of chocolates for me. We sat down and everybody was talking. Soon the young man was getting restless, looking towards the kitchen, and finally he asked me, 'When are we having tea?' I told him, 'Not yet', as we had only

53. Australian family, 1960s. From left: Ricky Inberg & companion, Edith & Albert Swieca, Betty & Sam Swieca, Booba, Peter Swieca, Rosine & Max Inberg, Francine, Bunny Inberg.

just eaten dinner. Finally, Betty took me aside and asked me if I had invited the young man for tea. When I said, 'Yes', she immediately served food to this hungry young man. She explained to me that I had confused him with word usage, as many people in Australia referred to the evening meal as 'tea' rather than 'dinner'.

Charly was married to June, an Australian work colleague of his, and they lived in Arncliffe, south of the city and near the Sydney airport. As always, he worked very long hours. June was pregnant when Booba and I arrived in Sydney and, two months later, their baby boy was born on 10 May 1959, the anniversary of the invasion of Belgium. Charly and I did not have many opportunities to socialise though I would visit them every couple of weeks to share a meal and enjoy their news. Charly's only child was named Ian to honour our father, following the Jewish custom of naming a child after a dead relative in order to perpetuate their memory.

Both Charly and I were still in mourning for our father. We also harboured regrets about the childhood that we could have lived if our father had survived to raise us in a stable family.

A career

After a few days in Sydney, it became evident that I must find some kind of employment to pay rent and for food. Auntie Betty found me a job in a friend's shop. I could not sell much in this electrical goods store because my English was not very good, so I was assigned to make refreshments and to clean. I hated being back at that low-level work. Improving my English became my priority so I could obtain interesting work. How much easier my start in Australia would have been had my mother taught me English.

Therefore, I came up with the idea of applying to the Alliance Française office in the city to find work where French literacy and fluency were advantages. There I learned of a vacancy at the French bank as the office assistant to the general manager. Monsieur Rista was very happy to have a French-speaking person on his staff. I loved my new position which was a challenge far above my typing pool days and I secretly felt proud of finally achieving higher status in the work place.

One day, a male acquaintance came to the bank and invited me to lunch. It was a very pleasant time even though the young man did not leave an impression on me – I have long-forgotten his name. When I arrived home that evening and told Auntie Betty that I was a guest at lunch and mentioned that we went to Romano's, she was horrified. 'How could you go to Romano's without a hat and gloves?' I obviously did not know that Romano's was a posh meeting place for the well-heeled in Sydney and had not learned about the proper local dress customs for women invited to a formal lunch. There was more than English to learn in this new land.

In pre-decimal money, I was earning fourteen pounds per week at the bank. Half was paid to Auntie Betty for room and 'full board', as rooming rates were known at that time. In addition to making that weekly payment, every night I had to wash the dinner dishes and I had to drive all the cousins to school during the week. The balance of my wages paid for public transport to work, clothes, personal grooming and any entertainment and gifts. Smoking was an added expense, so I was very often short of money.

As Christmas approached, I discovered that my Jewish family celebrated the practice of exchanging gifts. How could I manage to reciprocate when I was short of money? Fortunately, a work colleague told me that shops discounted last minute purchases; in truth, they were only reducing the prices for the sale that took place the day after Christmas Day, known as the Boxing Day public holiday. I put little notes in envelopes, telling recipients that I had not been able to get their size or a specific colour and purchased the discounted presents at the subsequent sales.

At a party for Bastille Day, the Belgian Chargé d'Affaires, Monsieur Stevens, complained to Monsieur Rista that he was short of staff and could not find a French-speaking assistant for the Sydney Legation Office. The men made their own agreement and I received an offer to change jobs. At first, I thought Monsieur Rista had fired me! Now, I was a member of the Belgian Foreign Service.

Imagine me, ten years after I was forced to leave formal schooling in Belgium when thirteen years old, now being the acting Belgian Chancellor, issuing passports, visas and a wide range of documents. This was a time of great upheaval in the diplomatic corps when all legations became embassies and were relocated to Canberra, the national capital of Australia. Monsieur Stevens, a poet and violinist, was the first Belgian Ambassador to Australia.

The plans for the embassy in Canberra, its furniture and furnishings were designed in Belgium and the contents shipped to Australia. As items arrived daily, I supervised the manifest up to the completion of the building and placement of its furnishings as they arrived from Belgium. Even the content of the library was meticulously selected by and shipped from Brussels.

Naturally, I felt proud that, due to yet another twist of fate, I was able to help other people by working for the Belgian government. I was engrossed in this very exciting, busy and rewarding position. It was an exciting and scary time, when Belgium gave independence to its former colony, the Belgian Congo, now Zaïre. After the murder of Lumumba, who was destined for a great leadership role in the new Congolese government, there were demonstrations outside our offices and security personnel escorted staff in and out of the premises.

At this time, I wrote to my former school principal, Mademoiselle Simonis in Brussels, to inform her that, despite her hindering my education (by forcing me to repeat fourth grade), I had achieved the position of Chancellor of the Belgian Embassy. I omitted the adjective, 'acting'. Perhaps she did not recognise my irony as she replied with her congratulations without any reference to her interruption of my education.

One advantage of the position was that I could buy a little Mini Morris car, tax-free, paying less than £700 for a new car. An unpleasant expense loomed, however, because my teeth had never been checked in Belgium. Combining two decades of poor nutrition and neglect of my overall health, my teeth were in quite bad condition. Extensive dental repair was necessary, incurring agony as well as requiring vast payments that I could not afford.

After the Embassy was fully established, I returned to Sydney and continued working for the Belgian Government and a series of Consuls-General. The office was in Trelawney Street in Woollahra, a lovely leafy street that held many foreign missions.

Booba in Australia

The housing decision made before our arrival in Sydney was that Booba would live in an apartment purchased with the proceeds of the sale of her and Zeida's house in Brussels. The initial plan was that I would live with Booba but, of course, Auntie Betty had invited me to stay with her. Auntie Betty took care of Booba's needs. Finally, I no longer had to clean and scrub, shop and carry for my grandmother. Bunny was moved to live with Booba, leaving his boarding house room. He had warmly welcomed me on arrival and extended his generosity by treating me to outings that he could ill-afford. I saw him frequently at family events and now I wish I had spoken up in his defence when family members made fun of him.

When she left Belgium, Booba carried with her many beautiful and valuable pieces of jewellery, gifts from Zeida over the decades. While still in Brussels, she showed me a pair of large diamond earrings and told me, 'One for you and one for Rosalyn.' When we stayed with Auntie Fay in London en route, Booba gave her granddaughter Rosalyn one of the diamond earrings but the one she promised to me she gave to her other granddaughter, Joy.

On arrival in Australia, Booba was exceedingly generous in her distribution of the remaining jewellery to Betty, Rose and Max's wife, Rosine. Another piece that Booba promised to me before we left Belgium was a diamond ring. She had said to me, 'When I die, this is yours.' She gave that ring to another cousin in Sydney. After their great welcoming of Booba, their mother and

54. Empty promises, empty earrings – worthless jewellery of Booba Inberg given by Auntie Betty Swieca née Inberg to Francine, received 1975.

grandmother, and collecting their gifts, the aunts, uncles and cousins spent very little time with her. Betty supervised Booba's care. After the death of my grandmother, Auntie Betty gave me just 'a keepsake', the unwearable bent metal frames of Booba's everyday diamond earrings, already stripped of their valuable stones. They are a perfect symbol of my damaged relationship with Booba.

Booba breaking her promises had very little to do with whether or not I received one of her baubles. Her jewellery was a symbol of incomplete transactions between us. My disappointment centred on her never relating to me with love or affection nor showing me any thanks or appreciation for everything I did for her and Zeida. Further hurt and disillusion developed when I observed, in England and in Australia, that I was not treated as equal to her other grandchildren. Yet I was the only grandchild who had helped her daily for over a decade.

Oddly, Booba did not give any jewellery to Minnie or Helen before she left Belgium nor did she give any memento to Charly on her arrival in Australia. From that deliberate omission, I presume that Minnie and her three children were not equal, in Booba's eyes, with her other children and grandchildren. Minnie, Charly and I had foregone a decent life to meet the demands and endure the spite of this ungrateful woman.

Truly, the same relationship with Booba continued as years passed. Booba remained distant and uncaring towards me. The only outward change was that she was no longer dependent on my ministrations for her care once we left the ship in Sydney.

When I reflected on all the things I did for Booba, I realised that there had been no alternative as my mother had forced me to look after her and Zeida. Booba regarded my primary purpose as being to meet her needs and wants. Ours was a mistress-servant relationship. I wondered if she had treated my mother in the same selfish manner and so thwarted Minnie's emotional development or ability to care for others, including her children.

Booba was not kind and loving but I believed that I was the cause of her failing to love me. I even thought that I provoked her relentless nastiness and her subsequent disregard for me. Booba was hard-hearted, selfish and ungrateful; she did not even demonstrate a thread of grace when imposing her will on me.

Yet I did not want to see my grandmother as she really was. I yearned to gain Booba's approval or, dare I say, her love. Even for a while after I was married, I still regularly visited her. Sometimes I took my babies and gave her money, flowers, chocolates (gifts that I could ill-afford) or food that I had prepared. As the children grew, Booba said that the noise of her great-grandchildren gave her a headache. I visited her less often after that remark. My grandmother died in Sydney on 15 January 1975, in her eighty-sixth year. Not once have I visited her tombstone in Sydney.

Social life

Despite not having earned tertiary qualifications, I had the temerity to join a Jewish social group of young adults that called itself 'The Graduates'. Most of the members were, indeed, university graduates but I was never queried about my academic credentials. I enjoyed the company and relished the intellectual and convivial conversations. Although I must have dispensed some ill-informed comments, I prefer to think that the other members perhaps thought that I did not make sense due to my inadequate English.

My first aeroplane trip was to a family wedding in Melbourne in the 1960s. I was anxious for days beforehand but tried not to reveal that it was my first flight or that I was apprehensive about flying. In Melbourne, I met the sister of Sam Swieca, once again, who had introduced me to the pavlova dessert when I arrived in Australia. She asked me to take raw carp back to Sydney where it was not available. Auntie Betty would make gefilte fish (a Jewish delicacy) for Passover with it. While the others remained on holiday in Melbourne, I flew back to Sydney to return to work, so I was charged with carrying the raw fish aboard the aeroplane (without refrigeration). When a Sydney acquaintance on the same flight suggested that there was a bad smell of fish near my seat, he urged me to move to another seat. Red-faced, I had to admit to holding this contraband, with great embarrassment about its smell and the unwanted attention I received.

Within a year of arrival, I was engaged to a French-speaking man, likewise a war orphan, Leon Wise. I discontinued the relationship soon after, realising it was not the right time for it. Later, when working at the Belgian Mission I would meet my husband-to-be.

Chapter Sixteen

Revisiting Survival

What is it all about? Where can I find me? Where is the road home? Who are these people? What are these happenings? ... All I want is the smell of home ... Give me some proof of me! ... Give me my mother! Give me (my father)'s grave ... give me my secrets back.

Mervyn Peake,
Titus Alone[53]

The desire to know more about my own forgotten childhood always remained deep in my psyche, a primal need to understand and to recall more of my early life during the hidden years and after the war. I began to acknowledge this need to search for my past and yet I felt trepidation about what I might learn. In addition, I was seriously afraid that nobody would believe what experiences I had to tell. As Delpard wrote, 'What I have lived in the time of my childhood during the Second World War is within me like a shameful secret.'[54]

Tentative recall

Through fragments of memory, reading official documents and even clues from my nightmares, I spent decades trying to recover details of my early life. Tentative attempts to recall, reclaim and understand my early life began in 1960. More than fifty years passed before I could compile everything I have remembered, discovered or been offered as proof.

Seeking documentation of my childhood was an initial tactic to refresh my memory. I wanted basic official papers that documented details of my early years and which validated the few memories I retained. Simplistically, I thought that documents from schooling or foster carers would provide me with a mirror into which I could look and possibly see parts of my childhood, maybe even a few happy memories.

For many years, it appeared that no records remained from my childhood, whether details of my hiding places, the multiple foster carers or the many schools I attended. The absence of documentation drove a fear in me that none of my teachers, carers or indeed anybody valued my existence enough to record my name. Of course, most of my childhood documents were either lost during the war or never formalised in the post-war chaos.

Gradually, I began to find the small remnants of documentation that still existed, largely provided by the obsessive Belgian records on foreigners. I did find a few addresses at which I lived with my family and just one foster carer's address. Gathering facts was not enough for me, however, as small morsels of information did not provide any sense of what my life was like at any of the recorded addresses.

Chapter Seventeen

Was my Father still Alive?

The hope of finding one's parents again is central in all the testimonies of other hidden children. It is probably that, without this hope, they might not have found the strength to fight for their survival

Sylvain Brachfield[55]

Let me backtrack ... to the point fifteen years earlier, when Charly was thirteen and I was six years old and we were both hiding from the Nazis. Our father was arrested by the Germans, held in the Caserne Dossin and we never saw him again.

In my heart, I always believed that my father was alive in Russia, imprisoned behind the Iron Curtain. My hope revived when the Auschwitz authority reported that it held no record of my father in its archives. As the Russians liberated Auschwitz, I imagined he might have been taken to Siberia after the end of the Second World War.

Another hope I held was that, perhaps, he had jumped off the train to Auschwitz just as Moishe Lewin had (twice) and this hope was reinforced by the advice that the camp held no record of my father arriving or going to his death. Somewhere, somehow he may have survived. Maybe his memory was impaired but I had not lost my memories of him or my wholehearted love for him.

It continued to make sense to me that my father was alive in a place far away, given that I was now living far from Belgium. Anything was a possibility in the wide world into which I had been flung. Therefore, in 1960, I requested from the Belgian government an extract of my father's death registration. The document I received illustrated the vague records of the post-war Belgian government in relation to murdered Jews; it was so nebulous that it appeared evasive. It included the comment that 'he died for Belgium in an undetermined place'. The apparent facts were that he was arrested on a Brussels street because he was a Jew and that he had died in Auschwitz because he was a Jew.

My renewed doubt that he had been murdered increased because I now knew that there was no record in Auschwitz of his arrival or of his death. The only clear record about his death was in my aching heart and my brother's sad face. My hope resurged that my father had survived and was alive, somewhere on this planet.

One of the Belgian police documents included a note about my father's arrest by the Germans being the reason for his absence from the family in November 1944. Six decades later, I read with horror the detailed papers that recorded his departure from Malines for Auschwitz, thoroughly documented by the Nazis and their Belgian collaborators.

Every so often, I wondered if I had invented a wonderful father. I really did not know him well, as we had not lived in the same home from the time I was four years old. Despite or perhaps because of being separated when I was hidden in Saintes and around Brussels, in my imagination he remained kind, loving and caring. At other times, I wondered if, had he lived, he really would have loved me, given the self-doubt I endured under my mother and grandparents. Was he the person I had built in my mind, heart and imagination? I always hoped that he would have cared for me and upheld me with his love.

If my father had not perished in the Holocaust, I believed that he would have been my foundation rock, secure and unwavering in his love for me. He would have been a reliable parent who loved me, guided and advised me wisely and always held my best interests in his heart. He would have defended me against real and imaginary enemies, just as he found a safe place for me to hide during the dangerous war years. His love would have been unconditional and my welfare would have remained his foremost consideration.

I would have been able to ask for his opinion on a myriad of topics and we could have had father and daughter time during which we could have exchanged opinions, ideas and hugs. The impact of losing my father remains incalculable.

Had my father lived, though, I may never have come to Australia. Momentarily, the realisation felt sad because I love Australia with all my heart. Australia became my safe harbour in the world and in my life.

Immediately after the war, my mother and all my adult relatives admonished me in an attempt to make me forget whatever had happened to me, whether in hiding, separated from my family, hungry, fearful or in poor health. As Vromen conjectured in *Hidden children of the Shoah*: 'Although they [the parents] were immensely relieved that their children had survived, there was little room for gratitude. New lives had to be forged as quickly as possible ... they had no place for the past.'[56] As a little girl, perhaps being silent soothed me, as 'many used silence as a coping mechanism to deal with situations ... in order to survive'.[57]

As a result of all this, I could not thank my saviours after the war. As a six-and-a-half-year-old girl, I certainly could not have known how to find Marie and Catherine who saved my life by keeping me in Saintes and sheltering me from murderous soldiers. As for the many homes where I was sheltered for a few days at a time, they were too numerous, too brief, occasionally abusive and long-forgotten. I never knew the names of the various people who took me in or the names of the brave women who risked their lives walking me in the streets.

In adulthood, I wanted to thank every one of them for saving me. I wanted to shout out every name and to recognise every person who helped my family and me. Now, I longed to nominate everyone for recognition – if only I knew each person's name. Jews recognised and honoured people who were instrumental in saving lives, formalised in Yad Vashem in Jerusalem as the recognition order called the Righteous Among the Nations. By 1 January 2016, 1,707 Belgians had been awarded the distinction of Righteous Among the Nations by the State of Israel for risking their lives to save Jews from persecution during the occupation.[58]

Over the years, I contacted several organisations for details about my hiding places between my fourth and sixth years of life. So far, results have been sparse. All I knew was that somebody was orchestrating my constant movement between safe houses. Each time I heard of another Resistance heroine or read a child Survivor's tale of reunion with a rescuer, I immediately grasped any facts, like falling leaves, to examine if I could have been in the same position, the same house or with the same rescuer taking me to the next house. Having read research and social analyses as well as hearing speakers at conferences, my adult mind has become informed about what was being done to save Jewish children in Brussels and throughout Belgium. Occasionally I have remembered glimpses of my hidden childhood. My sense of instant recognition of an incident or response has been so powerful that I have involuntarily said aloud, 'Oh, that was me!'

Given that the Nazis issued orders to kill the entire family of anyone caught aiding a Jew, I was struck by how deeply committed my rescuers were in risking their lives. That insight heightened my sense of guilt and loss that I never thanked the people who hid me at enormous risk to themselves and their families.

Visiting Belgium, 1977

Eighteen years after I left Belgium, I returned for a brief visit with my Australian husband, Phillip. Thirty-five years beforehand, in 1942, Brussels was a killing ground for Jews and others condemned by the Nazis. The roof where I clung would have been repaired, the haystack where I hid in Saintes was replaced by industrial buildings and the Masons' apartment was probably the home of another family.

My first act was to take a pilgrimage to Saintes by catching a train to Tubize and then a taxi to Sainte Reineldis church. It was unchanged since the time when I had visited it every day when hidden on the farm. Alas, I did not know the last names of Auguste and Marie, Jean and Catherine, so the young local priest could not assist me in identifying and locating the two women. I wanted to thank Marie and Catherine for saving my life. Inside the church, I lit candles in memory of these kind and generous people who hid me when the Nazis would have murdered me. They put their lives at risk to shelter and save me. Maybe Auguste and Jean died because they were in the Resistance. They hid me at their farm due to their high moral values and political will to resist the Nazi evil, encouraged by a bordello Madam to whom they owed a favour. If I knew their last names, I could formally honour these people who saved me as Righteous Gentiles. I will always honour my saviours in my heart and provide public recognition by recording their great deeds in print.

However, I could not find the farm where I was hidden because, by 1977, urbanisation had changed the landscape. No longer was Saintes a quiet little village with small market garden plots, though some farms still surrounded the village. When I asked residents if they could identify the building in the photo of me as a child at the farm, no one could help me.

When I had uncovered the information that I owed a bordello Madam such gratitude, I checked whether she was recognised as a Righteous Gentile by Yad Vashem. She saved five members of our family, firstly by arranging my shelter with the farmers in Saintes as well as by providing a hiding place for my parents where, occasionally, Charly and Moishe slept. In addition, the Madam twice arranged Zeida's release from the Gestapo. Sadly, she probably failed a few criteria for being counted as a Righteous Gentile, one being consorting with the Nazis.

In Brussels, I stayed with Moishe and his wife Claire for two nights. Moishe drove me to see Zeida's grave which he had commissioned at the Cimetière Israëlite Kraainem in Wezembeek on the outskirts of Brussels. I was pleased to see Mrs Lewkowicz. I remembered that she lived in the same building as my family before the war and she always enjoyed talking English with my mother. She had possibly saved Charly as she warned him to leave Malines when he tried to see our father there in 1944.

Once again I walked along the familiar streets to my grandparents' house and along rue Camusel where I had walked with my father. I came away, however, still not satisfied with what I had learned and achieved on that trip.

Chapter Eighteen

My Name is Survivor

In trying to forget, we Survivors had repressed our identity of being hidden children: we were still 'emotionally in hiding'

B Shenitz[59]

A major part of my early years was in hiding, followed by a harsh post-war middle childhood. I felt overwhelmed by numerous sad and bad experiences that I wanted to forget or, at least, to repress.

However, I never considered myself as a Survivor as defined by the Jewish usage of the term Holocaust Survivor. I identified my mother and my grandparents as Survivors, despite all of us having been in hiding and surviving. It seemed unnatural to even contemplate the question of whether I was a 'true' Survivor. I accepted and totally believed the script of myself as a lucky child who should forget what happened to her during the Nazi occupation: 'nothing happened'. Firstly I denied and lied as a child, gradually I forgot and then I repressed the remainder.

Even when I participated in the International Gathering of Jewish Holocaust Survivors at the University of New South Wales in Sydney Australia in 1985, I convinced myself that I was attending solely for the intellectual stimulation and to participate in an important discussion for the Jewish community. Also, I wanted to support my brother-in-law, Gerald Falk, who was a member of the organising committee. I was playing it very safe, keeping the topic of Jewish Holocaust Survivors, my feelings and every discussion at 'arms-length', thus maintaining a separation between what had happened in my hidden years and my new adult life.

Until this first Survivors' forum, I had not known that fewer than 10 per cent of Jewish children in Nazi-controlled countries had survived. I felt stunned to be part of the statistic – barely 100,000 Jewish children had lived and over 1,500,000 children were killed. As a small fraction of a tiny percentage, Charly and I were two of fewer than 6,000 Belgian Jewish children who survived the *Shoah*. We were two of the 3,000 Belgian Jewish children who lost one or both parents. This information brought home to me a sharp realisation of the enormous odds against either of us surviving.

I remembered the mantra which I was told repeatedly after the war, 'You are the lucky ones', as though nothing else except luck had contributed to my being alive at the end of the war. Whilst there were other factors, indeed, luck had played a large part in my survival.

Soon after this Survivors' forum, at an annual memorial for Yom Hashoah, all Survivors were invited to stand. Auntie Betty's sister-in-law, Edith (hidden in France) and brother-in-law, Albert Swieca (who survived the Warsaw Ghetto) both stood. They looked down at me, still seated and urged me to stand up with them. I told them that I was not a Survivor. I felt theirs was a preposterous suggestion and an affront to those whom I considered 'real' Survivors. They convinced me and as I stood up in the congregation, I felt enlightenment and connection with my early years. For the first time, I had a name for my experiences as a hidden child during the Nazi occupation. I was a Survivor.

This was the beginning of a long and painful recovery and readjustment. After that momentous occasion, I recalled more of my childhood and the hidden years, as though I was freeing my memory to reveal all it contained. Gradually I opened up more and became willing to speak with people who were close to me and supportive of my stories of suffering and surviving.

The Sydney Child Holocaust Survivors Group was formed in 1987.Each of us, as members, treasured the realisation that we were not alone in our early experiences nearly fifty years previously. We never compared or graded our relative sufferings but offered total acceptance of and support for each other. This group proved a catalyst for emotional growth for many, myself included. Members met regularly to talk to each other and to listen without judgement. We became involved with the established network of adult and child Survivors of concentration camps and many other community organisations. Our Sydney group became part of the World Federation of Jewish Holocaust Child Survivors and Descendants. That organisation embraced all children who survived the *Shoah*, in the ghettos, in the camps, under a false name or hiding, and now, their descendants.

The drama of the hidden children was the least known or documented component in the stories of victims of the Nazi regime. There were few adults who could help children rebuild their lives. Fifty years later those long-held fears, anxieties and terrors emerged from our emotional depths. We had tried to bury our feelings deeply while pretending to be like everybody else and getting on with life, work and families. 'Everyone was talking about Anne Frank', one Survivor recalled, 'so we kept quiet because we were considered the lucky ones'.[60] I accepted that I am a Survivor of the Nazis' intent to kill every Jew. I still carry immense sadness for all those children who did not survive the *Shoah*.

Professor Sarah Moskovitz, the creator of the term 'Child Survivor', was a speaker at that 1985 International Gathering of Jewish Holocaust Survivors in Sydney when I first realised that I was a Survivor. She had started a support group for Jewish Child Survivors in Los Angeles with subsequent groups being established around the world. On her 1991 visit to Sydney, she asked to meet child Survivors of the *Shoah*. Through word of mouth, a few of us met with her informally. We finally started to talk about our experiences, our lives and survival during the Nazi occupation. Suddenly in a safe environment, the floodgates of my memory were unlocked.

When she invited us to complete a survey, I did so and then added my heartfelt thanks to Professor Moskovitz:

> I am still trying to unravel my thoughts and memories from nightmares. For the first time in my life, I felt I was amongst people who shared experiences similar to mine and they could understand me, and now I was free to express my stories. None of us needed to feel ashamed or embarrassed by our experiences. I felt closer to my brother although we seldom discussed the war issues with each other. For many of us our feelings of rejection did not end with the war. For instance, on many occasions my mother, a young widow who desperately wanted to get re-married said, 'If it were not for you two (the man's name) would have married me, but who wants to be saddled with other people's children?' Many a time I felt then and perhaps later that she would have been happier if I had been taken too. In fact I had felt a moral, intellectual and emotional cripple.

Hearing Sarah Moskovitz speak was wonderful balm for healing my emotional wounds from the war.

Now I realised that I was not the only child Survivor who had hidden and kept secret all the things that had happened during the Holocaust. We were not as lucky as we were told we were; we all suffered trauma. It was a simple but powerful discovery. This triggered a lot of painful memories and many sensations returned to me. The sources of some of my strange mannerisms were revealed to me and I began to explore why I always felt different and experienced very negative emotions. I embarked on reconciling my early years with my needs and problems as an older adult. I found an exclusive affinity with other child Survivors.

In January 1993, I attended the Inaugural Australian Conference of Child Survivors of the Holocaust. The Melbourne Child Survivors of the Holocaust organised the Conference at the Melbourne Holocaust and Research Centre. Professor Moskovitz was, again, our keynote speaker. It was memorable in many ways. It was a relatively small gathering at which I was able to interact with most of the other participants. We shared friendly get-togethers following the formal sessions. These gatherings, however cathartic, always brought back mostly-unwelcome memories.

On the last evening, I felt moved to write a letter to the members of the organising committee. Later, the Melbourne Child Survivors of the Holocaust published an extract:

> Dear All (and you are dear to me)
> As I lay awake in my hotel room this morning reviewing the past days' events I suddenly had the urge to write to you my friends whom I had not even met last week.
>
> I wanted to thank you for everything: organisation hospitality friendship that I encountered in Melbourne amongst my 'extended family.' I know Litzi thanked you on behalf of the whole Sydney contingent but I wanted to share a thought: my husband who is a 7th generation Australian has been going to school reunions (he attended the same school from kindergarten to matriculation).
>
> When we went to Belgium in 1977 he could not understand that I could not remember a single 'school mate' nor the name of my school (they were too numerous). Last night, sitting at the farewell dinner-dance, I suddenly had the wonderful feeling that this was my class reunion – my 50th class reunion– and I felt so happy! I just wanted to share this thought with you all thank you.
>
> For the first time in my life, I felt what 'belonging' meant through unconditional acceptance as a member. It was such a simple word for such a human need, just like the need for food and shelter.

Opening up in Brussels

Over fifty years after the Liberation, I met many more people who had been hidden when children during the Second World War when I attended the First European Meeting of hidden children in 1995. It was organised by *l'Association belge de l'enfant caché* (Belgian Association of the hidden child), the first worldwide conference of hidden child Survivors. That occasion was a journey to my childhood, emotionally and literally as, fortuitously, the Université Libre de Bruxelles hosted us in a glorious Brussels springtime. The 609 representatives came from 16 countries including USA, Canada, South Africa, Israel and Germany, various South American countries and many from the former East European block. I was both flattered and, at the same time, felt lonely when I was singled out in the welcoming speeches as being the sole Australian attendee. Each Survivor's story reinforced that one was not alone in harbouring one's 'secret' for decades. Every individual had a unique story. At long last, we were free to tell our stories in all their seeming surrealism.

55. Emblem of *L'Enfant caché*, Brussels, on badge worn by Francine at the First European Meeting of Hidden Children, Brussels, 1995.

Until this time, I had not allowed myself to think about my childhood and this marked the beginning of my open and frank recall of long-buried memories. I was able to express my grief and, yes, anger. I began to believe that I could commence living more fully and more wholly as an individual now integrating my war and teen years with my mature self.

The emblem of the Conference represented a child standing in the forefront, bathed in light, bearing the Star of David, and an adult figure standing in the shadow behind the child. It poignantly represented the absence of an adult and the feeling of abandonment which many of us encountered in our childhood under Nazism, wherever we were hiding. It also captured the adults we had lost, especially parents.

The Chancellor of the Université Libre de Bruxelles welcomed us. The guest speakers were among the Who's Who of European politics, arts and academia, most of them child Survivors. It appeared that many of the hidden children had reconstructed their lives and perhaps tried even harder to become achievers and leaders in their chosen fields. They made us feel proud.

'Formerly hidden children were put in their place by people who had been in the camps: "what are you complaining about? you have not suffered, you don't know what hunger means, you cannot even imagine the constant fear, the beatings, the humiliations or the physical and mental pain; you don't know what it is to be in constant fear of death"'.[61]

One of the recurrent themes during our discussions was the unfairness of the 'gradings' of suffering during the *Shoah*. Clearly, we accepted that the most brutalised victims were the Jews who were killed. Yet people considered that those who survived the camps had suffered the most, followed by those in the ghettos. That type of recognition omitted to consider those who had escaped to safe countries and those who hid in occupied countries. Hidden children were often told that they had not suffered, simply because they were not sent to the camps. Research over eleven countries confirmed this hierarchy in the aptly-named '*The Politics of War Trauma*'. During the Conference, some activists campaigned for moral recognition of hidden children and compensation for their suffering, physically and mentally.[62]

Now it was time to accept that all who had survived, whether in camps, ghettos, hidden, living under aliases or escaping bullets to another country, had suffered. Participants asserted that there were no degrees of suffering among Survivors and that discrimination amongst those who survived should cease.

After reading Pavlova's biography as a teenager in concentration camps, *I Am from the Holocaust*,[63] I felt tempted to revise that view of treating the suffering of all Survivors as equal. I could not compare my experiences to the horrors that she endured as an adolescent. Faniya lived through the *Shoah*, suffering terrible privations and torture, cheating death many times in ghettos and camps only to find that her whole family had been murdered, along with the entire Jewish population.

As children, we could not make independent judgement of good or evil. We were not sufficiently mature at the time to recognise the pressures and risks surrounding us nor were we able to process our emotions and experiences. We never received psychological assistance. As most of us were told to forget, these experiences that were repressed and denied remained in the recesses of our minds, inaccessible but not forgotten.

Through shared understanding and mutual support, we could begin to reclaim our memories, expose them and analyse them in order to reconcile our early years with our adult needs and problems. We could, firstly, recognise our own sufferings. Secondly, we might achieve recognition of our traumas and the lasting emotional impacts that stayed with us. Finally, perhaps, we might live long enough to resolve inner conflicts and, eventually, find peace.

Professor Maxime Steinberg, an historian and former hidden child, horrified me with his definitive research on the place of the child in the history of genocide and in our particular experience, the *Shoah*. To the Nazis, the main priority in their war was not to manufacture tanks, win a battle, secure territory or feed their people. The most important Nazi goal was to kill all the Jews. The *Shoah* was unique in that not only were children annihilated, they were the top priority, both because they were a burden once their parents had been liquidated but, more importantly, because the Nazis feared that, if left to live, the children would be witnesses and avenge their parents. Professor Steinberg's statistics summarised the evidence that the Nazis had no mercy as far as children were concerned. Even if the effort cost the Nazis the war against the Allies, the Jewish children had to be murdered first.

Therefore, our saviours ensured we could tell the world about Nazi horrors seen by our own eyes. As the youngest, we are the last remaining victims of the Nazi madness who can speak and write as eyewitnesses. More than just my life was saved: the truth of my observations was saved and placed on public record for posterity.

Polish attendees were keen to talk about payments of German compensation monies to hidden child Survivors. The Polish government steadfastly refused to allocate any part of the reparation monies to them and, consequently, the Polish Jews felt angry. Some expressed feelings of resentment in terms that shocked most of us. They abused the Jews living in Western countries, in terms similar to the anti-Semitic insults yelled by Belgian schoolgirls at me in the late 1940s. Their attitudes made me feel extremely uneasy. They did not need our 'old rags' (second hand clothes), only their share of what they believed we (collectively) enjoyed. I tried to reason with them, explaining that I for one did not receive any reparation from the German government or any other source. At that time, I did not know that my mother had collected the funds provided for Charly and me as war orphans.

The moving ceremony on the last day of the Conference gave public recognition to many Righteous Gentiles who had saved the lives of one or more Jews, honoured by the Ambassador of Israel to Belgium and recognised by Yad Vashem.

Despite the presence of hundreds of international visitors celebrating our survival as Jewish children, there was no mention of Jewish heritage in Belgian or Brussels travel media and tourism information. John Felt noted that only as recently as 2001 did the Belgian Tourist Office issue a Jewish heritage guide, as a token reference to its former population of 66,000 people.

This Conference and my meetings with other hidden children gave me confidence that my memories and feelings were real. I was beginning to recover and discover the foundations of my life.

Comité de Défense des Juifs, Belgium

At the 1995 Conference in Brussels, Madame Yvonne Jospa received a standing ovation. She was in charge of the children's department of the *Comité de Défense des Juifs* (Jewish Defense Committee or CDJ) and she was personally responsible for placing hundreds of children in safe havens at great risk to her own life. I saw her hugged as a saviour and as a mother figure with much love and respect. At the time that I met her, I was not aware that I owed her gratitude but now I realise that this Resistance group likely ensured my survival after I had to leave the farm in Saintes.

Formed in mid-1942, the secret CDJ created rescue strategies for Jews threatened with deportation. It formed a secret network among children's services, private individuals and faith-based organisations and, through them, found safe places for Jewish children and raised money to pay for their upkeep. 'It is noteworthy that this French name has two meanings – a committee to defend Jews, and a Jewish defence committee. In other words, the name implies that there was a need both to defend the Jews and to give them the opportunity to defend themselves. The committee attempted to fulfil both roles. Almost all the Jewish organisations were represented on the committee'.[64]

Yvonne Nèvejean-Feyerick, head of the *Oeuvre Nationale de l'Enfance* (National Agency for Children or ONE) served on the CDJ executive. Through her organisational and institutional authority, she controlled many orphanages and recreational camps in Belgium. She arranged that ONE sites were available for short stopovers for Jewish children and longer placements. ONE falsified their lists of occupants to disguise the extra Jewish children secretly hidden at its locations. Nèvejean selected appropriate CDJ people, who were assigned to visit families hiding Jews and to pay them for the upkeep of the children in their care and, at the same time, to check on the care and living condition of the Jewish children, assisted by Ida Sterno and Fela Perelman.[65]

Nèvejean successfully lobbied for funds to support these efforts from the Société Générale Bank and the Belgian government-in-exile, in London. Towards the end of the German occupation in August 1944, the Nazi-established AJB learned that the Germans planned to arrest all the Jewish children remaining in Brussels and send them to concentration camps. Despite collaborating with the Nazis, the AJB informed the CDJ and urgently requested that Nèvejean find new safe hiding places for all the Jewish children under its care.[66] Nèvejean coordinated that rescue mission by finding additional hiding places in homes that were already overfilled, far beyond capacity.

Madame Jospa praised Nèvejean's dedication to the rescue of Jewish children. 'Driven by her love for children, her antipathy towards any form of discrimination, and her being in defiance against the Nazi occupation. Her paramount concern was to provide the same opportunities for Jewish children as for non-Jewish ones.' On 16 February 1965, Yad Vashem recognised Yvonne Nèvejean as Righteous Among the Nations.

'Some children had to pass through several "hands" until they found safe haven with the help of the CDJ, i.e. mostly through Ida Sterno and her catholic co-worker Andrée Geulen'.[67] 'When fetching the children, we would never tell the parents where we would hide them. I am aware of how cruel this must have been for the parents to hand their children over to an unknown person (naturally we couldn't tell them who we were and only introduced ourselves as members of the Resistance) and who wouldn't even tell them where they were taking their child (Geulen-Herscovici, Yad Vashem).' 'In this way, between 3,000 and 4,000 Jewish children were saved' in Belgium, as estimated by Paldiel in Michman.[68]

Now I could put my frequent movements when hidden in Brussels into the context of the work of the CDJ, as I was moved repeatedly until a longer-term placement was found. Andrée Geulen-Herscovici kept coded records of the movements of approximately 300 Jewish children whom she had personally moved into safe houses. A few of her books of children's names are preserved in the Yad Vashem Holocaust History Museum in Jerusalem and digital copies are available on request.

Upon receiving copies of her records, I read every name on each page searching for my own. I saw the names of my close friend Henri Gurman, his sister and his two brothers. After the surprise and joy of recognising a person from my childhood, I began to experience a sense of sadness because we had never talked about our respective war years but now I could not ask them anything as three of them had passed away and I was unable to contact the fourth. I did not find my name in those pages. In 1989, Andrée Geulen-Herscovici was recognised as Righteous Among the Nations.

According to Vromen,[69] a large part of the money needed by the CDJ to feed and hide Jewish children came from the Belgian Government-in-exile in London which asked the nation's banks to supply the money against the Government's guarantee of reimbursement. The American Jewish Joint Distribution Committee also provided significant amounts of money. Occasionally, parents could make payments and the CDJ took over paying expenses if the parents could not pay or, worse, had been arrested and deported. I know that my father and grandfather spent their life savings trying to keep all of our family alive.

At least once the CDJ carried out an armed action.[70] The attack by three young Belgian resisters on the twentieth convoy of Jews deported from Belgium bound for the Auschwitz-Birkenau concentration camp allowed 231 Jews to escape from the train, including my cousin Moishe Lewin.

Caserne Dossin

Visiting the Caserne Dossin was my priority after the Conference concluded. My father and most other Belgian Jews left from there to their deaths. I was surprised and appreciative that the old barracks now hosted a fine museum of remembrance of the many victims who had passed through on the way to their deaths. The King opened the *Mémorial, Musée et Centre de documentation sur l'Holocauste et les Droits de l'homme, Belgium* (Memorial, Museum and Documentation Centre on the Holocaust and Human Rights in Belgium) one month before my visit. At the front were two pieces of rail track, symbolising the tens of thousands of people who departed in cattle trains from that place to the death camps.

For the first time, I had certainty of the dates of departure of my father from Caserne Dossin and his arrival in Auschwitz. His name was ticked repeatedly on the manifest of the train convoy into which he had been herded, along with hundreds of others. It goes without saying that I found this information challenging and traumatic.

We were taken to Fort Breendonck, where countless political prisoners were interrogated and tortured. Most of them were then killed. A former Jewish inmate guided us through, one of only two Jews who survived this camp. I felt privileged to meet him.

56. Israel Kamerman's name on Victims' Memorial, Brussels, Belgium, 1995.

Finally, we went to pay our respects at the new memorial in Brussels to the Jews deported from Belgium to their death, The National Monument to the Jewish Martyrs of Belgium, located at rue Emile Carpentier and rue de Goujons in the district of Anderlecht on the 'Square of the Jewish Martyrs'. The memorial was in the shape of a Magen David, the Star of David. In its centre was an urn containing ashes retrieved from Auschwitz. This was the only place where many could feel close to their murdered relatives. This could be a place to recite a Kaddish, a prayer that is always recited at memorials and funerals, praising G-d and expressing yearning for the establishment of G-d's kingdom on earth.

Here I felt I could commune with my father on a spiritual level in this consecrated place. I read my father's name, engraved for posterity and fittingly honoured as a victim of the Nazis, the first time I had seen his name memorialised. I kissed my fingers and then touched his name as my gesture of love. It felt insignificant compared with the abiding grief that I had harboured for so many years. I felt reassured that his name will be remembered for all time in this place, among the 23,838 names inscribed on the wall.

Jewish Resistance fighters were recognised in another section. Proportionately, Jews were the most numerous of any social group to participate in underground movements and many perished in their endeavours. These facts dispelled the erroneous allegation or myth that Jews went to their deaths meekly and without a fight.

At the Parc du Cinquantenaire, I viewed a comprehensive exhibition on the Second World War, entitled '*J'avais 20 ans en '45*' (I was twenty years old in 1945), in honour of the fiftieth anniversary of the Liberation of Brussels. There were full sized reproductions of, astonishingly, Hitler's bunker through which visitors could walk if they wished; a London tube station during the Blitz; a bombed classroom and many other realistically recreated Second World War sites. Among key artefacts and original documents were the signed instruments of surrender by Germany and transcripts from the Nuremberg trials of Nazis. I was totally absorbed in this exhibition for the entire day, even though I was only seven in 1945.

Returning to Australia, I had mixed feelings. Each trip back to my past seemed to raise more questions than answers to my persistent yearning to know and to understand my earliest years of life. Hence, this trip had been both disturbing and satisfying. Recovering a few details from my past helped me begin to fill some gaps in my memory.

Child victims are Survivors too

Hidden children were not recognised as *Shoah* Survivors until the late 1980s.[71] It was as though our suffering was underestimated, not recognised for a long time, even by our families and the Jewish communities in our various countries. Besides, we were told we were 'lucky' in comparison to concentration camp Survivors. Another child Survivor, Samuel Lauber, explained this viewpoint. 'For many years I never spoke openly about my background. I felt that the Holocaust Survivors were those people who were either in labor camps or concentration camps or escaped from concentration camps – hence, I never openly shared my story'.[72]

'Similar to concentration camp Survivors, hidden Jewish children were threatened by death. The main difference was that because of having to remain hidden, we were constantly in a state of fear of being discovered.'[73] All hidden children had to hide their Jewish identity, while some were given new names: such subterfuge may have saved our lives. I learned the Catholic prayers in Saintes and my name passed as Belgian but I always felt a disturbing sense of dislocation through my life. The key part of me that was denied and covered up was my Jewish heritage.

'Imagine a child in early years who had repeated traumatic and abrupt separations during and after the war that made no sense to the child; of course, our emotional growth was impeded and we lacked secure attachments, missing key developmental steps in early childhood'.[74] As hidden children, we had to adapt to unfamiliar environments. Some children were locked within institutions. The long aftermath, using 'silence as a survival strategy … and the non-recognition of their experiences in the aftermath of the war, discouraged them from disclosing their suffering for more than 40 years'.[75]

While I was sheltered in multiple places during the war, I subsequently lived in many foster homes and moved to many rented apartments with my mother. Each of these settings was punctuated by repeated separations and left me with an underlying traumatic impact.[76]

There was comfort when reading similar feelings if published in academic research, as though those feelings were more real and more valid, if acknowledged by learned people, than my own painful yet identical anxieties.

The years passed quickly but now I was certain that I would never be afraid of accusations of false memories or so-called childhood imaginings. Furthermore, I was confident that I could tell the awful truth of one hidden child in Belgium. Gradually I began to feel liberated from keeping secrets, firstly of being hidden as a Jewish child and, secondly, about the unconscionable rejection and neglect by my mother when we were reunited after the war.

In the remaining years of our collective lifetimes, all child Survivors should record their memories and stories, however much sorrow they initiate. Holocaust research must not marginalise us or our qualitative research simply because of the academic preference for 'hard' data. Every single Jew of the six million murdered was a person, over one and a half million of them children. Each testimony from a Survivor stands as a record of the evil perpetrated and as a memorial to those who could not escape.

By placing our stories of survival on the public record, future policymakers may not deny history nor ignore our suffering and will be able to read our eyewitness statements about the *Shoah*. We must counter the revisionists and deniers and provide evidence for the historical record. Hopefully, we may prevent repetition of genocide against children, Jewish or otherwise.

My vision is that child Survivor history will be integrated into research and studies on the Holocaust.

Discovering clues

In August 1999, I attended another Child Holocaust Survivors' Conference, this time in Prague. Gathered in an open and safe forum, this was another cathartic experience. Here I could affirm my early life memories and experiences without denial or censorship by others. This Conference provided a safe environment that reinforced all attendees' realisations that they were not responsible for what happened to them and any resulting traumas. Should sadness surface, we were encouraged to consider that we might feel better once we shared our sorrows with others who had similar experiences. Noticeboards invited participants to place notes in the hope that, maybe, one person in their family had survived and they could meet after so many years.

If a concentration camp can be considered the best part of a tour, a definite highlight was our day trip to Terezin camp. Local Jewish children performed Brundibar after the completion of our tour of the camp. This children's opera was composed in 1938 by Hans Kràsa and Adolf Hoffmeister. Kràsa was imprisoned in this concentration camp where he taught the incarcerated children to perform. As those young singers were transported to their deaths in Auschwitz, new cast members stepped in to replace them. I saw drawings by those children of what they saw daily, and what they were dreaming of while interned there was heart wrenching. I often think about those sad children who never had a chance to live a long or fulfilled life.

Visiting Auschwitz

In 1995, I had felt so close to my father's last days of life when I had visited the Caserne Dossin and as I walked around Brussels where I had lived with him. Visiting Auschwitz became my pilgrimage to the site of the deaths of my father and all my relatives from Poland who perished there. I will grieve for my father forever as well as for my extended family killed by the Nazis.

Following that 1999 Conference, I flew from Prague to Krakow in Poland, the nearest city from which to visit Auschwitz. Emotionally, I needed a quiet and solitary visit, preferring not to be crammed in a bus full of other visitors, so I hired a driver to take me to Auschwitz, alone, for one day. When I arrived, a sinister aura hung over the entrance and buildings.

There were few visitors in sight and it felt as though I was the only person in the former camp. I knew and definitely felt that terrible things had happened here and being on my own was, at times, frightening and challenging.

A large field in the former camp was respected as sacred because there, many bodies had been buried.

While walking alone, I started talking aloud to my family. Realising that my father and grandparents would not have understood English, I spoke to them in French and Yiddish to let them know that I loved them and I missed them. I felt I was walking with my father who had died there. Across the chasm of death, I hoped I had made him proud of the life I had lived. I wished I could have looked after him, the way he protected me. I would have cared for him in his ageing years. I told him that we had survived and I also spoke about his grandchildren in Australia. However, when I caught myself talking aloud, I felt quite a shock. I was glad I was alone, uninterrupted and not subject to scrutiny or judgement by anyone.

Visitors could walk and explore everywhere at that time, including the gas chambers and the crematoria. I climbed down the steps into the gas chamber. The Nazis had detonated the Auschwitz gas chambers and barracks on 2 November 1944 as the Wehrmacht (the German army) was being steadily pushed back by the Russians. The Nazis forced 66,000 inmates to march west towards Germany and those too weak to continue were executed on the spot. Nearly ninety days later, Russian troops opened the doors of the camp on 27 January 1945. Although a fraction of the prisoners who were left behind were still alive, Survivors were too weak to rejoice at their liberation and many succumbed to death within days of their freedom.

Near the former gas chambers, I met a small group of Israeli youths who were placing an Israeli flag there, as they had elsewhere throughout Auschwitz. They took part in my recitation of a Kaddish, the Jewish memorial prayer, and stood as I lit memorial candles that I carried from Australia. I had carefully selected memorial candles made in Israel as a calculated gesture to associate my beloved relatives with Israel. At the time of all their suffering, they could not have imagined that there would exist an independent Jewish nation such a short time after the *Shoah*.

I learned so much from the experience. I developed an unshakeable appreciation of what my father and millions of Jews, young and old, endured until they were murdered. Still there were no other people around me; all was quiet, peaceful and respectful. Eerie and emotional responses were unavoidable on that day. The Polish Jewish poet M.J., whose full name remains unknown and who died in the Warsaw Ghetto, eloquently expressed my feelings for my father:

A Funeral

The coffin – a crematorium furnace,
Lid – transparent, made of air,
Human body turned into smoke,
Blown through the smokestack of history.

How shall I honor your passing,
Walk in your funeral procession?
You, homeless handful of ashes
Between the earth and heaven.

How to cast a green garland
On the grave dug high in the air –
An ark of the world's four corners
Under the invader's fire.

Your coffin, which is not,
Will not slide from roaring cannons,
And only the column of air
Illumines your death with sunrays.

And here is such a great silence
On earth, like a trampled banner,
In the mourning smoke of corpses,
In the crucified outcry.

This poem was translated from Polish by Yala Korwin (1933–2014) and first printed by Warsaw's Jewish-Polish underground press and, later, smuggled on microfilm to London's organisation of Polish Jewry. It was finally published in 1945, *The Ghetto Poems – From the Jewish Underground in Poland.*[77]

Approximately one million Jews were killed in Auschwitz, plus at least one hundred thousand Polish and Roma and, in addition, many Soviet prisoners. According to Andreas Eichmüller, a German historian in Munich, 6,500 SS members who served at the camp, survived the war. Of these, fewer than a hundred were ever tried for their crimes in German courts and only fifty were convicted.

A subsequent visit to Auschwitz in July 2007 was far less gratifying as visitors were only allowed access to a few restricted barracks, and then only in a group with a guide. Lighting memorial candles was no longer permitted to avoid possible fire hazards but visitors could purchase red roses to leave on the tracks of the railway line. There were dozens of buses and thousands of tourists, many laughing, talking and giggling which I found extremely disrespectful. This interrupted my reverie and prayer. I was so grateful for the previous, quieter opportunity when I felt able to commune with my loved ones in peace, without the theatrical arrangements that were overwhelming this sacred site.

Despite evidence of my father's transportation to, and death in, Auschwitz, the Polish authorities that administer the camp Museum have found no record of him. In the last few weeks of Nazi control the Germans perpetrators continued killing as many Jews as they could without maintaining their usual impeccable recordkeeping. They lost count and had no details of the Jews they murdered. For the many members of my family who were lost in the war there were no tombstones at which I could pay my respects.

In 2015, my grandson, Jared Levy, visited Auschwitz and there read the name of Israel Kamerman in a book supplied to the former concentration camp by the Yad Vashem Holocaust Museum. I am glad that my father's name and memory are preserved where he died. Jared recited a Kaddish, the prayer traditionally said for the dead, in honour of his great-grandfather, providing me with great comfort.

It was not remarkable that it was so difficult for me to come to terms with my father's death. I never learned anything definitive about his murder and, consequently, I have never been able to express my grief adequately or fully.

Chapter Nineteen

My own Family to Love

Just as man cannot live without dreams, he cannot live without hope.
If dreams reflect the past, hope summons the future.

Elie Wiesel[78]

Auntie Betty went for a few days' rest to stay in the Blue Mountains, about 150 km west of Sydney, staying at the Carrington Hotel. There she met an old friend whose nephew was single. They conspired for him to meet me. The nephew invited me to go out with him. However, he wanted the approval of his old school friend and took me to meet him.

Phillip Lazarus, the friend, was very handsome. The next day, he telephoned me on the pretext that he wanted information on commercial possibilities for importing goods from Belgium. By coincidence, we met again at the Graduates social group where I discovered that Phillip had not attended university either. On our first date in 1961, Phillip took me to dine at a Japanese restaurant that seriously impressed me – it was completely beyond my life experience. He had lived in Japan for three months and showed me how to eat the Japanese delicacies, seeking to demonstrate that he was a man of the world. He had the most beautiful sonorous voice. I fell deeply in love with this friend rather than Auntie Betty's friend's nephew for whom I was intended.

Auntie Betty and Sam did not want me to go out with Phillip who had a reputation for being a playboy. When I would not stop seeing him, they gave me an ultimatum – either I must stop going out with Phillip or I would have to leave their home. I chose to leave and moved into a little house with three New Zealand women, the first time I had lived independently. It was such a happy period in my life. I look back fondly on that carefree period of independence.

My new home was full of fun. We decided to host a wine and cheese party which we thought was very sophisticated. As all our plans were dictated by how much money we could spend, or how little, I bought several dozen bottles of the cheapest wine on the market which tasted very much like vinegar and the cheese was not much better, though our guests had a fabulous evening. Over time the winery whose bottles we had consumed that night became quite respected, as I hope did my catering skills! Our little home was bursting at the seams with so many people who visited and enjoyed our urbane hospitality.

There was no romantic marriage proposal from Phillip, just a statement of the fact that we would marry and, as I was blindly in love, I did not object

57. Francine on the day after her engagement to Phillip, Sydney, 28 September 1963.

to his suggestion. I felt jubilant about proving that my Auntie Betty was wrong in her pronouncement about Phillip's character. We became engaged on the eve of Yom Kippur (Jewish Day of Atonement), on 27 September 1963.

One of my future sisters-in-law, Joyce, and her husband, Gerald Falk, gave us a wonderful party. Guests mingled in the spacious gardens of the home of Phillip's parents in Rose Bay near Sydney Harbour. They had ordered a big marquee to be raised where a band played lovely dance music. Only then did I find out that, despite the lessons Phillip took as a young man, he still could not dance!

Planning for our wedding, I met with the Rabbi who would conduct our ceremony at the Central Synagogue in Bondi Junction. It was then that I realised that I needed a Hebrew name for my wedding in an Orthodox Synagogue. However, my mother had never told me my Hebrew name. When I asked her, she could not remember if I had even been given one. I explained my predicament to the Rabbi and my true desire to have a Hebrew name. The Rabbi asked me what name I wanted and what it meant to me. King Solomon's *Song of Songs* is a wonderful poem in which he sings of his undying love for Shulamit (שולמית), I chose that name because she was loved, as I always hoped I would be loved.

Another necessary detail that I lacked was my mother's wedding certificate or *ketuba*, to prove that I was Jewish. It had been destroyed in the war. The Rabbi agreed to accept the *ketuba* of Auntie Betty as she was my mother's sister, providing satisfactory evidence that my mother was Jewish. Of course, I wanted my mother to be at my wedding. However, she had travelled to Australia earlier that year to assess her possibilities for migrating and she had already returned to Belgium.

In her usual authoritarian way, Auntie Betty took over the organisation of my wedding. She selected the fabric for my short dress and her dressmaker ran up a dress, not a beautiful gown – no veil, no train, no travelling between bridal salons excitedly. There was no offer of a bridal shower in my honour. I had some doubts about marrying Phillip at that time, which I could not identify and I explained them away as being bridal jitters but, as was the case with my one-way ticket to Australia, there was no turning back.

Next, Betty appointed a cousin with whom I was not close as my only bridesmaid. Betty printed the invitation without me seeing the wording. To my shock, I read that I was incorrectly identified as the daughter of 'Minnie and Maurice Blumberg.'. There was no mention of my late father on the invitation to my wedding. My joy was shadowed by sadness and renewed grief that my father had been struck from my life by his wife's relatives as well as by the Nazis.

My wedding was not a grand affair. We married on 22 December 1963 at the beginning of the long summer holidays in Australia, a convenient time when Phillip's business was less demanding. Auntie Betty restricted the guest

Mr. & Mrs. Sam Swieca

request the pleasure of the company of

----

to celebrate the Marriage of their Niece

Francine Kamerman

daughter of Mr. & Mrs. M. Blumberg

of Brussels, Belgium

to

Phillip

son of Mr. & Mrs. Z. Lazarus

at the Central Synagogue,

Bon Accord Avenue, Bondi Junction

on Sunday, 22nd December, 1963

at 6 p.m.

Reception at the home of

Mr. & Mrs. Sam Swieca,

44 Wolseley Road, Point Piper

following the ceremony

58. Wedding invitation from which Francine's father was omitted, 1963.

list to family members and I was allowed to invite just one friend. Betty and Sam stood with me under the *chupa* (wedding canopy) in the recently built Central Synagogue. The small reception was held in Betty's new apartment. The money that Minnie had sent with me from Belgium and which I had entrusted to Betty's care four years earlier paid for my wedding. We flew to New Zealand for our honeymoon, touring and then returning to Sydney in early 1964.

The Lazarus family offered me a sincere and warm welcome. Life with and around my in-laws was much happier. I felt respected and genuinely appreciated by Phillip's family. I acquired Phillip's three wonderful sisters as my own, Joyce and Marian, living in Sydney, and Beverley, living 1,000 km south in Melbourne. They embraced me and lovingly accepted me into their

59. Wedding of Francine Kamerman and Phillip Lazarus, Sydney, 22 December 1963.

families as they still do today. We continue to have wonderful outings on a regular basis, especially when we celebrate our birthdays. They are very warm friends and I love them dearly.

Zadea and Doris Lazarus (née Isaacs) were my parents-in-law. Phillip was the seventh generation born in Australia on his mother's side, Doris' forbearers having arrived in the 1860s.[79] The Lazarus family maintained a strong tradition of community service and philanthropy. Phillip's grandfather, after whom my husband was named, served on the Board of Sydney Hospital and was instrumental in the founding of the Picton Lakes Village, a settlement for the treatment of people affected by tuberculosis. My father-in-law, Zadea, was President of the Legacy Council, a charity that supports war widows and orphans. Doris was President of the Sydney Women's Auxiliary of Legacy for many years and she initiated Legacy's provision of a holiday house for war widows and their children.

It took a while to form a friendship with my mother-in-law. When Doris discovered that I shared a birth date with her favourite brother, there was great progress in our relationship. I called my mother-in-law 'Mum' and she eventually considered me to be one of her daughters and treated me equally with them, even in her will. She always made me feel so welcome and I loved her very much; I still miss her. Her sister, Ada, lovingly co-opted me into her family, always introducing me to her friends as 'our daughter-in-law'. My father-in-law, Zadea Lazarus, was somewhat more remote.

The understated elegance of Mum's meals and entertainment, whether a formal dinner or an alfresco garden lunch, was more charming than an experience at Minnie's table, where one pot was produced for self-service. Mum was a superb cook and set her table with exquisite serviettes, often with crystal finger bowls in which floated beautiful rose petals and always with a floral centrepiece that she arranged herself. Auntie Fay's lessons in manners once again helped me to select the silver implements correctly.

Now I knew that, for the first time since the Second World War, I was not taken for granted. I was enthralled by my in-laws' warm greetings, quite a contrast with the indifferent reception when I visited my own mother and grandmother. I was happy that no one asked me to do chores as though that was my expected role as it had always been in my own family. Whenever I visited her, Mum would always welcome me with a smile, saying, 'Thank you for coming.' This was in sharp contrast to my visits to Booba, my grandmother, who did not welcome me and then complained about an endless list of irritants.

Zadea, my father-in-law, was the master of the backyard cricket game played by most of the grandchildren and some of the adults. His sister, Valerie, known as Ba, was a talented award-winning painter. She was a finalist in Australia's prestigious Archibald Portrait Prize ten times between 1937 and 1969, as well as nine times in the Wynne Prize (landscape) and twice in the Sir John Sulman Prize at the Art Gallery of New South Wales. Every Thursday my new aunt and her group of friends painted together *en plein air*, after which they returned for lunch at her home to which she invited me. The painters doted on my little baby, Michael, and I enjoyed their company and her lunch, which was always curried egg sandwiches and lemon tea. Ba had looked after her mother when she was younger and had remained single. Marian, my sister-in-law, and I went frequently to art shows, spending happy hours together.

Two weeks before my first child, Michael, was born, Marian gave birth to her second son, Daniel, younger brother to Mark Forstmann. Doris invited us new mothers to a sumptuous lunch every week. After we fed our babies and put them to sleep in their little baskets, Mum and her sister Ada minded them and gave us two precious hours of child-free time to do errands or just to walk in the sunshine. Sadly, Danny who became Michael's best friend, passed away when he was just nine years old. Another sister-in-law, Joyce, also went through the heartache of losing her precious only son, Antony, who was universally loved.

Each of these deceased nephews has been grieved for a long time and we miss them at every anniversary, birthday and family occasion. My son Michael was very badly affected by the death of Danny, who was his own age, and then by the passing of Antony who had been a true role model to Michael. Seeing my two sisters-in-law going through the sadness of their irreparable losses of their sons made me even more grateful for my wonderful, precious children.

In later years, I made a habit of taking my children to visit their Lazarus grandparents every Sunday. It was such a pleasure to visit Mum. She taught my youngest son, Jason, to play Scrabble and, in all her activities, showed great patience and kindness to all visitors.

When pregnant for the first time, I continued to work at the insistence of the Consul General who had requested replacement staff who had to journey from Belgium. Only days remained to prepare before I gave birth to our first child, Michael. By that time, Phillip and I were living in a lovely apartment on Trelawney Street, Woollahra, thanks to Phillip's old friends, Tamara and Andrew Adler, whose uncle rented us his newly refurbished apartment. It did not take me very long to arrive at work as I only walked across the street, which I continued to do until late September 1964, just before I gave birth.

Our first son, Michael Phillip Lazarus, was born on 12 October 1964. He was a beautiful baby and the nurses marvelled at how perfect he looked with his straw blond hair. Cindy Jo Lazarus was born on 20 October 1966. She has my father's nickname, Jo, as her second name. In Hebrew she is called Israëla, also in memory of my father. Our second son, Jason Edward Lazarus, was born on 29 August 1973. He was a gift, as I no longer expected to have another child.

While I was not salaried, I was a Director of Phillip's business, importing china and glassware into Australia and wholesaling it all over the South Pacific. I was in charge of costing items to set the wholesale prices. Eventually I did

60. Michael, Cindy and Jason Lazarus, Sydney, Australia, 1975.

this on an early home computer. I still ran the home and looked after the children as Phillip began to travel overseas more often to source new products to import; sometimes he was away from home for up to two months at a time.

For the first ten years of our marriage, we rented two-bedroom apartments but, after Jason was born, we managed to pay a deposit on a house in Towns Road in Vaucluse into which we moved in 1974. Here we brought up our family and lived for thirty-two years. At the back of that house there grew an enormous plane tree that was Michael's special hideout; he would perch in its branches out of my reach.

Phillip was a generous provider within our means and, as the business grew, we could send the children to good schools and, later, universities. However, Phillip maintained a remote approach to parenting, similar to his father, Zadea. When at home, he played tennis several times each week, including each Saturday and Sunday afternoon as well as mid-week, just as he had always done in his bachelor days. Despite accepting his plans without any objections, I still wished he spent some weekend time with our three children and me.

Eventually, I learned to enjoy spare time to pursue my own interests.

Chapter Twenty

Resuming my Education

As a result of only completing a truncated primary education, I always felt inferior to people who were well educated. My educational deficit hurt me deeply, partially because I blamed myself. From childhood, I developed a deep-rooted sense of shame about how I endured primitive conditions during the war and afterwards, when I was neglected and lacked protection. At school, I felt stigmatised and, worse, I feared that others did or would hate me. This negative self-image reduced my confidence as I experienced hatred and expressions of contempt from students and teachers, driving my humiliation deep into my core.

In adulthood, my shame was linked to a related fear that, if people found out about my lowly education, they would dismiss me with derision, in the same way that I had been disparaged since childhood. I was taught that every perceived failing or alleged deficit of mine was my own fault and an innate part of who I was. Yet most disappointments I had experienced were the direct results of what others had caused: deeds of shame, hate, contempt and abandonment were done to me. I had to lie about my inadequate schooling.

Never was it my choice or my decision to stop formal education at primary school. Unfortunately, I had not fully accepted those facts that I was forced to leave school, unable to overturn my mother's decision. I had proven my learning abilities and my school offered me both the opportunity and the means to pursue the highest level of secondary education in Belgium.

Rationally, a longer education would have developed my latent talents and my life might have been very different. My father was my one parent who would have ensured that I was educated but, of course, he did not survive the war. In fact, the brevity of my school years was in sharp contrast to my own father's education. Every one of my cousins completed high school and nearly all went to university whether in England, France or Australia.

Learning was important to me as was the attainment of a formal educational credential. Already I had read a great deal and the more I read, the more I realised how little I knew.

Completing high school

At the age of forty years, I made a two-pronged plan to advance my formal education. At first, I was afraid that I would not have the ability to tackle the task and I did not want to fail. Tentatively, I enrolled at the local adult education centre, a primary school where adults studied at night. I studied a couple of high school subjects, just to test my ability. Success in that first year boosted my confidence so, the following year, I enrolled in Technical and Further Education (TAFE), a government-run institution that offered very interesting and challenging instruction. My new peers were adults who had not completed their schooling, all of us with similar goals to learn and improve ourselves. At TAFE, I completed the high school curriculum and I also sat for the 'mature' university entrance exam.

By 1984, I had passed all the examinations to achieve the Higher School Certificate (HSC), completing all of the high school requirements in two years, another 'come from behind' educational achievement. Both of the two major universities to which I applied offered me the coveted entry to tertiary studies, for which thousands of hopeful students competed.

Aiming to achieve more of my own life goals, at the age of forty, I also learned to swim. This was a basic skill and an essential ability for safety and survival around the Sydney beaches and harbour. I achieved this thirty years after I was barred from participating in the school's swimming classes at the St Sauveur piscine in Brussels. Firstly, I did not own a swimsuit and my mother had refused to buy me one. Secondly, she did not spend money on school expenses, let alone any extra-curricular activity as frivolous as learning to swim, so I could not pay for any of the lessons. When the other students excitedly left school to go to their classes, I walked directly to clean my grandparents' house as I did every day. My mother's chief objective for me was to do the family chores; her needs outweighed any extra learning for me.

This circuitous argument provided me with insight into how I could never obtain what I needed from my mother – her wishes for me were far from my own interests and ambitions and if ever I expressed these she would accuse me of being unreasonable and obstructionist. When I was young I was very confused by my mother's reasoning. In hindsight, I recognise that she was unconcerned about me. By contrast, my mother could swim very well so swimming, per se, was not the issue.

As a parent and later a grandparent, I knew that swimming was a safety skill, essential for survival in lakes, rivers and on beaches in Belgium, just as it is in Australia. Now I could swim and save myself or anyone else in trouble in the water, achieving another of my life goals.

University studies

Education became an important cornerstone for my midlife personal development. With modest university goals, to study Arts and to complete a Bachelor's Degree, I enrolled at the University of New South Wales and, over several years, completed my undergraduate degree majoring in French and

61. Francine's Bachelor of Arts graduation, University of New South Wales, Sydney Australia, April 1990, with Michael, Jason and Cindy.

62. Francine's Master of Arts graduation, congratulated by her mother, Minnie Blumberg, husband, Phillip Lazarus, and their three children, Michael, Cindy and Jason, University of New South Wales, Sydney Australia, May 1993.

Sociology in 1989. This achievement was not as satisfying as I anticipated. It was too easy! Therefore, I applied to do a Master's degree in French literature, completing some coursework and writing a thesis. I learned to think critically, to gather and to analyse information.

Now I genuinely felt that I could hold my head high forever, as the spectre of shame faded from my life for being under-educated and for believing that I had to lie to hide my brief early education. Through courage and hard work, I overcame a deficit that only happened because my mother (and supposedly my stepfather) wanted me to earn, not to learn.

Hard-earned research skills, critical thinking and dogged fact-hunting abilities were honed in time for me to pursue and seek completion of my research on my hidden childhood in Belgium and the broader impact on all hidden child Survivors. I reflected on what I might have accomplished if I had acquired university degrees when I was young.

My personal journey gathered pace as I began to research how other peoples' decisions, starting with Hitler's, had affected me. I sought to reconcile the impacts of others on my life. I began to trace how I became the person I am today from meeting and overcoming many diverse challenges over decades.

Chapter Twenty-one

Family Reunited
in Australia

My mother, Maurice and Helen migrated to Australia in April 1969. They arrived in Perth on 25 April, which is Anzac Day, Australia and New Zealand's joint national holiday to honour all who have served in war and peacekeeping missions.

Over the years since I left Belgium, we had remained in touch through regular correspondence. Every fortnight I had written a letter to my mother, signing it 'love, Francine'. In reply, my mother wrote similar newsy letters, signing them, 'love, Mum'. I rang her once each month but we said little to each other of personal importance.

After their arrival, a guarded peace was established between my mother, Maurice and me, creating a semblance of family unity. They lived in Birrell Street in Bondi Junction, a few kilometres away from my home. My children quickly became attached to them. They were now surrounded with extended family from both sides of the family, something that I did not have after so many relatives were murdered. My desire for a close, loving family was being realised in my next generation. Eventually my grandchildren would also know and grow up with their broad extended families.

When Helen arrived in Australia, we resumed our close relationship. Her English was poor, so she spoke in French and we both laughed happily at her jokes. Once a stranger on a bus told us nastily, 'speak in English', a xenophobic retort frequently directed at migrants in Australia at that time, and we were so embarrassed that we left the bus and waited for the next one on which to continue our journey. This was before Australia embraced multiculturalism, even though the policy did not end the ignorance and prejudice of individuals towards speakers of other languages.

Once I offered to teach Helen how to bake in my kitchen. I put a dozen or so egg whites in a bowl and turned on the electric beater to whip them until they were light and fluffy. We started to talk and I ignored the whizzing of the machine until finally I turned around and there were amazing flocks of egg white 'snow' floating throughout the kitchen, some rising to the ceiling, others depositing themselves on shelves, on top of the fridge, table, stove and our hair. There was even some on our reading glasses. It took us forever to clean up the kitchen but we laughed so joyously.

After a short time in Australia, Helen decided to move to Israel where she stayed in the Beit Hashitah Kibbutz. We wrote letters sporadically while I was busy with my young family and she was exploring her new life. When Helen returned to Australia, she soon met Alex Berger. They married on 3 June 1973. It was quite a society wedding, with so many attendees that I doubted that Helen, my mother or Maurice could have known all the guests personally. I was disappointed not to be invited by my only sister to be one of her bridesmaids or Matron of honour, a private hope that I had always held.

Helen and Alex had two boys, David and Adam, who are first cousins to my children from Minnie's side (Inberg-Rosenblum). When our little boys were still young, David, Adam and Jason were very close. We met at my mother and Maurice's home. It was nicknamed our 'halfway house' as it was approximately midway between Helen's and my own home.

63. Helen Blumberg and Alex Berger's wedding day with her mother Minnie and father Maurice Blumberg, Central Synagogue, Sydney, Australia, 3 June 1973.

Together we explored Sydney. Helen, Alex and I invited my mother, Maurice and sometimes our children to go on Sunday afternoon outings. Helen selected a place of interest and we would all drive to the destination with an ample picnic basket. We went to every historic and natural attraction and hundreds of community events on great family outings. That was a good time in all our lives and enriched our children's development and family closeness.

Every week my children and I visited my mother and Maurice for lunch, along with Helen and her boys. These were really enjoyable times together. Maurice was a very good cook, preparing all the foods of 'the old country' including chicken soup, borscht, onions and eggs and always serving delicious stewed fruit. Even after being diagnosed with diabetes, Maurice continued to prepare lovely meals. Occasionally we caught him tasting the forbidden food in the kitchen where he thought he could eat without being seen. My mother reigned as the queen of the apple pie. Hers was the best in the world and the children gorged themselves on her pie regularly.

Helen and I always loved being together, sharing quality time no matter how busy we were. With our children grown, we still meet regularly for lunch when we reminisce, gossip and laugh a lot. Recently we were recalling a movie we saw together in Sydney just after she arrived, now more than forty years ago. The plot of *Buona Sera Mrs Campbell* (1968) starring Gina Lollobrigida was so impossible that we laughed so much we had tears running down our faces.

I have known Helen since she was born. I resented having her foisted on me and having to take care of her. Our relationship was more like that of a mother and daughter rather than that of sisters. When she came to Australia she was grown up and, again, we knew absolutely nothing of personal importance about each other but managed to establish a loving, caring, stable relationship. Helen has a wonderful sense of humour and that often brings us closer. She makes me laugh and I enjoy this feeling. Helen is a kind and considerate person. We share good times when we are together.

In the early period of Helen's arrival, Charly met us only on special occasions. His second wife, Rachel, rarely invited any of his family to their home, which was within walking distance of ours. I managed to have long chats on the phone with Charly in between visits. Jennifer, his third wife, shares her liveliness with all the family and provides Charly with wonderful support.

I believe it was a very good time for my mother, surrounded by her son and two daughters and their growing families. Ian Kamerman, Charly's only child, visited his grandmother when his medical studies and career permitted. Ian and his wife Margaret have two children, James and Sophie (recently married to Jason Bromage), who are great-grandchildren of my father.

64. Charly Kamerman and his wife, Jennifer Cheyne, at the wedding of Sophie Kamerman, his only granddaughter, Tamworth, NSW, Australia, 2014 (courtesy Simon Scott Photo).

65. Ian Kamerman, son of Charly and nephew of Francine, with his wife Margaret, celebrating the wedding of their daughter, Sophie Kamerman to Jason Bromage, along with their son James, Tamworth, NSW, Australia, 2014 (courtesy Simon Scott Photo).

66. Minnie, Francine's mother, and Maurice Blumberg dancing, Belgium 1961.

Maurice Blumberg

The second husband of my mother migrated with her to Australia when over sixty years old, leaving Europe for a brash new country that was overflowing with opportunities. I appreciate how difficult it would have been to migrate in one's later years. When I arrived aged twenty years, ten years earlier, Australia had little cultural or commercial sophistication. Maurice must have felt so much more contrast, being older and speaking little English.

When I was married and a parent, I could better appreciate the enormous loss of his first wife in the death camp, along with most of his family in the *Shoah*, as well as his post-war challenges and adjustment issues, including taking responsibility for me for nine years. He had survived multiple concentration camps by luck or cunning. It is not for me to judge nor should anybody else who has not been in a life and death position. Who knows how we would have acted if faced with the same circumstances.

In Australia, we established a truce, eventually bordering on friendship. Maurice knew Jason since birth and doted on him just as much as on Helen's two sons. Jason recently told me that, until he was an adult, he had never known that Maurice was not his 'real' grandfather. It had never occurred to any of us to talk about my father or to tell him that Maurice was my mother's second husband.

Once when Phillip was away on business, I offered to take Maurice to a Sydney Symphony concert with me, using my husband's ticket. The look of pure enjoyment and pleasure on his face was a revelation. Maurice had had a very tough life, not much schooling and certainly very few moments of happiness. He had worked very hard all his life. Observing him thoroughly immersed in the music at the concert, I was surprised to see his joy and appreciation of classical music and I discovered a commonality with my stepfather. We enjoyed a few more such outings together and I am glad that I was able to give him this small pleasure.

Maurice did not feel settled immediately and complained that things were better 'over there'. I acknowledged his many challenges, starting with the obvious, that Australia was not Europe nor was it as cultured. In addition, he was not happy being retired with very little to do. Fortunately, Phillip suggested he might like to help at our warehouse. Maurice loved that job and worked there for a few years, largely because he was happier going somewhere each morning and feeling that he had a purpose.

Minnie and Maurice went back to Europe to visit their friends and relatives. On his return to Australia, Maurice seemed quite subdued. He no longer complained about Australia or Sydney. Eventually, he became mellow in Australia. Following a diagnosis of diabetes, Maurice became quieter and did not converse as much as when he was younger. There was no longer any animosity between us. We developed our relationship to a safer level, sharing a guarded friendship. I remained in a relationship 'triangle' with Maurice as I could not forgive him for having unwittingly taken my father's place, something neither of us could ever undo.

Maurice died on 30 May 1996, aged eighty-one years. While I felt very sad when he died, I realised only then what he had done for me. Too late, I recognised that he took me in when others refused or were unable to support me. He raised me through my teens as well as he knew how, even though he did not show me any affection such as a kiss or a hug. In Australia, he began to offer me vast amounts of my favourite foods, seemingly as his substitute for emotion. I think of him often and sometimes I smile when I see a product at a reduced price in a supermarket, as he so much enjoyed buying a bargain, especially food.

Mother widowed again

Once again, my mother adapted to living as a widow after Maurice passed away. Helen, Charly and I took turns to look after her while she remained in her own apartment. She was proud of her independence. Although now in her eighties, she did not consider herself elderly and vehemently declared that she did not want to spend time with 'old people'. It took a great deal of coaxing to persuade her to join activities at the nearby Jewish meeting place for elderly people, the Burger Centre.

So my mother sat in her lounge, always ready and happy for any visitors to arrive. We hired professional carers to help her dress and to prepare her meals. At that time, my mother's hair was snow-white which complemented her magnificent sapphire eyes, mirrored in the eye colour of my two elder children. Meanwhile, my mother charmed every visitor and all the people

67. Minnie Inberg Kamerman Blumberg, with her daughters Francine Kamerman Lazarus and Helen Blumberg Berger, and son Charly Kamerman, Sydney, Australia, 1993.

whom she met at the Burger Centre. Helen, at that time, took me to hear a lecture about dementia; I was horrified that she might be suggesting that our mother was losing some of her mental faculties.

I was oblivious to her gradual loss of memory or her small mishaps. My mother misplaced or hid items and then accused her carer of stealing them. We spent hours looking for the missing items, always finding them in the most incongruous places, causing us to laugh, privately. I could even smile at her lifelong habit of blaming and demeaning other people for her displeasure as, by now, she had just forgotten.

Helen looked after Minnie's physical needs and I did all her paperwork, such as paying her bills. We took turns to take her to various appointments and social engagements. Helen and Alex continued to host her for *Shabbat* dinners most Friday nights. By then, she could not walk up the steps to my home. Occasionally, Charly invited her to an event at his home.

One day we discovered Minnie very unwell at home. She must have had a stroke. We found her lying in her lounge room. She could not have been there long as all three of her children never let a day go past without visiting her home or telephoning her. She was hospitalised and subsequently moved to a nursing home. Charly, Helen, Alex or I were present at each meal to help her eat and to keep her company.

She started refusing to eat but, as she loved ice cream, that was what we happily fed her. We provided a few luxuries, such as manicures and a special chair in which we wheeled her outside into the garden. I sung her the old songs that she liked and had sung to me, including those made famous by Vera Lynne after the war, especially one of her favourites, *Jealousy*: 'Why did I make that big mistake, I wronged you right from the start'.[80]

Eventually, though my mother still knew her name, Minnie, she no longer responded to being called 'Mum' nor did she recognise me. Even then, I kept on hoping that she would say just once, 'I love you.' She never did. After a few months in care, she died on 24 November 2000. I did not cry.

Family secrets revealed after her death were unsettling for Charly, Helen and me. Telling the truth was always difficult for my mother, as was expressing affection to Charly and me. I have no regrets about my part in my relationship with my mother. I know that I was always a good daughter. However, I felt that she was not a good mother to me in many respects though I grant that her life may not have been an easy or a good one.

I have tried to forgive my mother.

Chapter Twenty-two

Recovery

Fear is the main source of superstition, and one of the main sources of cruelty. To conquer fear is the beginning of wisdom.

Bertrand Russell[81]

My children and grandchildren provide me with my greatest joys in life. Nothing gives me more pleasure than to have them around me, talking, listening and laughing. They hug and freely express their affection for each

68. Francine and Phillip, Michael, Cindy and Jason Lazarus, at the wedding of Sophie Kamerman, Tamworth, NSW, Australia, 2014 (courtesy Simon Scott Photo).

69. Michael Lazarus and Kim Byrne, Tamworth, NSW, Australia, 2014 (courtesy Simon Scott Photo).

other and for me. Whenever I am with one or more of them, I feel complete and fulfilled.

Michael

My eldest child is one of the most kind-hearted people I have ever met. He has always protected me, even if he had to put himself in harm's way when still very young. Michael's passion is rugby. He always accompanied Phillip to the Wallabies and Waratah games

His wicked sense of humour enlivens every occasion. He expresses affection easily and I enjoy spending time with him. He has never married but enjoys a fine relationship with Kimmaree Byrne who is bright, fun, very caring and a superb cook.

Michael always exhibited above-average intelligence and he was invited to join Mensa, which is a society whose members qualify by having an IQ in the top 2 per cent of the population, when still in school.

Cindy

My daughter is my best friend, as well as being my confidante and helper. She is a wonderful mother and a friend to many. Always thoughtful, Cindy speaks

70. Wedding of Cindy Lazarus and David Levy, with her parents, Francine and Phillip Lazarus and her brothers Jason and Michael Lazarus, Sydney, Australia, 3 September 1995.

on the phone almost every day with me and I enjoy spending time with her over a cup of coffee. I feel fortunate to have an outstanding relationship with my daughter and to have ended the cycle of exploitation of women in our family.

She earned her Bachelor of Commerce degree and subsequently earned a Bachelor of Laws with Honours while working full-time as a chartered accountant. Then she obtained a Master of Business Administration when living in South Africa following her marriage. Cindy chose a new career path when she then qualified as a personal trainer.

David Levy, my son-in-law is a wonderful loving father to my grandchildren. He doesn't care much for social conventions but that is fine with me. He always offers to include us in their holidays and activities, as when Phillip and I went to South Africa, met his relatives and he guided us through several of his favourite game parks.

Jason

My younger son, Jason, and I studied at the same university at the same time. He felt embarrassed when I was in a lecture with his school friends. Secretly, I think that he was proud of me. When Jason planned a trip to Turkey, he

71. Cindy Lazarus and David Levy, Joshua (sixteen), Jared (fourteen) and Jessica (six) Levy, Sydney, Australia, December 2014 (courtesy Joel Symonds).

invited me to fill a vacancy due to one traveller cancelling. That trip and especially the time we spent together ranks as a highlight of my life.

Professionally, Jason is a barrister, an independent legal advocate who argues in the higher courts. I take pride in Jason's achievements, even though he does look a little bit silly in his wig and gown! I always value his advice and I am amazed at the scope of his knowledge. I tell Jason that he never caused me any sadness, only created joy. When he announced his impending marriage to Carly Ross, I was elated because I knew that he had found his true soulmate. Carly is warm and caring, qualities that befit her career as a clinical psychologist. I feel blessed that she has come into my life as well as that of my son. Jason and Carly were married on 11 September 2016 in a beautiful ceremony. Thankfully Phillip was able to attend. I am so happy: my cup runneth over.

Love of grandchildren

After all my hardships and unhappiness, my wonderful grandchildren provide me with inspiration and love. Their personalities and abilities are far greater than I could have imagined for myself at their ages. Please indulge this doting grandmother.

72. Jason Lazarus and Carly Ross at their wedding, 11 September 2016 (courtesy Chris Prestidge).

Cindy's children are Joshua (nineteen in 2016), Jared (sixteen) and Jessica (nine).

Joshua commenced university studies in 2016, enrolled in commerce and mathematics, following years of excelling at high school. In 2013, he created a video about my Holocaust experiences, known as the Hans Kimmel project, for which he won a school prize. He is a high achiever.

Jared excels in English, mathematics and science, debating and acting. He attended weekly *shiurim* (lessons) with the school's Rabbis to discuss philosophical issues pertaining to Judaism. He plays trumpet in the school band and is completing the Gold Duke of Edinburgh award. His Hans Kimmel project about my life experiences also won a prize.

Jessica is beginning to enjoy the educational aspect of school, where she shows leadership skills, assisted by her extroverted personality. She is very affectionate, with a genuinely helpful and spirited manner.

Luckily for me, all our family lives within a five kilometres radius. We try to get together every Friday night to share the Sabbath meal. This tradition keeps us together as a family, allowing everyone to share their news and discuss any concerns over the meal. I place less emphasise on the religious associations of the Sabbath than on the joy of being together with my family.

Jewish in Australia

One event from my children's schooling raised a deep realisation. Cindy was singing with her Jewish school choir on a city plaza. When I went to hear her sing, to my amazement, the choir stood holding an Israeli flag and singing Hebrew songs, right in the middle of Sydney's central business district! I was so taken aback, seeing the freedom and the openness with which we live in Australia that I began to cry tears of joy. That evening, I wrote to the school headmaster and thanked Mr Harold Nagley for unintentionally showing me that there was no reason to hide my Jewishness any longer.

Only after migrating to Australia did I first sit at a Sabbath table, in Auntie Betty's home. In my Belgian family, I never saw Sabbath candles being lit nor observed any of the commandments relating to the Jewish holy days.

I barely follow the religious services because my Hebrew remains elementary and I have still never learned the meaning within the rituals; I admit that I am not a regular attendee to synagogue. I go primarily on holy days and occasionally on a Sabbath. I would like to be a believer, after observing how other people find great strength and peace when they turn to their religion for solace. As much as I would like to feel enveloped by a mystic certainty of a superior being, my rational mind does not want to accept its existence. Here too, I feel like an outsider as in many aspects of my life.

I am a member of the Great Synagogue in Sydney, continuing over a century of tradition in my husband's family of belonging to the congregation. I attend because I was born Jewish and I wish to maintain the traditions for my children and grandchildren in order to encourage them to continue the customs.

Chapter Twenty-three

Ending Intergenerational Victimisation

Booba's most shameful secret was that she could not read. To avoid detection of her illiteracy, she excused herself from reading by saying that she had forgotten her glasses. She made me her reader and letter writer when we lived in Brussels. Many times over, I heard her grievance that her brothers received a good education while she and her sisters had none. Yet she did nothing about learning to read or write, despite almost limitless leisure time in later years. After all, she had me to clean and do all her chores every day. Being unable to read all her life was one obvious fact that made me doubt the family fable of her travelling when pregnant across Europe alone except for her tiny children: she would not have been able to read a ticket or a train station sign.

Other sources of Booba's inveterate unhappiness stemmed, most probably, from her arranged marriage in Poland as a teen bride, then taken far away from her family to live in England. There she did not understand the local language and was bound by the responsibilities of raising her children with no family assistance. Next, she moved to Belgium when her three youngest children were still dependent, when Betty was thirteen, Rose was nine and Bunny was eight years old. She continued her role as an unhappy mother in another country with yet another new language to learn while still far from her family.

Could she have had a happy marriage with Zeida? I never saw signs of love or affection or even basic happiness between them. Booba was always arguing about trivial matters and Zeida tried to stay away from her for as much time as possible. She claimed to have many illnesses and afflictions, probably to get attention and sympathy and to excuse herself from mundane activities. She expressed her unhappiness to those around her, principally by praising her absent relatives as an implied criticism of the person she was talking with, especially me when I was looking after her.

Booba compensated for the unhappiness she claimed to feel by demanding selfish indulgences. She left her children and husband for many days when she stayed in expensive spas in other countries. Her only visible expression of love and affection was when she said she loved and missed her family members who were living far away. She would wail 'Betsa, I miss my Betsa' (Auntie Betty in Australia).

Her ultimate device to create some form of happiness for herself was delegating her mothering and housekeeping duties to her second daughter. That girl was my mother, who was neither allowed to complete her education nor to make her own decision to leave school. Booba mistreated my mother by curtailing her education precisely to use Minnie as the housekeeper and nanny for her younger siblings. I never saw Booba express kindness to Zeida or to my mother and never to me.

My mother's marriage to my father was, I felt almost sure, also an arranged one. Perhaps she agreed to marry this older man to escape her parents' authority and cease doing housework for Booba. My father controlled their finances and she neither earned nor had any money of her own. She had not received any from her parents nor had she been able to save from her meagre wages. When she went shopping for basic goods, she had to ask him for the exact money and to explain what she was intending to buy. In many ways, regardless of this financial control, he gave her a better life than at her parents' home, with his gentle loving manner.

Probably the only really happy period my mother experienced in her long life was the brief time between her two husbands, after my father's death. She enjoyed her independence, working, managing her own money, dating and dancing after the war. It was the only time in her life that she was free of anybody holding sway over her or with whom she had to compromise. After sending me away to my grandparents and later to foster carers and sending Charly to work, she indulged herself as a free woman.

After Helen was born, my mother made me mind her baby and do the housework, just as she had been forced to look after her younger siblings in England. Every free day that she could, my mother spent her time curled up in a lounge chair, sucking her thumb, eating chocolates and reading popular English women's magazines. She worked three months at the markets in summer, then one day per week for the next nine months. She kept tight control of the market income and Charly's wages, as well as her three pensions about which I was kept ignorant. Meanwhile, she assigned me to clean, scrub and do many other chores for my grandparents. She certainly did not spend any money on me beyond essentials, memorably just one pair of shoes each year.

My mother repeated Booba's abuse of her, upon me. She duplicated her own limited education by restricting my educational opportunities, as I commenced appallingly late and finished unnecessarily early. Like her, I was forced to work as a housekeeper, kitchen help and nanny for three generations, namely for my grandparents, my mother and Maurice, and my little sister, Helen.

My mother also used me as free labour in her market business, overloaded by additional domestic duties. When she made me quit my paid position every

73. Three generations of women: Minnie Inberg Kamerman Blumberg, Francine Kamerman Lazarus and Cindy Lazarus, Sydney, Australia, 1993.

year to work for her with no wages throughout the summer, my mother effectively curtailed my career opportunities and restricted my private earnings.

Against feeling deep dissatisfaction with and loathing for how I was treated, I always obeyed, even if I was a completely unwilling victim. I was desperately unhappy but could not see an escape from my mother's controlling devices and could not find a way to live more independently. I had already seen how other women at work managed their time, money and affairs, so I hoped that I could be in charge of my life one day, preferably soon.

While not intended as a favour, my mother sending me to Australia offered me a fresh beginning when a young adult. Even there, Auntie Betty had tried to impose a subordination role on me by controlling my finances and dictating my relationships.

Despite my difficult and near-deadly early years, a core of resilience had remained that helped me build a productive life and develop social skills. However, I had learned to concede to dominating people as I knew no other way of relating to people. In relationships I neither expected any reciprocity nor knew that I had rights not to be abused or exploited. With great satisfaction, I have learned to reject attempts by others to make me their victim.

My marriage was to a man I chose rather than one who had been imposed on me, in direct contrast with the marriages of my mother and Booba.

However, I found it natural to follow the conventions of the time, to defer to my husband's opinions and to accept his decisions without any discussion and without voicing my ideas. Phillip and I followed the traditional gender separation of power (his) and submission (mine) in all our family decisions. My family is a happy one and my relationships with my children are warm and caring, unlike in any household in which I lived as a child.

In my middle years, when my youngest child was about to complete high school, I saw clearly that I had the time and opportunity to recommence my education, a goal that I had held for the previous thirty years. I seized my first chance to learn, to re-engage in lost opportunities and to explore ways in which I could realise and express my genuine self. A key reason for seeking further education was to gain self-confidence and the respect of others. Gradually, my regrets about my early years, especially for my limited education, diminished.

My beautiful daughter, Cindy, was born strong and wilful as my second child. I inculcated in her the need never to be a victim as I had been. There would always be perpetrators about but I taught her not to obey them. I encouraged her to stand up for her rights and to maintain her integrity, fight for it if need be and never, ever be reliant or dependent on anyone besides herself.

Cindy chose a university education to meet her own goals. My daughter always provides much joy and loving support to me and to Phillip, as well as to her brothers. Her marriage to David Levy was based on their mutual choice of each other. It did not curtail her own goals or personal development, rather it encouraged her. Together they are a great partnership and they have created a loving family.

Recently, Jessica, Cindy's only daughter retorted to her mother, 'You're not the boss of me', which is not really true but indicates the independence and assertiveness of the youngest generation. Attending her school recently, I cried. My tears were both for joy at her achievements and tears of regret for my early truncated education and interrupted personal development.

Unlike their forbearers, my daughter and granddaughter are strong, independent and nobody's victims. They will pursue their own dreams and achieve as well as they can in whatever they set out to accomplish. I am so happy and grateful that future generations of women in my family will be able to determine their own futures.

A new strong, beautiful and accomplished woman has joined our family. Her name is Carly Ross who has recently married my son Jason. Their union is based on love and mutual respect. Already she has endeared herself to all of us. I wish Jason and Carly happiness always.

The cycle of abuse, neglect and victimisation has ended. This is one of my greatest achievements: to have ended the cycle of exploitation of women in our family.

Chapter Twenty-four

Emotional Scars

Like many formerly hidden Jewish children, I still suffer symptoms that are related to traumatic experiences, seventy years after coming out of hiding. 'Their life stories highlighted important impairments related to their war experiences (e.g. feelings of guilt, familial and social difficulties, emotion restrictions ...)'.[82] My traumas were caused by antisemitism, Hitler and the Nazis, the war and subsequent neglect and abuse.

When sanctions are imposed externally, such as by family elders and community leaders, or by customs and laws, guilt can develop if one breaks such admonitions or taboos. Because many children had not survived, I was told I was 'lucky'. I could not comprehend if I was supposed to feel guilty because I lived or guilty because others died. I genuinely felt very sad about all the children who were murdered by the Nazis and I felt ashamed that I never attempted to find Catherine and Marie to thank them for saving my life on the farm in Saintes, though, of course, I was not allowed to speak about them or find them after the war.

Now, I feel guilty, after being told never to mention what happened to me in the war in terms of how and where I was hidden. I have shared events that happened to my brother, my mother and my father, grandparents and my cousin Moishe, before, during and after the war.

Early on, I was given a big dose of 'blame' for many difficult situations and, subsequently, I began to feel guilty about anything that went wrong. I could not judge how irrationally I was linking myself to a difficult situation over which I had neither influence nor any possible control.

Besides imposing mental controls on what to say or feel after the Second World War, many people subjected me to abuse and neglect, leaving lasting physical and emotional scars. I was used, exploited and abused by carers, strangers and family members. Strangers at school teased, insulted and hit me. One technique that helps me integrate myself with that sad, lonely and unloved little Francine, is that I imagine that I am hugging her, reassuring her that she is loved to help her feel better.

Even before being abandoned to foster care, I had ceased to have any family life. It was very disorienting being moved so often, reinforcing the 'villain' script that I was so naughty that no one wanted me or loved me. My few possessions would be packed in a cardboard box and I would be taken away and deposited at another stranger's door. In foster homes, I was subjected to living without safety or genuine support as a child deserved. All those perpetrators admonished me to hide and keep secret the bad things they did to me. My suffering and the victimisation made me feel guilty too, ashamed because I thought I must have deserved the abuse and neglect. Yet I never attempted to run away from a foster home, having no money and no possible destination. My only options were my mother's home where I was not wanted or that of my grandparents, who kept me with them for no more than a month or two at most.

A deep sense of shame developed about the way I lived during the war and afterwards, with poor clothing, in primitive conditions and with nobody to love or protect me. Perversely, I blamed myself, yet war conditions and the Nazis caused my grim childhood years. Piers and Singer emphasised that, 'Behind the feeling of shame stands out not the fear of hatred, but the fear of contempt which, on an even deeper level of the unconscious, spells fear of abandonment, the death by emotional starvation'.[83]

Why would I still feel shame about the wild ignorant child that I was, thinking that I knew everything and putting on a show of bravado? Then, I had no adult to guide me when I did not know how to interact. Now, I try to cease shouldering blame. Often I have experienced great difficulty in playing games with my grandchildren. To be fair with myself, at their ages, I was in hiding or in post-war chaos, living for years without playing or laughing, talking or crying, every day hoping for enough food and safe shelter. I watch them and their competencies and feel again my social and educational inadequacies through childhood and into early adulthood.

Research findings confirmed that hidden Jewish children still report severe post-traumatic symptoms sixty-five years later, often considered 'as high or higher than children who survived the camps'.[84] 'It is possible that the inability to disclose their experiences may partly explain this phenomenon, as disclosure of traumatic experiences is related to better mental and physical health among Holocaust Survivors ... This could suggest that nondisclosure and non-recognition as Holocaust Survivors may have impaired the ability of hidden children to adequately process their traumatic past'.[85] Without a doubt, my living situation continued to undermine my emotional stability.

Another factor that did not help my ability to come to terms with my traumatic childhood was probably having insufficient education. Fohn et al. found that education helped child Survivors work through trauma, improved emotional stability as well as providing employable skills and flexible adult options.[86]

Such results succinctly summarise why I felt like a perpetual outsider and considered myself to be marginalised in society. At first, for my survival, I was isolated from other children, family and friends. After the war, I was emotionally isolated because I knew no one who talked about war experiences like mine. Further, I was isolated from my peers by not being enrolled in school at the legal age. When sent to school aged eight years, I was enrolled in the earliest, baby class. I was never dressed suitably or provided with books and other educational tools and experiences to keep up with peers. Being Jewish, no longer having a father, finally being put in foster care, all combined to multiply my social deficits and isolation in post-war Brussels.

The limited education I had was, of course, another source of shame, about which I lied, saying that I had an advanced education. Then, I was ashamed of lying ... It was very difficult to get off this sad merry-go-round once shame, fear of contempt and rejection and mere lies started to catch up with each other.

Fear drove my decisions and reactions for decades. Early on and as time went by, I developed a pervasive sense of fear after extremely frightening death-defying experiences in the war and from risky and abusive situations after the war. My fears grew from repeated exposures to traumatic events as a hidden child, compounded by post-war abuse and neglect. I feared a repeat of those situations, such as wicked strangers, separation from my family, loud noises, germs and disease, hazards and accidents, destruction and death. Similar events still frighten me.

While Kestenberg and Kohn described how some child Survivors frequently blamed their parents for abandoning them or giving them away into hiding, I longed to be with my parents and brother, never blaming them for being somewhere else.[87] Eventually, I began to blame myself for being alone. Surviving that death-defying mix of childhood despoliation did not end my story of pain and suffering, fear and guilt, shame and self-criticism. At times, I am still that little girl, desperately trying to please everybody and earn their approval.

Possibly I never learned to say 'No'. Eventually, I pleased nobody, least of all myself. Imagine my internal schism. I wonder how long, if ever, until I find peace and self-acceptance. Each year I have regained a little more control over my life and the decisions affecting me.

My life has been marked by cumulative grief and trauma. After my heart was wrenched out when my father was arrested in Brussels and sent to Auschwitz to be murdered, I dumped a mountain of blame and guilt on myself. Always I thought I was the cause of my father's capture and deportation, haunted by fears that he was caught in a round-up on his way to see me in my hiding place. I carried irrational blame for his arrest and death for decades.

Of course, it was Hitler's fault.

Friendship

In childhood, I learned to be content, if not happy, with my own company. With no child or adult to play with, that is how I learned to adjust, whether in hiding, roaming the streets or, later, having no free time to make new friendships. Very early in life, I learnt that nothing would be permanent for me as I was moved from one hiding place to another, from one foster carer to another carer, from one school to another school and from one job to another. I felt, or more likely rationalised, that it was better for me not to become attached, lest I feel disappointed or experience hurt feelings.

As a hidden child and too soon afterwards, a foster child, I concealed my feelings and could not express my emotions of affection or love for others. I also stopped to seek affection or to ask for emotional support because these signs of caring for me were unlikely to be provided. If I expressed my feelings or indicated my needs to my mother or grandmother, I was chastised and denigrated for my emotional outpourings. Altogether, this provided a weak basis for achieving sound attachments and emotional security throughout my life.

What I have always yearned for is a real friend, someone who wants to be my friend. I imagined that a true friend would be a warm person who understands my foibles, who is willing to listen, who understands me and accepts me as I am. I still hope to meet somebody with whom I can share my innermost thoughts. Of course, I hope I can offer the same to that person.

The vision of what friendship meant was the easy 'give and take' that I observed between my mother and Betty Carlier in Brussels. I always longed for such a close connection with another person, male or female. I once considered someone a friend but she terminated the relationship over a misunderstanding and I could not comprehend how friendship could be so fragile. obviously I was not her friend. Friendship is a two way street. I lost confidence in my capacity to make friends and have not trusted myself to form new relationships, other than the everyday exchanges of small talk. This is another way in which I feel like an outsider. Now, I find it difficult to open up to new acquaintances, lest I risk being misunderstood or possibly feel rejected. Over the last few years, I have felt accepted by some groups of people and perhaps I will form deeper friendships.

Aged sixty-four years, I joined an aqua aerobics class. One participant started a 'water sprites' group of women and I was invited to join. Belonging to a group – to me, this phrase has a wonderful sound and special meaning. While I am part of a family and part of a community, now I feel that I belong with a group of people from diverse backgrounds whom I see several times each week at classes. The aqua ladies meet monthly for lunch in each other's homes when we defeat all the benefits of our exercise with a delicious lunch prepared by the hostess. We laugh a lot, we eat, we enjoy each other's company and we express, even celebrate, our developing friendships with each other. The more serious aspect of our meetings is to raise money towards curing cancer, as sadly two of our members died from cancer in quick succession in 2013.

We are a diverse group united in enjoying each other's company. We discuss life's challenges, sometimes share our pasts and support each other in any present endeavour.

Is this a universal trait of hidden children who learned to hide, physically, mentally and emotionally? This yearning for friendship is true for me, due to my particular circumstances of experiencing criticism and rejection, time and time again.

Enjoying life

Soon after I arrived in Sydney, I spent more money than I could afford on one ticket to hear the Sydney Symphony Orchestra performing at the Sydney Town Hall. The acoustics may have been poor but my ear did not assess perfect pitch; I heard the concert with my heart and drank in all the beauty of the music. My love affair with performing arts has continued uninterrupted.

Fortunately, Phillip shared my love for opera and together we heard many works and saw great performers of our time such as Dame Joan Sutherland, Luciano Pavarotti and Placido Domingo. We enjoyed ballet and were thrilled to watch Rudi Nureyev and Dame Margot Fonteyn dance in 1964 at the old Elizabethan Theatre in Sydney. Over the decades, I have marvelled at the performances by many visiting international ballets and fantastic Australian companies. We tried to see almost every Sydney performance in theatre, ballet and the Sydney Symphony Orchestra and supported several artistic companies.

Retirement came after our children had left home and Phillip closed the business. For more than forty years Phillip was my partner when we played bridge at the local club. We achieved some successes and some embarrassing defeats, and we enjoyed the challenge. We moved to an apartment located near our family. We took quite a while to get used to communal living. For years we played – or rather our sons played music as loudly as they wished; now we could not bombard neighbours living next door.

Until Phillip's health deteriorated, we enjoyed travel, particularly cruising and visiting Israel many times, mostly with various study groups. We travelled often to Europe where we enjoyed seeing the amazing collections of art from many centuries. On cruises, one meets many people who are friendly holiday companions but mutual interests do not extend beyond the holiday period. Two such holiday friendships have become steady friendships. Arlene and David Multz live in Florida and have visited us in Australia; I hope to have a reciprocal visit to Florida one day. Marilyn and Alan Lazarus (no relation) live in London, so we have met them several times when visiting England. I wished that both couples lived here so I could see them more often as I find their company and conversation very enjoyable. They are our long distance friends, our Skype friends.

Israel will always be my favourite destination. It was a beacon of hope for me after the war and it still holds part of my heart.

Chapter Twenty-five

Healing

Gradually I am accepting my experiences of surviving the *Shoah* by being hidden. I cannot forget or heal every emotional or physical scar. Part of me remains 'emotionally in hiding'.[88] Learning from other child Survivors, in meetings and through research, has helped me to validate my memories and to express my feelings honestly and courageously. The harsh truth of the dynamics of my life after the war, no longer with my father and without a loving home, still shocks my innate sense of what is right for children.

I, who was not supposed to survive the evil round-ups and murders of Jews, reared three beautiful children. Now, I see my wonderful grandchildren and feel satisfaction that my father has continuity. The greater tragedy was that he never lived to see Charly and me grow up nor to enjoy his four grandchildren and his great grandchildren.

As I relax and muse over all my life's challenges and deficits, I am suddenly struck by the fact that I thought I was unique and tainted and the only one who had to hide and keep secrets. Now I recognise that all the Jewish children whom I met in Belgium after the war lived somewhat like me. We all went through the Holocaust, lost many loved ones and lived a bizarre, fearful childhood, always on a knife-edge. How else could we have been Jewish children and still be alive after the war in Belgium?

Silent no more

Never did any of us mention a single thing about our war survival experiences to one another. Obviously, those Jewish children who survived had all been hidden in one way or another. I feel a loss in that we did not speak openly about how we lived and survived when we were young and few have spoken subsequently. Yet 'many used silence as a coping mechanism to deal with situations ... in order to survive'.[89] I did, and I also used to pretend in order to fit in with others after the war. So many of us lived some kind of lie, to push our sadness and fear far away from our consciousness when coping with our daily post-war life. We were anticipating being 'found out' as Jewish child Survivors, as we had so recently feared being found out as Jews by the Nazis.

Few former hidden children had someone whom they trusted sufficiently to speak with and with whom to share details of their sad and scary early lives. Increasingly, during the past two decades, hidden children have spoken and written about their experiences and been acknowledged as Survivors of the *Shoah*. When I read others' memoirs and testimonies, each former hidden child's revelation strikes awe into me. All their stories, voices and feelings have helped to affirm my memories and to revive my feelings from childhood.

Recently Jacques Lewkowicz, a childhood friend still living in Belgium, sent me a short essay about his years in hiding during the *Shoah*. I never suspected and never knew the pain and suffering he endured. Our families had lived in the same building, rue Gendebien 14, since I was born. Just two years older than me, he seemed to be my protector and a friend. His father was appointed the legal guardian for Charly and me, following our father's arrest by the Nazis. Jacques' mother gave Charly potentially life-saving advice when my brother tried to visit our father in Malines after his arrest by the Nazis prior to our father's fatal transportation to Auschwitz.

Likewise, although I had known Henri Gurman since I was twelve years old, never did either of us mention anything about our war experiences or where we were hidden, with whom or by whom. I knew nothing about him and he knew nothing about me. It never occurred to me to ask him more details about himself or to share with him my hidden years. It certainly was not that I did not care about him. I think I feared to awaken sad memories and thoughts, for me and for him. I so wanted to ask him a myriad of questions but I waited too long to ask, as he died in 2013. I felt a compound loss at multiple levels, losing someone who had known me for decades and losing another of my tenuous links with my war years.

Sydney Jewish Museum

Possibly, I was unconsciously waiting for my immediate family to ask me about my early life. When he was a teenager, Michael asked me questions about my youth in Belgium but I was unable to share any details even though I was already in my forties. Almost fifteen years later, I invited my children to attend when I was filmed for the Spielberg project in 1995 (Survivors of the Shoah Visual History Foundation). Somehow I was still tongue-tied and I could only speak in general and vague terms because I had not begun to trust my memories and own my history. I was so happy that Cindy observed my interview being recorded.

My gradual release from secrecy and imposed guilt flourished after I became a guide at the Sydney Jewish Museum. There I tell visitors about my childhood, hiding and surviving Nazi occupation. Being able to recount my secrets to strangers in a safe environment provided a new channel for acknowledging my survival, to myself as well as to others. It was almost a confession, a way of 'coming clean' as I repeatedly described hiding, worsening conditions and fears that were implanted in my psyche and tarnished my adult life.

Furthermore, this guide role created an impetus for my family to ask more about my early life, as by now, strangers knew more about me than did my own children. My grandchildren have shown interest. They ask me questions in a family setting and I have shared my hidden childhood experiences. The eldest two have written papers for school based on my experience. Telling my life story to others has been a self-healing process. I am grateful I have these opportunities to tell, hear myself and process the many mixed feelings and bizarre events of my formerly forgotten childhood.

The Museum has been an important destination in a personal journey that commenced three decades ago with the Sydney Child Holocaust Survivors Group in the mid-1980s. For Jews, the admonition to remember is a core principle of religious belief. It is essential and an act of piety to keep alive the memory of the millions who were murdered. My role at the Museum serves that purpose.

The Australian State in which I live, New South Wales, requires the Holocaust to be taught in high school, as do most Australian educational authorities. I am impressed by the diverse means by which teachers incorporate the Holocaust into subjects in addition to history, such as sociology, psychology and literature. The Museum hosts over 25,000 children annually for tours, organised through their schools. If available, a Survivor speaks initially to a group of students before another guide takes them through the exhibitions. Many of the Museum visitors declare this to be a highlight, perhaps because each of us who escaped death when the Nazis planned to murder us is a living exhibit in some form.

Talking to students at the Museum, I mention my childhood experiences as a Jewish girl in Nazi-occupied Belgium and as a hidden child. They are mostly very attentive and some cry in sympathy. I tell them that they have to bear witness as they have seen and heard a Survivor. They must tell the world, when we are gone, of the horrors of the *Shoah*. Now they have looked into the eyes and heard the words of a person who saw it, the students cannot forget. We are both believable and unforgettable, and possibly more influential than any textbooks.

Specifically, I reinforce for every student two key ideas. Firstly, that they should never bully as the Nazis did and, secondly, not to be a victim as were the many millions affected by the *Shoah*, me amongst them. I particularly stress never to be a collaborator and definitely not to stand on the sidelines when an injustice occurs. Up until very recently, I was unaware that I was paraphrasing Yehuda Bauer's 2000 poem, *Never Again*:

Thou shalt not be a perpetrator
Thou shalt not be a victim
And thou shalt never
But never be a bystander.

At the end of each presentation, I stress to the students the importance of gaining education as well as how lucky they are to live in Australia with all its opportunities, rights and freedoms. I encourage them to make the most of their chance to create a better world. Students' questions are mostly well thought out and relevant. Still, on a regular basis, a child has asked me, 'Did you meet Mr Hitler?' I refrain from smiling, knowing that this is a universal query that Survivors hear, echoed by Trude Levi in *Did You Ever Meet Hitler, Miss? A Holocaust Survivor Talks to Young People*.[90] I know that they cannot possibly imagine the magnitude of the *Shoah*.

Students have written profound and touching letters of thanks to me, many of which I treasure as evidence that they understood and remembered my messages, both in their heads and in their hearts. Some write that they feel my talk has changed their lives. Many students tell me that they went home that day and hugged their mother. I feel more than rewarded; I feel I have made a small difference to the way that a few individuals will treat each other and strangers throughout their lives.

When I pass through the Museum's ghetto display and see photos of little children sitting in the gutter, begging for a crust to stay alive for one more day, I feel very distressed. Any food scraps in my kitchen, even vegetable and fruit peels always remind me of the camp inmates who were grateful to eat a blade of grass. Pictures of children dying and others walking confidently towards the gas chambers, unaware of their fate, leave me painfully sad.

Recently, I was confronted by the absence of mention, indication or any display about hidden children at the Sydney Jewish Museum, other than one photo of Anne Frank. Therefore, I donated my sole memento of my hidden years, a child's porcelain coffee set given to me when I was hidden. In 1959, I brought it with my few belongings to Australia, unable to separate myself from its intrinsic charm. It also represents people who kept me alive and allowed me to enjoy playing secretly. I have donated that child's coffee set to the permanent collection of the Sydney Jewish Museum to ensure that something representing hidden child Survivors is exhibited.

The Museum has its first permanent display on the plight of hidden children. We were hidden and we remained hidden in many ways, from our families, from the Jewish community and from the broader worldwide stories about the *Shoah*. Survivors are ageing. Soon there will no longer be living witnesses to the *Shoah*. There will be no one alive to recount the truth or describe the trauma of the Holocaust in person.

In mid-2015, I was the guest speaker for The Remember Me program which takes place at the Museum once a month. Here a Survivor speaks in detail about his or her war experiences. My son Michael shared a voice recording on the internet.[91] I also speak to professional symposiums for medical practitioners, high school teachers and other groups.

74. Child's coffee set, given to Francine when in hiding in Belgium during the Second World War. Donated to the Sydney Jewish Museum, 2014.

Peace within my grasp

The damage was done, my father murdered, my life disrupted irreparably and my fragile ego was under siege from fear and guilt, shame and self-loathing. My enforced silence about a hidden childhood was a measure of how much I still suffered.

On my seventy-sixth birthday I felt an urgency to begin writing down my memories of the *Shoah* and about my father. Possibly I feared that I would forget the details of that terrible time as, after all, I had been told to forget everything. I also felt a responsibility to testify against antisemitism and racism. Over the past two years of research, each day has provided a revelation of my new mental strength, with clarity of thought, self-confidence and clearer decision-making that I have never felt before in my life.

I have shared now what I remember from my early life as a hidden child in Nazi-occupied Belgium and the aftermath of that horrific catastrophe on my Jewish family and connected fragments in my memory with feelings, images and sounds that I remember. I traced my hidden childhood by finding scraps in my heart and images in my mind, supported by details in books, journals and archives. The testimonies of other hidden children and anecdotes from my brother augmented and stimulated my fragmented recall.

My account benefitted enormously from other authors and official documents that validated and filled small gaps in my memory. My analyses and inferences are as complete as the facts that I have gathered and I have made my own conclusions.

For the first time in my life, I understand that people want to read, hear or know about that horrible period. Without those brave, selfless people who hid me, I would have been murdered along with the many who never returned. Researching and writing my story has allowed me to express my feelings.

Through writing this historical account, I provide a voice to the millions who perished in that terrible time and who cannot tell their own story. This is my legacy as a witness to the Holocaust, in memory of my extended family members who perished, especially my father.

Already I have lived more fully than I could ever have hoped when I was six and a half years old in 1944. Now I am free from being abused and exploited, shamed and blamed, rejected and demeaned. I have lightened my load of guilt imposed on a young child who did nothing out of the ordinary but survive against extraordinary odds in a hateful and murderous time.

Research continues as I seek more documentation. While I still hope that my hidden years will be more fully revealed from records of schools, foster carers, relatives and neighbours, as well as being recovered from the depths of my memory, I will not cease examining my feelings and recall of events that were suppressed for so long. I will prepare testimonies for Yad Vashem on my many murdered relatives for whom no record has ever been submitted. Of course, I will be testifying every time I speak to a wider audience beyond the Jewish community.

Paradoxically, if I need to find solace when stressed, I occasionally go to an old church. There I sit quietly in a pew and deeply inhale the remnants of the ceremonial incense in the air. I am transported away from daily worries and feel better in that moment. It is wonderfully potent and takes me back to when I was a little girl in Saintes, unaware of the tribulations that lay ahead for me. I felt protected in that church and still believed that I would one day be happy.

Postscript

When I first set eyes on Phillip across a crowded room, it was love at first sight. We have been through bad times and wonderful times, sad times and joyful ones. We have grown older together. Phillip is my life companion, the love of my life. While I planned that we would have a happy old age travelling, catching up with long-term friends, passing time sharing memories and surrounded by our children and grandchildren, the future does not hold such shared activities.

When he was diagnosed with vascular dementia two years ago, it was a terrible blow to him and to me. I had envisaged growing old together, enjoying the grandchildren, spending time relaxing together. It is as though he has embarked on a voyage to a destination where I cannot follow him. All I can do is to be with him try to catch the last glimpses of his sunset.

Recently, doctors placed my husband in full-time nursing care due to his failing health, ending my hope for a peaceful, quiet old age shared with my life companion since 1963. Sadly, only a shell of his personality remains and his spirit is slowly leaving him. When I sit with him, I wonder when it will be the last time that he recognises me. It is very sad to return to an empty home. For a few weeks Phillip's sister Marian was similarly admitted to the same establishment, on the same floor. They would spend much time affectionately holding hands. Sadly, Marian passed away on 11 November 2016.

It also dawned on me that, apart from a few months living with some girls prior to my marriage, I have never been independent, able to make all my own decisions. I do not have to ask anybody before making a choice. I must admit that this is a very liberating feeling. I am treading lightly, taking small steps, savouring this unexpected freedom. At seventy-eight years of age, I have been set free to rule my own life but also, sadly, relinquishing my shared life with Phillip. It is a bitter-sweet revelation.

I am aware of studies undertaken in recent years on the health of now ageing Holocaust Survivors. At the Jewish Aged Care Home where my husband now resides, there are many adaptations designed to alleviate any emotional stress and grief of elderly patients remembering their past traumas

75. Phillip and Francine Lazarus, 2015 (courtesy Giselle Haber).

and losses. Can I blame my living conditions during those terrible years for my present ailments? Probably not all of them. I have described the emotional devils that I have been battling most of my life. Added to these is a recent diagnosis of Parkinson's disease.

At times I am overtaken with the inevitable: I am now old and I will never be able to accomplish all that I would have wanted to, all that I dreamed of. I never had a childhood nor a youth. I became old before having lived.

One day I may be able to embrace the foundations of my life, totally. The unconditional love of my three children and enthusiastic grandchildren brings immeasurable joy to my life, constantly.

My father would have been so very proud of his family.

Appendix

Timeline: Francine Lazarus née Kamerman

Year	Belgian and world history	Kamerman & Inberg family history
c. 1870		Silver Kiddish cup first given to a Rosenblum descendent
1897		Israel Kamerman born
1906		Zeida and Booba marry in Biala Podlaska
1909		Minnie Inberg born, Biala Podlaska
1914–18	First World War	Israel Kamerman conscripted by Prussian army in 1914, captured by Russian troops and forced to fight against Germany
1918	11 November, Armistice declared	
1926		Chaim Pinkus Inberg moves to Brussels from London
1927		1 February, Minnie Inberg arrives in Belgium from London, England, accompanied by younger brother, Mordko (Max)
		22 June, Israel Kamerman arrives in Antwerp Belgium after leaving Przemysl Poland 15 May
1928		July, Israel Kamerman moves to Brussels
		26 November, birth of Phillip Ernest Lazarus, Sydney Australia
1929	October 1929, the Wall Street Crash signals beginning of the Great Depression	Mima Edis (Grunberg, née Rosenblum) visits Albuck and Chippa Rosenblum, her parents, in Biala Podlaska and is given the Rosenblum Kiddish cup

Year	Belgian and world history	Kamerman & Inberg family history
1930	Belgium affected by the Great Depression	20 August, Israel Kamerman and Minnie Inberg marry in Brussels
	Wallonia and Flanders become unilingual regions	
1931		15 August, Charles Max Kamerman born in Brussels Belgium
		August, Uncle Jacques Kamerman and his son Emile visit the Kamerman grandparents in Przemysl Poland from France 21 December, Israel Kamerman named by police as being among those foreigners selling at the Place Jourdan market
1933	30 January, Hitler comes to power in Germany	
	The fascist and anti-Semitic Flemish National League (Vlaams Nationaal Verbond) founded in Belgium	
1935	15 September, anti-Semitic Nuremberg Laws introduced in Germany	
1937-38		Francine's aunts and uncles emigrate to Australia: Betty and Sam; Rosine and Max; and Rose who emigrated unaccompanied
1938	12 March, Anschluss, the annexation of Austria by Germany	12 March, Francine Kamerman born in Ixelles, a suburb of Brussels, Belgium
	9–10 November 1938, Kristallnacht (night of broken glass) throughout Germany	
1939	1 September, Germany invades Poland	
	3 September, France and Britain declare war on Germany	

Year	Belgian and world history	Kamerman & Inberg family history
1940		12 March, Francine Lazarus two years old
	10 May, Germany invades the Netherlands, Belgium and France	May, Kamerman family escapes Belgium to France attempting to reach England via Spain
	16 May, German army enters Brussels	
	4 June, Britain withdraws troops from continental Europe	Kamerman family stays in Cepet, near Toulouse in southern France
	22 June, France surrenders to Germany	
	July, Battle of Britain	September 1940, Kamerman family deported from France back to Brussels
	28 October, Nazi proclamations are introduced against Jews in Belgium • Administrative definition of who is a Jew is established • Ban on return to Belgium of Jews who had emigrated • Jews are required to register with their local municipality • Jewish owned shops and businesses must display a sign that identifies their owners as Jewish • Jewish owned economic assets have to be declared • Professional exclusion of Jews	Israel Kamerman has to label his market stall as Jewish-owned
	• Letter J stamped on Jewish identity cards	18 December, family registration with local government by Israel Kamerman

Year	Belgian and world history	Kamerman & Inberg family history
	23 October, Nazi decree-banning ritual slaughter of Kosher animals	Kamerman and Inberg families deprived of Kosher meat
1941		12 March, Francine's third birthday
	14 April, destruction of Jewish businesses and two synagogues in the Antwerp Pogrom	
	25 April, Nazi decree – Jews forbidden to enter public parks	Francine no longer taken to parks to play
	31 May 1941, Nazi decree – ban on possession of a radio by a Jew	Zeida defies Nazis and hides his radio
	Night curfew for Jews between 8 pm and 7 am	Israel Kamerman unable to travel outside curfew hours
		September, Francine starts kindergarten (day care)
	25 November, Nazi Decree – creation of l'Association des Juifs de Belgique (Association of Jews in Belgium or AJB) to control the Jewish population, in order to facilitate arrest and then deportation	
	1 December, Nazi Decree – Jewish children not falling within compulsory school ages are banned from schools	December, Francine no longer allowed to attend kindergarten
	7 December, Japan bombs Pearl Harbor, USA	7 December, Phillip Lazarus celebrates his Bar mitzvah, Sydney Australia
	8 December, USA enters Second World War	

Year	Belgian and world history	Kamerman & Inberg family history
1942	29 August, Nazi Decree – Jews forcibly confined to one of four cities; Brussels and Antwerp, Charleroi and Liège.	
	17 January, Nazi Decree – Jews forbidden to change residence without official approval	
	20 January, The Final Solution, Wannsee Conference Protocol, the secret agreement to exterminate all European Jews	
	11 March, Jewish workers no longer entitled to bonuses, paid leave including sick leave; Jews to be isolated from other workers	12 March, Francine's fourth birthday
	22 April, Jews having fled Germany are stripped of their German nationality	
	8 May, forced labour imposed on Jews in Belgium	
	27 May, Nazi decree – Jews over eleven years required to wear the Star of David on all outer clothing	Kamerman and Inberg adults forced to wear Star of David
	9 June, Nazi Decree – exclusion of Jews in medical and paramedical professions from practising	
	Freedom of movement strictly limited for Jews	
	Comité de défense des juifs (CDJ) formed	

Year	Belgian and world history	Kamerman & Inberg family history
	29 July, re-opening of Caserne Dossin, barracks in Malines	July, Kamerman grandparents murdered in Przemysl or deported to death camps
	August–September, first round-ups of Jews; temporary internment of prisoners at Caserne Dossin	
	4 August, first convoy of prisoners deported from Malines directly to Auschwitz	
	August–September, beginning of hiding by Jews in Belgium	
	September, Nazi Decree – all school-aged Jewish children excluded from school (seven to fifteen years)	September, Charly Kamerman ordered out of his classroom; Inberg and Kamerman families go into hiding
		September, Francine hidden on farm in Saintes
1943		12 March, Francine's fifth birthday (in hiding in Saintes)
	19 April, departure of the twentieth convoy from Malines to death camps	19 April, Moishe Lewin escapes twentieth convoy, one of 231 deportees freed by the Resistance
		Francine escapes murderous soldiers, aged five and a half years
		Late summer, Francine returned to Brussels (hidden by CDJ)
1944		12 March, Francine's sixth birthday (in hiding in Brussels)
	6 June, D-Day; Allies land in Normandy France, 524 kms from Brussels	
		July, father Israel Kamerman arrested and held in Caserne Dossin
	31 July, the last convoy for Auschwitz leaves from Malines, Belgium (twenty-sixth convoy)	31 July, father Israel Kamerman taken on the 26th convoy from Malines, Belgium to Auschwitz

Year	Belgian and world history	Kamerman & Inberg family history
		3 August, murder of Israel Kamerman at Auschwitz, Poland
	3–4 September, Liberation of Belgium	September, Francine and Charles Kamerman watch General Montgomery's troops enter Brussels
	11 October, the Comité de défense des Juifs (CDJ) reformed to l'Aide aux Israélites Victimes de la Guerre	
	23 October, Paris liberated	
	24 November, Nazis blow up Auschwitz gas chambers	
	16 December –January 1945, Battle of the Ardennes	
1945		12 March, Francine's seventh birthday, out of hiding
	30 April, Hitler commits suicide	
	7 May, Germany surrenders to allies	
	2 September, Japan surrenders	
	20 November, Nuremberg War Crime Trials commence	
1946		Francine sent to foster care
		Francine, aged eight and a half years, goes to school for the first time
		Aunt Betty Swieca applies for Australian visa for Minnie, Francine and Charly
1948	15 May, State of Israel declared	Minnie Inberg Kamerman marries Maurice Blumberg, in a religious ceremony
1949		23 December, Helen Blumberg born to Minnie Inberg Kamerman and Maurice Blumberg

Year	Belgian and world history	Kamerman & Inberg family history
1950	12 March, Belgian popular vote to allow King Leopold III to return to throne from 'exile' in Germany; he appoints his son, Prince Baudouin to rule temporarily	12 March, Francine's twelfth birthday
1951	Prince Baudouin appointed King	Francine completes primary school in Spring; Francine enrolled in l'école Funck typing school for six months
1952		Francine's first paid job as a typist; Charly Kamerman emigrates to Australia, aged twenty-one
1954		Francine Kamerman becomes a Belgian citizen at age sixteen years
1955		Francine Kamerman has a nervous breakdown
1957		17 October, Zeida (Chaim Pinchas) Inberg dies, Brussels, Belgium
1959		March, Francine Kamerman and Booba (Binia) Inberg arrive in Sydney, Australia
		12 March, Francine celebrates twenty-first birthday in Australia
1960–4	Belgian government grants independence to the Congo – now Democratic Republic of Congo.	Francine serves as Belgian Acting Chancellor in Australia
1963		22 December, Marriage of Francine to Phillip Lazarus
1964		12 October, Michael Phillip Lazarus born, Sydney, NSW
1966		20 October, Cindy Jo Lazarus born, Sydney, NSW
1969		25 April, Minnie, Maurice and Helen arrive in Australia as immigrants
1973		3 June, wedding of Helen Blumberg and Alexander Berger

Year	Belgian and world history	Kamerman & Inberg family history
1973		29 August, Jason Edward Lazarus born, Sydney, NSW
1975		15 January, Booba (Binia Inberg) dies, Sydney Australia
1980–1	Prosecution of Kurt Asche, the SS responsible for all the anti-Jewish implementations in Brussels, held in Kiel, Germany; sentenced to seven years in jail	
1985		International Gathering of Jewish Holocaust Survivors, Sydney Australia (Francine attends)
1987		Sydney Child Holocaust Survivors Group founded
1990		27 April, Francine Kamerman Lazarus awarded Bachelor of Arts, University of New South Wales, Sydney, Australia
1991	October, Creation of L'enfant caché, the Belgian Hidden Child Association	
1993	King Baudouin dies, replaced by his brother, Albert II	January, the Inaugural Australian Conference of Child Survivors of the Holocaust in Melbourne (Francine attends)
		4 May, Francine Kamerman Lazarus awarded Master of Arts, University of New South Wales, Sydney, Australia
1995		30 April–1 May 1995, First European Meeting of Hidden Children, Brussels (Francine attends), organised by *l'Association belge de l'enfant caché* (Belgian Association of the hidden child)
		3 September, Cindy Lazarus marries David Levy, Sydney Australia

Year	Belgian and world history	Kamerman & Inberg family history
1997		25 November, Joshua Levy is born
1999		August, Child Holocaust Survivors' Conference in Prague (Francine attends)
		Francine's first visit to Auschwitz
2000		21 January, Jared Levy is born
		24 November, death of Minnie Inberg Kamerman Blumberg, Sydney
2001	Belgian Tourist Office issues the first Jewish heritage guide	
2007		May, Francine's second visit to Auschwitz
		24 September, Jessica Levy is born
2010		Francine qualifies as guide at Sydney Jewish Museum
2010-16		Independent research on hidden Jewish children in Belgium
2016		11 September 2016, Marriage of Jason Lazarus and Carla Ross, Sydney, Australia

Notes

1   Speech Delivered at the Dedication Ceremonies for the United States Holocaust Memorial Museum, 22 April 1993.
2   Patrick Lindsay, *The Spirit of Kokoda, Then and Now* (South Yarra, Melbourne, Australia: Hardie Grant, 2002), p. 72.
3   Michael Berenbaum and Fred Skolnik (eds), *Encyclopaedia Judaica*, 2nd edition (Detroit: Macmillan Reference USA, 2007), p. 148.
4   Rudi Van Doorslaer, 'Jewish Immigration and Communism' in Dan Michman (ed.), *Belgium and the Holocaust. Jews Belgians Germans* (Jerusalem: Yad Vashem, 1998), p. 77.
5   Marnix Croes, 'The Holocaust in the Netherlands and the Rate of Jewish Survival', *Holocaust and Genocide Studies*, V20 N3, Winter 2006, p. 474.
6   Raul Hilberg, *The Destruction of European Jewry* (Chicago: Quadrangle Press, 1961), paraphrased.
7   *Encyclopedia Britannica*, www.britannica.com/place/Gurs (last accessed 15/12/2016).
8   French National Archives, *la collaboration* (declassified on Monday 28 December 2015).
9   Contemporary Memory Foundation, Brussels, www.fmc-seh.be (last accessed 15/12/2016).
10 David Fraser, 'The Fragility of Law: Anti-Jewish Decrees, Constitutional Patriotism, and Collaboration Belgium 1940–1944', *Law and Critique*, 14 (3) (2003), p. 253.
11 *Ibid.*
12 Jewish Virtual Library, www.jewishvirtuallibrary.org (last accessed 15/12/2016).
13 Yehuda Bauer, *The History of the Holocaust* (NY: Franklin Watts, 1982), pp. 228–9.
14 Maxime Steinberg, 'The Judenpolitik in Belgium Within the West European Context: Comparative Observations' in Dan Michman (ed.), *Belgium and the Holocaust. Jews Belgians Germans* (Jerusalem: Yad Vashem, 1998), p. 216.
15 *Inventaire de la France et la Belgique sous l'occupation allemande 1940–1944* (Paris: Centre Historique des Archives Nationales, 2002).
16 Clothing industry, p. 40.
17 Textile products and clothing, p. 120.
18 Harper Collins Dictionary (New York: Harper Collins, 2016), http://www.collinsdictionary.com/dictionary/english/razzia (last accessed 15/12/2016).
19 Suzanne Vromen, *Hidden Children of the Holocaust: Belgian Nuns and Their Daring Rescue of Young Jews from the Nazis* (Oxford: Oxford UP, 2008), p. 10.
20 *Ibid.*, p. 3.
21 In John R Bowlin (ed.), 'Rorty and Aquinas on courage and contingency', *Journal of Religion*, July 97, Vol. 77 Issue 3, p. 403.
22 John Tagliabue, 'Belgium: $170 Million in Holocaust Compensation', *New York Times*, 3/12/2008, p. 6.
23 Sylvain Brachfeld, *A Gift of Life: The Deportation and the Rescue of the Jews in Occupied Belgium (1940–1944)* (Jerusalem: Institute for the Research on Belgian Judaism, 2007), p. 162.

24   In Tara Zahra, 'The Psychological Marshall Plan: Displacement, Gender, and Human Rights after World War II', *Central European History* (Cambridge: Cambridge UP, 2011) Vol. 44 Issue 1, p. 37.

25   Althea Williams, 'A Child in Time', *History Today*, April 2013, Vol. 63 Issue 4, p. 6.

26   Debórah Dwork, *Children With A Star: Jewish Youth in Nazi Europe* (New Haven & London: Yale University Press, 1991), p.69.

27   Dori Katz, *Looking for Strangers: The True Story of My Hidden Wartime Childhood* (Chicago: University of Chicago, 2013).

28   See Vromen, *Hidden Children of the Holocaust*.

29   Natan Durst, 'Child survivors of the Holocaust: Age-specific traumatization and the consequences for therapy', *American Journal of Psychotherapy*, 57 (4), 2003.

30   Adeline Fohn, *Traumatismes, souvenirs et après-coup: L'expérience des enfants juifs cachés en Belgique* (Louvain: Université Catholique de Louvain, 2011); Adeline Fohn, Delphine Grynberg and Olivier Luminet, 'Posttraumatic Symptoms and Thought Control Strategies Among Aging Hidden Jewish Children' in *Journal of Loss and Trauma*, 17, 2012, pp.38–55.

31   Charlotte Decoster, *Jewish hidden children in Belgium during the Holocaust: a comparative study of their hiding places at Christian establishments, private families, and Jewish orphanages* (Dallas: University of North Texas, 2006), p. 14.

32   *Ibid.*, p. 47.

33   See Durst, 'Child survivors of the Holocaust', pp. 499–518.

34   Gabriel Sheffer, 'Jewry as an Archetypical Diaspora', in Mark Avrum Ehrlich (ed.), *Encyclopedia of the Jewish Diaspora: Origins, Experiences, and Culture*, Vol. 1, pp 540–57 (Washington DC: Library of Congress, 2009), p. 819; Vromen, *Hidden Children of the Holocaust*, p. 55.

35   See Steinberg, 'The Judenpolitik in Belgium Within the West European Context, p. 219.

36   Israel Gutman (ed.), *Encyclopedia of the Holocaust*, (Detroit: Macmillan Reference USA, 1989).

37   See Fohn et al., 'Posttraumatic Symptoms and Thought Control Strategies Among Aging Hidden Jewish Children', p.38.

38   Josephine Ngo & Marije Roos, *Silence within a world of words: why it took almost fifty years after the Holocaust for 'hidden children' to speak out* in Netherlands: Humanity in Action, www.humanityinaction.org, 2014 (last accessed 15/12/2016).

39   See Durst, 'Child survivors of the Holocaust, pp. 499–518.

40   Judith S Kestenberg and Charlotte Kahn, *Children Surviving Persecution: An International Study of Trauma and Healing* (Westport: Greenwood Publishing Group, 1998), p. 4.

41   In Ngo & Roos, *Silence within a world of words*, p. 2.

42   M Bergmann & ME Jucovy (eds), *Generations of the Holocaust* (New York: Basic Books, 1982).

43   Sophia Richman, 'From hidden child to Godless Jew: A Personal Journey', *Women & Therapy*, 2010, p. 46.

44   *A Gift of Life: The Deportation and the Rescue of the Jews in Occupied Belgium (1940-1944)* (Jerusalem: Institute for the Research on Belgian Judaism, 2007), p. 102.

45   See Bauer, *The History of the Holocaust* (NY: Franklin Watts, 1982), p. 334.

46   Raphaël Delpard, *Les Enfants Cachés* (Paris: J.-C. Lattès, 1993), p. 211.

47   Edmund White, *My Lives* (New York: Harper Collins, 2006), p. 140.

48   See Brachfeld, *A Gift of Life*, p. 231.

49   John Tuohy, *No Time to Say Goodbye: A Memoir of a Life in Foster Care* (LLR Books: electronic book, 2015).

50   See Brachfeld, *A Gift of Life*, p. 231.

51   Rachel Lev-Wiesel, 'Source Posttraumatic Stress Disorder Symptoms, Psychological Distress, Personal Resources, and Quality of Life in Four Groups of Holocaust Child Survivors', *Family Process*, Winter 2000, Vol. 39 Issue 4, p. 445.

52 Dorothea MacKellar, *My Country* (London: London Spectator Magazine, 1908).

53 Mervyn Peake, *Titus Alone* (2nd edition) (London: Eyre & Spottiswoode, 1970).

54 See Delpard, *Les Enfants Cachés* (Paris: J.-C. Lattès, 1993), p 227.

55 *A Gift of Life: The Deportation and the Rescue of the Jews in Occupied Belgium (1940-1944)* (Jerusalem: Institute for the Research on Belgian Judaism, 2007), p. 102.

56 See Vromen, *Hidden Children of the Holocaust*, p 121.

57 See Ngo & Roos, *Silence within a world of words*, p. 2.

58 Yad Vashem Archives, Jerusalem Israel, yadvashem.org (last accessed 15/12/2016), yadvashem.org/righteous/statistics.asp.

59 B Shenitz, 'Hidden Children Speak Out', *Newsweek* 117.15, 1991, p. 59.

60 Ronnie Scheib's review of Slessin's documentary, *Secret Lives,* 2002.

61 See Brachfeld, *A Gift of Life*, p. 118.

62 Sonja van 't Hof, 'A Kaleidoscope of Victimhood in Withuisi' in Jolande & Mooij (eds), *The Politics of War Trauma: The Aftermath of World War II in Eleven European Countries* (Amsterdam: Amsterdam University Press, 2010), p. 74.

63 Faniya Pavlova, *I Am from the Holocaust. Memoir* (Liepaja: Open Public Foundation, 2014).

64 Lucien Steinberg, 'Jewish Rescue Activities in Belgium and France', in Yisrael Gutman and Efraim Zuroff (eds), *Proceedings of the Second Yad Vashem International Historical Conference* (Jerusalem: Yad Vashem, 1977), p. 603.

65 Mordecai Paldiel, 'The Rescue of Jewish Children in Belgium During World War II' in Dan Michman (ed.), *Belgium and the Holocaust. Jews Belgians Germans* (Jerusalem: Yad Vashem, 1998), p 310.

66 *Ibid.*, pp. 307–25.

67 See Paldiel, 'The Rescue of Jewish Children in Belgium During World War II' in Dan Michman (ed.), *Belgium and the Holocaust. Jews Belgians Germans* (Jerusalem: Yad Vashem, 1998), p. 311.

68 *Ibid.*, p 310.

69 See Vromen, *Hidden Children of the Holocaust*, p. 87.

70 See Steinberg, 'Jewish Rescue Activities in Belgium and France', p. 603.

71 See Kestenberg and Kahn, *Children Surviving Persecution: An International Study of Trauma and Healing* (Westport: Greenwood Publishing Group, 1998).

72 See Brachfeld, *A Gift of Life*, p. 200.

73 See Dwork, *Children With A Star.*

74 N Koren-Karie, A Sagi-Schwartz, T Joels, 'Absence of Attachment Representations (AAR) in the adult years: The emergence of a new AAI classification in catastrophically traumatized Holocaust child survivors', *Attachment and Human Development* 5(4), 2003, pp. 381–97.

75 See Fohn et al., 'Posttraumatic Symptoms and Thought Control Strategies Among Aging Hidden Jewish Children', p. 39, after Sharon Kangisser Cohen, *Child survivors of the Holocaust in Israel: Social dynamics and postwar experiences* (Brighton, England: Sussex Academic Press, 2005).

76 After A Fohn & S Heenan-Wolff, 'The destiny of an unacknowledged trauma: the deferred retroactive effect of *après-coup* in the hidden Jewish children of wartime Belgium', *International Journal of Psychoanalysis*, 92, 2011, pp. 5–20.

77 *The Ghetto Poems – From the Jewish Underground in Poland*, translated from Polish by Yala Korwin (New York: Association of Friends of Our Tribune, 1945).

78 Elie Wiesel, 'Hope, Despair and Memory', *Nobel Lecture*, 11 December 1986.

79 Beverley Davis, *Be fruitful and multiply: the family history showing direct and collateral relationships of John Mark Davis, a fourth generation Jewish Australian* (Adelaide: Lutheran Publishing House, 1979).

80 Vera Bloom (lyrics) & Jacob Gade (music), *Jealousy* (New York: Harms Inc, 1951).

81 Bertrand Russell, *An Outline of Intellectual Rubbish* (London: George Allen & Unwin, 1961).

82 See Fohn et al., 'Posttraumatic Symptoms and Thought Control Strategies Among Aging Hidden Jewish Children', p. 51

83 Gerhart Piers and Milton B Singer, *Shame and Guilt* (Springfield: C. C. Thomas, 1953).

84 R Yehuda, J Schmeidler, LJ Siever, K Binder-Brynes & A Elkin, 'Individual differences in posttraumatic stress disorder symptom profiles in Holocaust survivors in concentration camps or in hiding', *Journal of Traumatic Stress*, 10 (3), 1997, pp. 453–63.

85 See Fohn et al., 'Posttraumatic Symptoms and Thought Control Strategies Among Aging Hidden Jewish Children', p. 51.

86 See Fohn et al., 'Posttraumatic Symptoms and Thought Control Strategies Among Aging Hidden Jewish Children', p. 48

87 See Kestenberg and Kahn, *Children Surviving Persecution*.

88 See Shenitz, 'Hidden Children Speak Out', p. 59.

89 See Ngo & Roos, *Silence within a world of words*, p. 2.

90 Trude Levi, *Did You Ever Meet Hitler, Miss? A Holocaust Survivor Talks to Young People* (London: Vallentine Mitchell, 2003).

91 Francine Lazarus, http://youtu.be/1J8CON4MsKU (last accessed 15/12/2016).

Bibliography

Publications

Australian Association of Jewish Holocaust Survivors, *The Gift of Life, Commemorative Book of The Holocaust Gathering, May 1985*, Sydney Australia (Sydney: Australian Association of Jewish Holocaust Survivors, 1989).

Bauer, Yehuda, 'Never Again' in proceedings of *2000 International Forum Conference on the Shoah*, edited by Eva Fried (Stockholm: Government of Sweden, 2005), p. 9.

Bauer, Yehuda, *The History of the Holocaust* (NY: Franklin Watts, 1982).

Berenbaum, Michael and Skolnik, Fred (eds), *Encyclopaedia Judaica*, 2nd edition (Detroit: Macmillan Reference USA, 2007).

Bergmann, M & Jucovy, ME (eds), *Generations of the Holocaust* (New York: Basic Books, 1982).

Bloom, Vera (lyrics) & Gade, Jacob (music), *Jealousy* (New York: Harms Inc, 1951).

Brachfeld, Sylvain, *A Gift of Life: The Deportation and the Rescue of the Jews in Occupied Belgium (1940–1944)* (Jerusalem: Institute for the Research on Belgian Judaism, 2007).

Cohen, Sharon Kangisser, *Child survivors of the Holocaust in Israel: Social dynamics and postwar experiences* (Brighton, England: Sussex Academic Press, 2005).

Contemporary Memory Foundation, Brussels, www.fmc-seh.be (last accessed 15/12/2016).

Croes, Marnix, 'The Holocaust in the Netherlands and the Rate of Jewish Survival', *Holocaust and Genocide Studies*, V20 N3, Winter 2006, pp. 474–99.

Davis, Beverley, *Be fruitful and multiply: the family history showing direct and collateral relationships of John Mark Davis, a fourth generation Jewish Australian* (Adelaide: Lutheran Publishing House, 1979).

de Saint-Exupéry, *Le Petit Prince* (Paris: Éditions Gallimard, 1943).

Decoster, Charlotte, *Jewish hidden children in Belgium during the Holocaust: a comparative study of their hiding places at Christian establishments, private families, and Jewish orphanages* (Dallas: University of North Texas, 2006).

Delpard, Raphaël, *Les Enfants Cachés* (Paris: J.-C. Lattès, 1993).

Dostoyevsky, Fyodor, *Crime and Punishment* (1917).

Dumas, Alexandre père (senior), *Le Comte de Monte-Cristo* (1845–6).

Durst, Natan, 'Child survivors of the Holocaust: Age-specific traumatization and the consequences for therapy', *American Journal of Psychotherapy*, 57 (4), 2003, pp. 499–518.

Dwork, Debórah, *Children With A Star: Jewish Youth in Nazi Europe* (New Haven & London: Yale University Press, 1991).

Ehrlich, Mark Avrum (ed.), *Encyclopedia of the Jewish Diaspora: Origins, Experiences, and Culture*, Volume 1 (Washington DC: Library of Congress, 2009).

Eliot, T. S., *Four Quartets* (New York: Harcourt, Brace, 1943).

Encyclopedia Britannica, www.britannica.com/place/Gurs (last accessed 15/12/2016).

Felt, Paul, 'Tourist Office issues a Jewish heritage guide', *Travel Weekly* 02/22/2001, Vol. 60 Issue 16, pp. E11–14.

Fohn, Adeline, Delphine Grynberg and Olivier Luminet, 'Posttraumatic Symptoms and Thought Control Strategies Among Aging Hidden Jewish Children' in *Journal of Loss and Trauma*, 17, 2012, pp.38–55.

Fohn, Adeline, *Traumatismes, souvenirs et après-coup: L'expérience des enfants juifs cachés en Belgique* (Louvain: Université Catholique de Louvain, 2011).

Fohn, A & Heenan-Wolff, S 'The destiny of an unacknowledged trauma : the deferred retroactive effect of *après-coup* in the hidden Jewish children of wartime Belgium', *International Journal of Psychoanalysis*, 92, 2011, pp. 5–20.

Frank, Anne, *Anne Frank's Tales from the Secret Annexe* (Harmondsworth: Viking, 1985).

Fraser, David, 'The Fragility of Law: Anti-Jewish Decrees, Constitutional Patriotism, and Collaboration Belgium 1940–1944', *Law and Critique*, 14 (3) (2003) pp. 253–75.

Geulen-Herscovici, Andrée, Rescue Story in *The Righteous Among Nations* (Israel: Yad Vashem), http://www.yadvashem.org/righteous/ (last accessed 15/12/2016).

Geulen-Herscovici, Andrée, *Notebooks* (Israel: Yad Vashem).

Greene, Beverly and Dorith Brodbar, 'A Minyan of Women: Family Dynamics, Jewish Identity and Psychotherapy Practice' in *Women & Therapy*, 33.3–4 (2010) pp. 155–7.

Gutman, Israel (ed.), *Encyclopedia of the Holocaust*, (Detroit: Macmillan Reference USA, 1989).

Harper Collins Dictionary (New York: Harper Collins, 2016), http://www.collinsdictionary.com/dictionary/english/razzia (last accessed 15/12/2016).

Hilberg, Raul, *The Destruction of European Jewry* (Chicago: Quadrangle Press, 1961).

Iglinski-Goodman, Leah, *For Love of Life* (London: Vallentine Mitchell, 2002).

International Labour Organisation, 'What is child labour', http://www.ilo.org/global/lang—en/index.htm (last access 15/12/2016).

Inventaire de la France et la Belgique sous l'occupation allemande 1940–1944 (Paris: Centre Historique des Archives Nationales, 2002).

Jewish Virtual Library, www.jewishvirtuallibrary.org (last accessed 15/12/2016).

Katz, Dori, *Looking for Strangers: The True Story of My Hidden Wartime Childhood* (Chicago: University of Chicago, 2013).

Kestenberg, Judith S and Kahn, Charlotte, *Children Surviving Persecution: An International Study of Trauma and Healing* (Westport: Greenwood Publishing Group, 1998).

Koren-Karie N, Sagi-Schwartz A, Joels T, 'Absence of Attachment Representations (AAR) in the adult years: The emergence of a new AAI classification in catastrophically traumatized Holocaust child survivors', *Attachment and Human Development* 5(4), 2003, pp. 381–97.

La Direction Générale (DG) Victimes de la Guerre (Director General of Victims of War), Government of Belgium.

Lazarus, Francine, http://youtu.be/1J8CON4MsKU (last accessed 15/12/2016).

Levi, Trude, *Did You Ever Meet Hitler, Miss? A Holocaust Survivor Talks to Young People* (London: Vallentine Mitchell, 2003).

Levine, Karen, *Hana's Suitcase: A True Story* (Morton Grove, IL: Albert Whitman, 2003).

Lev-Wiesel, Rachel, 'Source Posttraumatic Stress Disorder Symptoms, Psychological Distress, Personal Resources, and Quality of Life in Four Groups of Holocaust Child Survivors', *Family Process*, Winter 2000, Vol. 39 Issue 4, p. 445.

Lewkowicz, Jacques, *La Vie d'une Enfance Juive* (Brussels: private publication, 15 May 2014).

Lindsay, Patrick, *The Spirit of Kokoda, Then and Now* (South Yarra, Melbourne, Australia: Hardie Grant, 2002).

MacKellar, Dorothea, *My Country* (London: London Spectator Magazine, 1908).

Menczer, Arie (ed.), *Sefer Przemysl* (Tel Aviv: Irgun Yotzei Przemysl, 1964).

Michman, Dan (ed.), *Belgium and the Holocaust. Jews Belgians Germans* (Jerusalem: Yad Vashem, 1998).

Millman, Isaac, *Hidden Child* (New York: Farrar, Straus and Giroux, 2005).

Nèvejean-Feyerick, Yvonne, Rescue Story in *The Righteous Among Nations* (Israel: Yad Vashem), http://www.yadvashem.org/righteous/ (last accessed 15/12/2016).

Ngo, Josephine & Roos, Marije, *Silence within a world of words: why it took almost fifty years after the Holocaust for 'hidden children' to speak out* in Netherlands: Humanity in Action, www.humanityinaction.org, 2014 (last accessed 15/12/2016).

Nicosia, Francis R, Henry Friedlander, Sybil Milton Garland, *Archives of the Holocaust* (New York: Yeshiva University Press, 1990) p. 68.

Oshrin, Joyce, Koden, *A Shtetl No More* (Koden, Poland), http://www.jewish-gen.org/yizkor/koden/koden.html (last accessed 15/12/2016).

Paldiel, Mordecai, 'The Rescue of Jewish Children in Belgium During World War II' in Michman, Dan (ed.), *Belgium and the Holocaust. Jews Belgians Germans* (Jerusalem: Yad Vashem, 1998).

Pavlova, Faniya, *I Am from the Holocaust. Memoir* (Liepaja: Open Public Foundation, 2014).

Peake, Mervyn, *Titus Alone* (2nd edition) (London: Eyre & Spottiswoode, 1970).

Piers, Gerhart and Singer, Milton B, *Shame and Guilt* (Springfield: C. C. Thomas, 1953).

Richman, Sophia, 'From hidden child to Godless Jew: A Personal Journey', *Women & Therapy*, 2010, p. 189.

Rorty, Richard in Bowlin, John R (ed.), 'Rorty and Aquinas on courage and contingency', *Journal of Religion*, July 97, Vol. 77 Issue 3, pp. 402–21.

Rosenberg, Rudy in Brachfeld, Sylvain, *A Gift of Life: The Deportation and the Rescue of the Jews in Occupied Belgium (1940–1944)*, pp. 224–32 (Jerusalem: Institute for the Research on Belgian Judaism, 2007).

Russell, Bertrand, *An Outline of Intellectual Rubbish* (London: George Allen & Unwin, 1961).

Sheffer, Gabriel, 'Jewry as an Archetypical Diaspora', in Ehrlich, Mark Avrum (ed.), *Encyclopedia of the Jewish Diaspora: Origins, Experiences, and Culture*, Vol. 1, pp 540–57 (Washington DC: Library of Congress, 2009).

Scheib, Ronnie, *Variety* 11/18/2002, Vol. 389 Issue 1, pp. 30–3.

Schreiber, Jean-Philippe, 'Les Juifs en Belgique: une présence continue depuis le XIIIe siècle', *Les Cahiers de la Mémoire contemporaine – Bijdragen tot de eigentijdse Herinnering*, n° 2, 2000, pp. 13–37.

Schreiber, Marion, *The Twentieth Train: The Remarkable True Story of the Only Successful Ambush on the Journey to Auschwitz* (London: Atlantic, 2004).

Shakespeare, William, *Henry the Fifth* (1599).

Shenitz, B, 'Hidden Children Speak Out', *Newsweek* 117.15, 1991, p. 59.

Steinberg, Lucien, 'Jewish Rescue Activities in Belgium and France', in Yisrael

Gutman and Efraim Zuroff (eds), *Proceedings of the Second Yad Vashem International Historical Conference* (Jerusalem: Yad Vashem, 1977), pp. 603–15.

Steinberg, Maxime, 'The Judenpolitik in Belgium Within the West European Context: Comparative Observations' in Michman, Dan (ed.), *Belgium and the Holocaust. Jews Belgians Germans* (Jerusalem: Yad Vashem, 1998).

Steinberg, Maxime, *La traque des juifs, 1942–1944* (Bruxelles: Editions Vie Ouvrière, 1987).

Tagliabue, John, 'Belgium: $170 Million in Holocaust Compensation', *New York Times*, 3/12/2008, p. 6.

The Ghetto Poems – From the Jewish Underground in Poland, translated from Polish by Yala Korwin (New York: Association of Friends of Our Tribune, 1945).

Tuohy, John, *No Time to Say Goodbye: A Memoir of a Life in Foster Care* (LLR Books: electronic book, 2015).

Valent, Paul, *Child Survivor. Adults Living with Childhood Trauma* (Melbourne: William Heinemann, 1994).

van 't Hof, Sonja, 'A Kaleidoscope of Victimhood in Withuisi' in Jolande & Mooij, Annet (eds), *The Politics of War Trauma: The Aftermath of World War II in Eleven European Countries* (Amsterdam: Amsterdam University Press, 2010).

Van Doorslaer, Rudi, 'Jewish Immigration and Communism' in Michman, Dan (ed.), *Belgium and the Holocaust. Jews Belgians Germans* (Jerusalem: Yad Vashem, 1998).

Vromen, Suzanne, *Hidden Children of the Holocaust: Belgian Nuns and Their Daring Rescue of Young Jews from the Nazis* (Oxford: Oxford UP, 2008).

White, Edmund, *My Lives* (New York: Harper Collins, 2006).

Wiesel, Elie, 'Hope, Despair and Memory', *Nobel Lecture*, 11 December 1986.

Wiesel, Elie, Speech Delivered at Dedication Ceremonies for the United States Holocaust Memorial Museum, 22 April 1993, https://www.ushmm.org/research/ask-a-research-question/frequently-asked-questions/wiesel (last accessed 15/12/2016).

Wilkomirski, Binjamin, *Fragments. Memories of a Wartime Childhood*. Translated from German by Carol Brown Janeway (New York: Schocken, 1996).

Williams, Althea, 'A Child in Time', *History Today*, April 2013, Vol. 63 Issue 4, pp. 6–7.

Withuis, Jolande & Mooij, Annet (eds) *The Politics of War Trauma: The Aftermath of World War II in Eleven European Countries* (Amsterdam: Amsterdam University Press, 2010).

Yehuda, R, Schmeidler, J., Siever, LJ, Binder-Brynes, K, & Elkin, A, 'Individual differences in posttraumatic stress disorder symptom profiles in Holocaust survivors in concentration camps or in hiding', *Journal of Traumatic Stress*, 10 (3), 1997, pp. 453–63.

Zahra, Tara, 'The Psychological Marshall Plan: Displacement, Gender, and Human Rights after World War II', *Central European History* (Cambridge: Cambridge UP, 2011) Vol. 44 Issue 1, pp. 37–62.

Archives and Databases

All-Galicia Database, http://search.geshergalicia.org (last accessed 15/12/2016).
American Jewish Joint Distribution Committee Archives, New York USA, Jerusalem Israel.
Anti-defamation League, www.adl .org (last accessed 15/12/2016).
Archives of the Holocaust: Central Zionist Archives, Jerusalem, 1939–1945.
Archives of the Holocaust, New York: Yeshiva University Press.
Auschwitz Fondation, www.auschwitz.be (last accessed 15/12/2016).
Commissariat Général aux Réfugiés et aux Apatrides (CGRA).
CEGESOMA (Center for Studies and Contemporary Society), www.cegesoma.be (last accessed 15/12/2016).
Centre Historique des Archives Nationales, Paris.
https://www.ushmm.org/learn/holocaust-encyclopedia (last accessed 15/12/2016).
French National Archives, *la collaboration* (declassified on Monday 28 December 2015).
General Office of War Victims in Belgium, http://warvictims.fgov.be (last accessed 15/12/2016).
Hidden Child Foundation, http://www.adl.org (last accessed 15/12/2016).
Institute for Holocaust Education, www.ihene.org (last accessed 15/12/2016).
International Tracing Service, www.its-arolsen.org (last accessed 15/12/2016).
Jewish Records Indexing – Poland, http://jri-poland.org (last accessed 15/12/2016).
Jewish Virtual Library, www.jewishvirtuallibrary.org/jsource/judaica/ejud_0002_0002_0_01172.html (last accessed 15/12/2016).
Kazerne Dossin / Caserne Dossin – Mémorial, Musée et Centre de documentation sur l'Holocauste et les Droits de l'homme, Belgium, www.kazernedossin.eu (last accessed 15/12/2016).
France's National Archives, www.archives-nationales.culture.gouv.fr (last accessed 15/12/2016).
Monitor Polski Court Announcements (The Government Gazette of the Republic of Poland).
National Archives of Australia, http://recordsearch.naa.gov.au (last accessed 15/12/2016).
Poland State Archives, http://archiwalna.archiwa.gov.pl/ (last accessed 15/12/2016).
Polish National Archives, http://agadd.home.net.pl (last accessed 15/12/2016).

State Archive in Belgium, www.arch.be (last accessed 15/12/2016).

The Central Israelian Consistorie of Belgium, www.jewishcom.be/wordpress/ (last accessed 15/12/2016).

The City Archive of Brussels, www.bruxelles.be/artdet.cfm (last accessed 15/12/2016).

The Commune of Ixelles, www.elsene.irisnet.be (last accessed 15/12/2016).

Yad Vashem Archives, Jerusalem Israel, yadvashem.org (last accessed 15/12/2016).

Index

Page references to photographs will be in *italic* print

A

Administration Communale, 4, 23

AJB *(Association des Juifs en Belgique)*
registration form, *25, 26, 27*

American Jewish Joint Distribution
Committee (AJJDC, known as The Joint),
101, 161

Anti-Semitism, 18–19, 22, 85

Anti-Semitism in Belgium, 1x, xiii, 18, 23-32

Antwerp, 24, 105

Anzac Day, 181

Aqua aerobics class, 202

Archibald Portrait Prize, 174

'arrêté par les allemands', 58

Art Gallery of New South Wales, 174

Association belge de l'enfant caché, Belgium,
156

Association des Juifs en Belgique (the
Association of Jews in Belgium or AJB),
24–25, 34, 53, 160

Auschwitz-Birkenau, 35 149, 150; Gas
Chamber in, *59*; Israel murdered in
(1944), 60; survivors of, 65–66; visit to,
165–168

Australia, 14, 23, 34, 95, 96, 97, 98, 101,
106, 119, 123, 133, 134, 135, 136, 138,
139, 150, 163; applied for visa, 101;
auntie Betty migrated to, 75; Booba in,
143–145; Bunny arrived to, 96; career in,
141–143; Charly left for, 108; family in,
139–141; Fay visited, 96

Australian educational authorities, 207

Australian family, 139–141, *141*; first
Passover with, *139*

Austro-Hungarian Empire, 1, 5, 11

Aznavour, Charles, 99

B

Balabustas, 8

Becks, Mademoiselle, 22

Belgian government, 23, 104, 106, 143;
extract of death registration of Israel, *58*;
records, 4; records of post-War, 149

Belgian government-in-exile, 160, 161

Belgian nationality, 18, 128

Belgian Nationality Option Certificate, *129*

Belgian Police file, Minnie's, 101–102

Belgium, 4–5; *Administration Communale*, 4;
Department of Security, 53; escape from,
33–34; Jewish hidden children in, 39–51;
Jews living in, 11; leaving, 135–136;
Nazi Decree in, 23–31; Nazi-instigated
registration of Jews in, 11; under Nazi
rule, 22–32; Place Jourdan, 5; visiting (in
1977), 151–152 –

Belmode Knitting Mills, 139

Belmode Millinery, 139

Belsele, 32

Berlinblau, Georges, 76

Biala Podlaska, 6, 7, 8, 9, 29, 63, 97, 99,
115

Birrell Street, 181

Birth Certificate, Francine's, *16*

Blankenberg: apartment in, 111; bands
played in, 113; summer in, *122*

Blumberg Helen (see Berger, Helen)

Berger née Blumberg, Helen, 104–105,
118, 136, 182, 196; Alex Berger's
wedding day, *182*; with Francine,
105, 199; moved from rue du Heysel,
107–108

Blumberg Kamerman, née Inberg, Masza
(known as Minnie, Francine's mother)
6-7, 10, 11, 13-17, 22, 28, *30-31,*34-36,
39, 41-43, 50, 53,57-58, 61, 64-67, 69,
71-73, 75-79, 81-89, 91, 95-98, 101,
103-104, 106-114, 116-119, 121-123,
126-128, 130-131, 133-137, 142, 145,
150, 152-153, 155, 159, 164, 171, 174,
177-183, 185-188, 196-197, 200

Blumberg, Maurice, 103–104, 105, 106, 108, 110, *118*, 126, 127, 133, 134, *136*, 171, 181, 185
Board of Sydney Hospital, 174
Bordello Madam. *See* De Heyn, Madame Jules
Boucherie chevaline, 69
Brugmann Hospital, 88
Brussels, 12–18; emblem of, 131; Sunday market in, 127
Buona Sera Mrs Campbell, 183
Burger Centre, 187-188

C
Camp Cove, 140
Canberra, 143
Car (stepfather's) 108, 130, 136
Carlier, Betty, 35, 89, 202
Carlier, Marius, 35
Carlier, Robert, 87
Carnet de Marriage, for Minnie and Israel, *15*
Caserne Dossin, 29, 30, 32, 35, *54*, 55, 57, 149, 161–163
Castel St Angelo, Rome, Italy, 130
Catherine, 41–42, 44, 61, 150, 151, 152, 199
Catholicism, 34, 40
Central Synagogue, 171, 172
Cepet, 21-22
Chava (Eva), 13, 97, 98, 99
Child Holocaust Survivors' Conference, Brussels, 156-159
Child Holocaust Survivors' Conference, Melbourne, 155
Child Holocaust Survivors' Conference, Prague, 165
Child Holocaust Survivors Group, Sydney, 154
Child's coffee set, 48, 138, *210*
Cimetière Israëlite Kraainem in Wezembeek, 152
Cohen, Rosalyn (see Higgins, Rosalyn)
College St Michel, 34
Comité de Défense des Juifs, 159–161
Commerçant ambulant, 71
Commerce de produits textiles et habillement, 26
Commissariat Général aux Réfugiés et aux Apatrides (CGRA), 102
Congolese government (Zaïre), 143
Crime and Punishment, 115

D
Debloos, Monsieur
De Heyn, Jules (Monsieur) 36

De Heyn (Madame Jules) 36-37, 41, 43, 53, 58, 64
De Noose, Henri, 34, 49
De Noose, Rosine, (see Inberg, Rosine)
Directeur-Général des Victimes de la Guerre, 79–80
Duke of Edinburgh Gold award, 194
Dumas, Alexandre, 87
Dunkirk, 21

E
Education: completing high school, 177; critical thinking, 180; dogged fact-hunting abilities, 180; educational deficit, 177; formal, 177; Hard-earned research skills, 180; level of secondary, 177; primary, 177; University studies, 178–180
    denying, 121–123; deprivation of, 123; fourth class, 86–87; late start at school, 81–85; nomination for *Greco-romaines,* 121; refusal by Minnie for secondary studies, 122
Eichmüller, Andreas, 168
Elizabethan theatre, 203
Emblem of *L'Enfant caché,* Brussels, *157*
Emotional scars, 199
Emotional security, 202
Emotional starvation, 200
Emotional suppression, 70–71
Employment, 125–127; conditions, 125; losing income, 126; in multinational enterprise, 126; in office typing pool, *125*; in Sydney,141–143; in *Unilever,* 126–127
Études modernes, 121

F
Falk, Antony, 175
Falk, Gerald, 153, 171
Falk, Joyce, née Lazarus 172
Family reunited in Australia: adjustment issues, 186; post-War challenges, 186
Feldman, Chippa, 97
Felt, John, 159
Fohn, Adeline, 46
Forstmann, Daniel, 175
Forstmann, Mark, 175
Fort Breendonck, 162
Foster care, Francine with, 79–92; birthday celebration, 87; in fourth class, 86–87; friendless, 90–92; introduction to music, 89–90; late start at school, 81–85; overview, 79–80; ups and downs during, 87–89

France, 18, 21, 22, 24, 25, 34, 39, 63, 64, 81, 95, 110, 127, 154, 177
Frank, Anne, 87
Friendless, 90–92
Funeral, A, 167
Für Elise, 90

G
George, Mary, 128
German Vergeltungswaffei (V1) missiles, 50
Ghetto Poems – From the Jewish Underground in Poland, The, 168
Government Gazette of the Republic of Poland (*Monitor Polski*), 98
Graduates (The), Jewish Social Club, Sydney, 146, 169
Great Depression, 33
Greco-romaines, 121
Greenberg, Mary, *112,* 113, *118,* 119
Geulen-Herscovici, Andrée, 131, 161,
Grunberg née Rosenblum, Edis (Mima Edis), 14, 97, 98, 99, 101
Grunberg, Max, 14, 97, 98, 101, 103
Gurman, Henri, 130–131, 206
Gurs, 22

H
Hague Convention, 23
Halfway House, 182
Harel, Rami, 101
Hatzor Israeli Air Force base, 100
Haute Garrone region, 21
Healing: coping mechanism, 205; Jewish children, 205; round-ups and murders of Jews, 205; Sydney; Jewish Museum, 206; War survival experiences, 205
Herling, Israel, 101
Herling Zeltzer, née Rosenblum, Miriam (Mima Miriam) 99-100
Herling, Zeev, 99, *100*
Herling, Zipporah, 100, *100*
Hidden children of the Shoah, 150
Higgins, née Cohen, Rosalyn, 112, *118,* 119, 122, 123
Higher School Certificate (HSC), 178
Hoch Deutsch (High German), 95
Hoffmeister, Adolf, 165
Holiday on Ice, 88
Holland, 87, 137
Holocaust, 18–19
Holocaust Survivors (see Survivors, Holocaust)
Home without love, 131
Horrahs, 130

Hunger, of survived children, 69–70

I
Inberg, Benjamin, 7
Inberg née Rosenblum, Binia (Booba) 7-11, 13-14`, 16-17, 22, 25, 31, 34, 51, 62, 74-77, 82, 87, 96-101, 114-118, 136-138, 141, 143-145, 174, 195-197
Inberg, Betsy (known as Betty, see Swieca, Betsy)
Inberg, Bernard (known as Bunny), 11, 13, 14, 95–96, 106, 119, 135, 139
Inberg, Chaim Pinchas (Zeida), 7, *51, 74, 75,* 96, 109, 110, 222; AJB registration, *25*; brothers changed last name to Greenberg, 7–8; in Brussels, 12–18; business card of, *13*; as grandfather, 117–119; hiding from Nazis, 33–37; left England, 12; migration of siblings, 14; purchased house in Brussels, *12, 13*; before Second World War, *13*; wedding of, 9–10; death, 117
Inberg family, 95–97, *141*
Inberg Frajda Etla (see Lewin, Frajda Etla)
Inberg Gary, *139,* 140
Inberg, Henri (known as Ricky), 140, *141*
Inberg, Masza, known as Minnie (see Blumberg Kamerman, Masza)
Inberg, Mordko Aron, known as Max, 11, 34, 95, *141*
Inberg, Rachel (known as Rose, see Lander, Rachel)
Inberg, née De Noose, Rosine, 14, 34, *52*
Intergenerational Victimisation of Women, 195
International Gathering of Jewish Holocaust Survivors, 153, 155
International Labour Organisation, 116
Ixelles, Belgium, 1, *16*

J
Jewish Child Survivors in Los Angeles, 155
Jewish Defense Committee (*Comité de Défense des Juifs*), 159–161
Jewish family, 210
Jewish identity, 109–110, 164
Jewish New Year, 24
Jewish Resistance fighters, 163
Jospa, Madame Yvonne, 159, 160

K
Kamerman, Blumberg, née Inberg, Masza, known as Minnie, (see Blumberg Kamerman, née Inberg, Masza)

Kamerman, née Shillinger, Chaja, 1, *2*,
     marriage entry for, *93, 94*
Kamerman, Charles Max, (known as Charly),
     17, *17*, 28, *30, 31*, 32, 34, 35, 36, 50,
     53, 67, *73*, 106–107, 109, 141, *184*;
     collecting abandoned ordnance, 72; in
     lounge room of grandparents, *51*; moved
     from rue du Heysel, 107–108; post War
     (1945), 68; punishment to, 73
Kamerman, Dora, 63–64, 95
Kamerman, Emile, *63*, 64, 94, 95
Kamerman, Georgette, *63*, 64, 95
Kamerman family, 93–95
Kamerman, Francine (see Lazarus, Francine)
Kamerman, Hersz, 1, *2*, 94; marriage entry
     for, *93*
Kamerman, Israel, Registration of Jews, 27
Kamerman, Israel, (Francine's father) *30*,
     168; arrested by Nazis, 53–60; Carnet de
     Marriage for, *15*; documentation of
     parents' arrival in Belgium, 4–5; entry in
     XXVI Transport, *55*; extract of death
     registration of, *58*; family, 1, *31*;
     Francine's Parents' wedding portrait, *14*;
     memorial candle shines for, *59*; murdered
     in Auschwitz (1944), 60; name on
     Victims' Memorial, *162*; parents, 2;
     portrait, *3*; report (Registration of Jews),
     27; signet ring, *4*; with wife and children,
     17; working on markets, 6
Kamerman, Jacques, 1, *94*, 95
Kamerman, Majer, 1, 94
Kamerman, Mali, 1, 94
Kamerman, Patricia (see Rosenbaum-
     Kamerman, Patricia)
Kershner, Howard, 32
Ketuba, 171
Kfir (Israeli warplane), 101
Korwin, Yala, 168
Kràsa, Hans, 165
Kremer, Esther, 90

L
La Monnaie, 128
Lander née Inberg, Rachel (known as Rose)
     95, 101, 141
Lauber, Samuel, 164
Lazarus, Alan, 203
Lazarus, Beverley (see McIntyre, Beverley)
Lazarus, Carla Michal, née Ross (known as
     Carly) 192, *193*
Lazarus, Cindy Jo, 175, *176, 179, 190, 197*
Lazarus, Doris, 174, 175
Lazarus, née Kamerman, Francine, 40, *75*,

118, 136, 197; anxiety and fear ruled
     childhood of, 64; becoming Belgian, 128;
     birth certificate, *16*; changing hiding
     places, 45–51; in cumulative trauma, 41;
     day after engagement to Phillip, *170*,
     213, *214*; dining aboard the MS *Oranje*,
     137; emotional suppression, 70–71;
     enforced silence of, 61–64; with family,
     31; family members exterminated, 62–
     64; fantasies and falsehoods of, 70; first
     family car, 108–109; in first new gown,
     132; with foster carers, *80*; in fourth
     class, 86–87; with her two dolls, *40*;
     hiding alone, 39–51; hunger of, 69–70;
     late start at school, 81–85; living in attic,
     107–108; in lounge room of
     grandparents, *51*; love for pets, 76–78;
     Nazis heavy marching footsteps, 45; with
     parents', *17, 30*; parents' wedding
     portrait, *14*; paternal grandparents of, *2*;
     post War (1945), 68; in primary school,
     81; refusal by Minnie for secondary
     studies; 122 returned to Brussels (1943),
     45; search for father, 149–152; summer
     in Blankenberg, *122*; treatment my
     wounds, 44–45; waiting for her father,
     65–66; wedding of, *173*; working in
     office typing pool, *125*, after-effects of
     hiding, 210
Lazarus, Jason Edward, 175, *176*, 189, 191-
     192, *193*
Lazarus, Joyce (see Falk, Joyce)
Lazarus, Marian (see Nisbett Forstmann née
     Lazarus, Marian)
Lazarus, Marilyn, 203
Lazarus, Michael Phillip, 175, 176, 189, 191-
     192
Lazarus, Phillip Ernest, 169, 175, 176, *179*,
     189, 214; wedding of, *173*
Lazarus, Zadea, 174, 176
Le Comte de Monte-Cristo, 87
Levy, David, 191-192, 198
Levy, Jared, 168, *192,194*
Levy, Jessica, *192*, 194, 198
Levy, Joshua, *192*-193
Lewin, Daniel, 8
Lewin, née Inberg, Frajda Etla
Lewin, Moishe, 29, 34–35, 149, 152, 199
Lewkowicz, Dina, 55
Lewkowicz, Jacques, 206
Liberation, 64, 84, 104, 110. 163
Little Prince, The, 88
Lustiger, Jean-Marie, 34
Lynn, Vera, 72

M

McIntyre, Beverley, née Lazarus, 172
Madama Butterfly, 128
Madame Jules (see De Heyn, Madame Jules)
Manneken-Pis, Brussels, 131
Mason, Mademoiselle, 48
Mason, Monsieur, 48
Melbourne, 138, 146
Melbourne Child Survivors of the Holocaust, 155–156
Melbourne Holocaust and Research Centre, 155
Mémorial, Musée et Centre de documentation sur l'Holocauste et les Droits de l'homme, 162
Menco, Frieda, 62
Mima Edis, (see Grunberg née Rosenblum, Edis)
Mima Miriam, (see Herling Zeltzer, née Rosenblum Miriam)
Mima Sarah (see Rosenshein née Rosenblum, Sarah)
Monitor Polski Court Announcements, 97-98
Montand, Yves, 99
Moskovitz, Sarah, 155
Moussa, 54
Multz, David, 203
Multz, Arlene, 203

N

NAAFI, 71
National Agency for Children, 160
National Monument to the Jewish Martyrs, 163
Navy Army and Air Force Institute (NAAFI), 71, 72
Nazi concentration camp, 87
Nazi rule in Belgium, 22–32; AJB registration form for Jews, 24–28; anti-Jewish Nazi Decrees, 23; anti-Semitic actions in Antwerp, 24; forced labour, 28; hiding from Nazis, 33–37; mandatory registration of Jews' family, 25–28; Nazi Decree in, 23–31; Nuremberg Laws (1935), 24; strategy of stigmatising Jews, 23
Nervous breakdown, 131–134
Netherlands. *See* Holland
Nèvejean-Feyerick, Yvonne, 160
Nisbett, Forstmann, Marian née Lazarus, 172, 175, 213
Nuremberg Laws (1935), 24
Nuremberg trials of Nazis, 163

O

Oakley, Haya, 99
Oeuvre Nationale de l'Enfance (ONE), 160
Opera, music and ballet, 203
Oranje MS, 137
Organisation Todt, 34
Orphelin de guerre, 121
Orthodox Synagogue, 109

P

Parc du Cinquantenaire, 163
Parkinson's disease, diagnosis of, 214
Passeur (people smuggler), 21
Passover Seder, 110
Pax Taverne (hotel), 36
Place Anneessens, 77, 123
Place Jamar, 127
Place Jourdan, 5
Perth, 138
Picton Lakes Village, 174
Politics of War Trauma, The, 158
Presley, Elvis, 99
Przemysl, 1, 2, 5, 94, 95
Puccini, Giacomo, 128

R

Razzia, 29
Recovery, 189
Registration 'arrested by Germans,' 56
Rejzner, Helen, 133
Revisiting survival, 147–148
Righteous Gentiles, 152, 159
Rista, Monsieur, 142
Roman Catholic Belgium, 83
Round-ups of Jews in Belgium by Gestapo, 29, 33, 43, 220
Rorty, Richard, 32
Rosenbaum-Kamerman, Patricia 95
Rosenberg, Rudy, 67, 84
Rosenblum, Albuck, 97, 98, 99
Rosenblum, Binia (Booba, see Inberg, Binia)
Rosenblum, Cupa, 98
Rosenblum family, 97–101, 119; kiddish cup, 98;
Rosenshein, née Inberg Sarah (Mima Sarah) 99, 101
Ross, Carla (see Lazarus, Carla, known as Carly)
Russell, Bertrand, 189
Russia, 149

S

Saindoux, 47
Sainte Reineldis, 42

Saint-Exupery, Antoine de, 88
Saintes, Belgium, 43, 44
Saintes farmers, 37, 39–40
Schillinger, Chaja, (see Kamerman, née
    Schillinger, Chaja)
Schillinger, Jente, 1
Schillinger, Mordko, 1
Seltzer, Menachem, 99
Servant to family, 111–119; grandmother's
    maid, 114–116; market hand, 111–114;
    Zeida as grandfather and, 117–119
Shabbat, 140, 194
Shadkhin, 9
Shiurim, 194
Shoah, 90, 95, 154, 155, 158, 163, 165, 166,
    186, 205, 206–207, 209
Shulamit, 171
Simonis, Mademoiselle, 87
Sir John Sulman Prize, 174
Sir Moses Montefiore Jewish Aged Care
    Home, 213
Société Générale Bank, 160
Song of Songs, 171
Spanish Civil War, 22
Star of David, 28, *29, 30, 31,* 43, 45, 157,
    163
Steinberg, Maxime, 158
Stevens, Willy, (His Excellency,
    ambassador)144
Survivor Proclamation, 97
Survivors, Holocaust, 65–66, 153–168; child
    victims as, 163–165; discovering clues of,
    165; Jewish Defense Committee for,
    159–161; opening up in Brussels, 156–
    159; visiting Auschwitz for, 165–168;
    visiting Caserne Dossin, 161–163
Swieca, Albert, *139,* 140, *141,* 154
Swieca, née Inberg Betsy (known as Betty),
    74, 75, 75, 95, 138, *139*–141, *141,* 142,
    169, 171
Swieca, Edith, *139,* 140, *141,* 154
Swieca, Peter, 75-76, 139, *141*
Swieca, Sam, 14, *139,* 140, *141,* 169
Sydney, 14, 96, 106; Booba in, 143–145;
    career in, 141–143; Child Holocaust
    Survivors Group, 154, 207; Harbour
    Heads, 138; Jewish Museum, 206;
    Legation Office, 142; love with, 135–
    146; social life in, 146; symphony
    concert, 186; Opera House, 138;
    Symphony orchestra, 203; Town Hall,
    203; Women's auxiliary of legacy, 174

T
Tagliabue, John, 32
Technical and Further Education (TAFE), 178
Terezin Concentration Camp, 165
Tosca, 129, 130
Transport XVII, 34
Transport XXVI, *55, 57*
Tubize, Belgium, 37-39
Tuohy, John, 79

U
United Nations High Commission for
    Refugees (UNHCR), 101, 102
University of New South Wales, Sydney:
    Francine's Bachelor of Arts graduation,
    179,
    Francine's Master of Arts graduation, *179*

V
Vascular dementia, 213
Vlaams Nationaal Verbond (Flemish National
    League), 31

W
Wannsee Protocol, 28
War conditions, 200
War reparations, German government, 107
Warsaw Ghetto, 166
Water sprites (Aqua group), 202
Wedding invitation, Francine's, *172;* Sophie
    Kamerman, *189*
Wichita Falls, Texas, 117
Williams, Patricia, 102
Woluwe-Saint-Lambert, *57–58*
World's Exposition (Expo 58), 118
World Fair tickets, *119*
World Federation of Jewish Holocaust Child
    Survivors and Descendants, 154
World Jewish Congress, 64
Wynne Prize, 174

Y
Yad Vashem Holocaust History Museum, 131,
    152, 161, 168, 211
Yom Kippur, 109, 171